WEST KILBRIDE c.1896

WEST KILBRIDE TODAY

# *Annals of an Ayrshire Parish*

## WEST KILBRIDE

---

BY

## THE REV. JOHN LAMB, B.D.
### MINISTER OF THE PARISH

---

*This Edition*

PAISLEY
The Grian Press
2007

Annals of an Ayrshire Parish
First Published in 1896


*This Edition*


Published 2007
©The Grian Press
Paisley PA1 1XU
www.grianpress.com


ISBN 10 digit: 0-9547996-8-2
ISBN 13 digit: 978-0-9547996-8-7

# PREFACE.

THESE chapters on an Ayrshire Parish, now published by request, were originally delivered as Lectures in West Kilbride Parish Church Mission Hall, during the earlier part of the present year. They are now issued in book-form, with a view to perpetuating the remembrance of not a few facts of local interest, which might otherwise pass into oblivion; as well as to illustrate the past life and history of a Scottish rural parish, which is now becoming a favourite Summer Resort. The information herein embodied has been derived from a variety of sources, both literary and local. The literary works consulted have been mainly these:—

"Pont's Cuningham," with notes both by Fullarton and Dobie; Robertson's "Cuningham," "Rural Recollections," and "Ayrshire Families"; Paterson's "History of Ayrshire"; Chalmer's "Caledonia,"; Scott's "Fasti Ecclesiae"; "Origines Parochiales Scotiae"; Volumes of the Ayrshire and Wigtonshire Archaeological Society; the Records of the Presbytery of Irvine; the Parochial Records of West Kilbride; Lytteil's "Guide to the Cumbraes"; M'Gibbon and Ross's "Castellated Mansions of Scotland"; Smith's "Pre-historic Man of Ayrshire," etc., etc.

For local aid and information, my thanks are due to Lieutenant Colonel and Mrs. G. Hunter Weston of Hunterstone; the late H. C. Hyndman, Esq., of Springside; H. F. Weir, Esq., of Kirkhall; Miss Boyd, Seaview; Mrs. Boyd, Highthorn; P. M'Conchie, T. Wilson, H. Hunter, and many others.

For the illustrations wherewith the volume is enriched, I have been specially indebted to the ungrudging labours of Mr. W. Leith.

Thanks are due to Mr. M'Conchie for his valuable services in revising the proofs, as they were passing through the press.

MANSE, WEST KILBRIDE,
    JUNE, MDCCCXCVI.

# PREFACE TO THE 2007 EDITION

WEST KILBRIDE possesses a singular charm. I have been a regular visitor to the town for a number of years and always leave feeling refreshed. The walk through Kirktonhall Glen is invariably pleasant and in May is truly charming. One of my favourite of walks is along the shore to Portencross (referred to as Portincross throughout in *Annals of an Ayrshire Parish*), a beauty spot which I believe to be one of the most picturesque in North Ayrshire, a view clearly shared by the constant stream of visitors to the area and by the fact that a car park and picnic area is provided for them.

The Rev. John Lamb's book, published in Glasgow by John J. Rae in 1896, a scarce item to source today, was instrumental in stimulating my interest in the area. The book was reprinted a few decades ago but it too appears to be as elusive to find as the original work.

This edition is not a facsimile but a new one which follows the original text closely. The illustrations have, in some cases, been turned around and inserted in the text at the places to where they are referred. The maps, which were poorly reproduced in the original work, have been re-done. A few new illustrations have been included. Some obvious misprints have been corrected but otherwise, in house style, the original text has been followed. We regret any typos that have crept in.

THE EDITOR
THE GRIAN PRESS
www.grianpress.com
Paisley, December 2006.

# CONTENTS

# WEST KILBRIDE

## CHAPTER I.
### PHYSICAL FEATURES OF THE PARISH.

THE parish of West Kilbride is situated towards the North-West of the Bailiwick of Cuningham, which is the name given to the portion of the county of Ayr lying to the North of the river Irvine—a name variously interpreted as meaning, "King's-home," "Milk-home," or "Rabbit-home," according to its derivation from "Köning," a king; "Cuinneag," a milk-pail or churn; or, "Cünning," a rabbit.

The name of the parish is generally believed to have been derived from St. Bride or Brigid, a distinguished pious Irish virgin of the fifth century, to whose memory so many chapels and churches, both in Ireland and Scotland, have been dedicated, and of whom we shall have more to say when we come to treat of the Ecclesiastical life of the parish. H. F. Weir, Esq., of Kirkhall, a well-known antiquarian, is, however, inclined to think that "Kilbride," rather means "A Wooded Stream," than, "The Cell or Church of St. Bride"; and this, because he holds that Saints more frequently derived names from the places where they were held in special honour, than gave names to them. This theory is supported by St. Kentigern's assuming the name of St. Mungo, when he migrated to the West and erected his rude Cathedral in that district. In further support of his view, Mr. Weir advances the existence of a Kilbride stream near Dunblane. The prefix "West" has been added in order to distinguish this parish from other places of similar name; such as the parish of Kilbride in Arran, and in Kilfinan, Argyleshire; East Kilbride in Lanarkshire; Kilbride, to the South-East of Mull,—which includes Oban and the island of Kerrara, and is now incorporated with Kilmore; Kilbride as name of post-towns near Lochmaddy in the Outer Hebrides, and near Lochgilphead in Argyleshire; and from Kilbride, as name of ancient chapelries in the parish of Strath in Skye; in Kirkcudbright, to the South-East of Kirkmabreck, which once had a chapel near Wigton Bay, called Kirk Bride; in the parish of Inverary, and in Nether Lorn, now in Kilbrandon.

The parish of West Kilbride is bounded on the North by the parish of Largs, on the East by the parishes of Dalry and Ardrossan, on the South by the parish of Ardrossan, and on the West by the Firth of Clyde. In its widest acceptation, the parish stretches from Fairlie Burn on the North, to a point about half a mile beyond Gourock Burn on the South. A range of hills stretches along its Eastern side variously known from North to South, as Kaim, Caldrongattel, Glentane, Crosbie, and Knockgeorgan hills. Its ecclesiastical bounds are, however, somewhat more restricted, only reaching from Glenside Barn on the North, to Gourock Burn on the South, but also including the island of Little Cumbrae. These bounds have not always been the same, as previous to 1650 the baronies of Southanen and Corsbie formed part of the parish of Largs, whilst the lands of Boydstone, Monfod, and Knockewart, now in Ardrossan parish, were then attached to West Kilbride. The following extract from the Records of the Presbytery of Irvine will show one reason, in addition to their greater proximity to the Church of West Kilbride, for the disjunction of South-anen and Corsbie from the parish of Largs; inasmuch as between the parish kirk of Largs and these districts here ran a stream (the Gogo), "Whilk after rain any space becometh impassable for horses, etc., and it runneth wt sik violence yt yr is no possibilitie to get a bridge upo it." When, in 1876, Fairlie was formed into a *quoad sacra* charge, the part of Southanen Barony to the North of Glenside Burn, was detached ecclesiastically from West Kilbride, and annexed thereto. The following extract from the Presbytery records will show that the idea of a church at Fairlie, though not then carried into execution, is by no means of yesterday. February, 8th, 1648.—"The perambulators did agree that the most commodious place for a new church, both for situation and neir by a like distance from both extremities of the paroches (Largs and West Kilbride) was in the laird of Fairlie, his lands, upon ane piece of ground callet the Sand-flatt on the North syd of Fairlie-burn foot, at the distance, or neir by half ane myle from the place of Southanen, the Lord Semple his residence. The Presbyterie agree that the lands to be attached to this church sall be these:—The lands of Southanen and Gogoside, belonging to my Lord Semple: the lands of Corsbie, belonging to Auchenames; the lands of Fairlie and the lands of Kelburn, belonging to the laird of Kelburn; the lands of Ryesdale Moure, belonging to the Lord Boyd; the lands of Craiglie, belonging to the laird of Heslet; the lands, Blair Hali, belonging to Gawan Blare of Hali."

In its widest or *quoad civilia* acceptation, the parish of West Kilbride contains about 7,924 acres, Scotch, or 10,032 acres, imperial, which with foreshore would bring its superficial measurement up to about 11,000 imperial acres, or rather over 17 square miles. Of these acres nearly two-thirds are arable, and the remainder principally hill and moorland. The surface may be generally described as undulating, with a narrow level strip lying along the sea-board and a valley of considerably greater width traversing the middle of the parish, and enclosed on its Eastern and Western sides by the Crosbie and Campbelton hills, respectively. Until about the middle of last century, or even later, the greater part of this central valley was a swamp or morass, over which pedestrians threaded their way on stepping stones or kept to the ridges on the hill-sides, whilst the carriage roads wended their way around its edge. Mementoes of this fact are to be found in such names as Ladybog, and Bogriggs, as well as in the dark and mossy character of much of its soil, the gravel found at no great depth in the neighbourhood of Highthorn, and the trunks of ash and other trees disinterred from it during the past century. The part of this valley, not marshy, was largely covered with scrub and whins, especially Kilruskin braes, but extensive tile-draining, for nearly a century, has entirely changed its aspect and transformed it into one of the most fertile portions of the parish.

In addition to the hills lying along the Eastern boundary of the parish, there are scattered throughout it, several detached or isolated heights, such as Blackshaw, Law, Drummilling, Tarbert, Campbelton, and Goldenberry Hills. The configuration and structure of these hills point to volcanic agency as raising them, and glacial action as shaping them, the more abrupt slope being generally to the north. They are rounded and verdant to the top, and from their summits, under favourable weather conditions, extensive and pleasing prospects by land and sea may be had. Amongst the higher points are, Kaim Hill, 1,270 feet; Caldrongattel, 1,090 feet; Crosbie Hill, 960 feet. Glentane, 870 feet; Knock Georgan, 757 feet; Blackshaw Hill, 709 feet; Campelton Hill, 706 feet; Lawhill, 551 feet; Tarbert Hill, 446 feet; and Barr Hoy, in Little Cumbrae, 409 feet. The Eastern range is largely covered with heather, bracken, etc., interspersed with grass, and thus at once supplies a good run for sheep and a good preserve for grouse and other game. To the millstones of close-grained Brescia, or white sandstone mixed with quartz, for which Kaim Hill is remarkable, we shall have occasion to refer when treating of the industrial life of the parish. On Blackshaw Hill there is a good sandstone quarry, out of which many houses in the parish have been built. This stone is somewhat hard and difficult to work. Being strongly impregnated with iron, it is apt to become of a rusty red colour on exposure to weather. From the summits of Kaim Hill, Crosbie Hill, and Knock Georgan the views are particularly extensive, ranging from beyond Ben Lomond in the North to Ailsa Craig and Wigtonshire in the South, and from the Dumfries and Lanarkshire hills in the East to the Paps of Jura on the West Parts of seventeen counties are said to be visible from the summit of Caldongatel. In its geological structure the parish bears considerable evidence of glacial action in striated rocks at Bank End etc., and in scooped out valleys behind Auld Hill. The general geological formation or basis is coarse sandstone declining 1 in 20 to the South-East; red at shore, white, ochred with iron, in the higher parts. Through the sandstone, veins of basaltic and porphyritic trap frequently crop, as may be seen at Ardneil Bank and the Three Sisters, where we find porphyry obtruding and overhanging the prevailing red sandstone. Conglomerate of red sandstone and quartz, or puddingstone, as it is sometimes called, is also found along the coast to the North of Portincross One small patch of rock crystal, or coarse mica, near North Bank, shows a formation of parallel strata, when an effort is made to break it. The isolated hills are generally composed of whin, which may also be seen in the large boulders deposited along the shore near Seamill, apparently under ice and water action.

As a whole, the parish is well watered, though as the hills lie at no great distance from the coast, the rivulets draining it never get beyond the magnitude of streams of three or four miles in length. Of these the three principal are Glenside Burn, Kilbride Burn, and Gourock Burn. Glenside Burn drains the valley between Kaim and Glentane hills, and in its short course forms three cascades, one of which, known as Biglees Fall, throws its waters full fifty feet into a pellucid pool amid leafy shade and tangled brushwood, and then bickers on to form a few yards further down a third fall of a more broken but scarcely less picturesque character; after which it meanders through thicket and glade and reaches the sea at Fence Bay. Kilbride Burn rises to the West of Glentane Hill, flows to the South-West, and enters the sea at Seamill, after a short course of little more than four miles; yet, with sufficient volume of water in its last mile to supply motive power to more than one mill. Gourock Burn drains the Western slopes of Knock Georgan, flows through Kirkland Dell past the side of a hamlet, or clachan, and mill which once bore its own name, and mingles its waters with the sea at Glenfoot. In these streams a few trout of very small size are occasionally found whilst minnows and greybeards abound, water rats

BIGLEES WATERFALL

also are by no means unknown. The slopes drained by Kilbride Burn supply the Crosbie reservoir, whence is drawn the water supply of West Kilbride, Seamill, Portincross, etc.

With the exception of slight chalybeate impregnations in a few of the streamlets and a well on the Western slope of Kaim Hill, no mineral or medicinal waters are known to exist in the parish; but, like the Promised Land, it is a land of fountains and of springs of water, of which perhaps the purest and most abundant is Dornell Well on

South Kilruskin. A copious fountain on the Western slope of Lawhill has changed the name of Underhill to Springside. Amongst the several wells of greater or less repute in the village before the introduction of a water supply by gravitation, there was probably none more famous than one still to be seen amongst the shrubbery down Kirktonhall Glen, It was known as the "Toddy Well," from the frequency wherewith many of the villagers resorted thither with a view to obtaining a supply of water supposed to be peculiarly adapted to the making of a beverage which so many think to he a cure for all human ills and woes. Then below Ardneil Bank, there are three wells of some note; one close upon the shore a little beyond North Bank, know as Moses' Well, or Horeb, because it springs out of a cleft in the naked rock and fills a small bowl-shaped basin and thus reminds one of the scriptural incidents wherewith these names are associated. Another, near the entrance to Auchenames House, is known as Joseph's Well, because an object of peculiar care to one Joseph Weiss, who once lived at no great distance. The third is the "Wishing Well," near a cave or rock-shelter in the face of the cliff immediately above Bank End, or, as it is commonly called, the Deil's Elbow. "Wishing" is here a corruption of the Saxon "Visa-an, Wisian or Wissian," a philosopher or sage, wiseman or instructor, and therefore the Wishing Well means "The Instructor's Well." There is no authentic or well supported tradition of any particular wiseman being associated with this well; there is, however, abundance of circumstantial evidence to show that the contiguous cave had in early times been used as a shelter or habitation. We are also informed by skilled antiquarians that Scottish wells were largely frequented by Celtic saints from Ireland, and that one of St. Ninian's pupils, who had fled from his master because of the excessive use of the rod, came to Scotia in a vessel of wicker-work, where he was hospitably welcomed and led to a shelter. Here he planted his staff, which became an ash tree, with a fountain of limpid water welling up near its root. May not this have been the spot where he landed and found a shelter This is all the more probable as Briguid Point close by was for long a favourite place for anchorage.

We are further informed that caves with wells were frequently resorted to on the first Sunday of May, for the cure of certain diseases, and that there, baptism was not seldom administered by some pious recluse or saintly cleric. Who then might he be who, long centuries ago, came to this rock-shelter, drank of this Wishing Well, and here dispensed the initiatory rite of our most holy faith. We know not for certain, but this we are told, that St. Kentigern retired for a time to a desert place and that he was fond of bathing. Now, such a retreat as this could well supply both desiderations; and this we know that the name of Kentigern was afterwards found in the Hunterstone family, the proprietors of the estate; and that in the person of Quentigern Hunter, who fell at the battle of Pinkie in 1547. Is it then too great a stretch of the imagination to conjecture that St. Kentigern may have been at least one of the wisemen who found here a safe retreat far from the busy haunts of men, and that he may even have given the well its name?

The cave contiguous to this well has a total length of twenty-seven feet, with an average width and height of about six feet. The entrance is at first wide and open, but suddenly contracts to a recess nine feet in length, four feet in breadth, and six feet in height. The floor is damp,

the roof, weather and water-worn. The large number of
shells found in the rabbit burrows close at band, first
called attention to the possibility of excavations there
yielding some useful results. Accordingly, a few years
ago, in presence of Lieutenant Colonel G. Hunter
Weston, Dr. Cochrane Patrick, and Prof. Cleland, a
thorough exploration of the cave was made. By digging
down to a depth of six feet to the native rock near its
mouth, evidence was found of three distinct floors, at the
respective depths of eighteen, thirty, and thirty-nine
inches, with layers of shells, whelk, mussel, and cockle,
between the ordinary trodden sand. Above the lowest
floor, there were found chiefly amongst the ash deposit,
pieces of charcoal, two stone objects—one of flint and
the other of slate—a few specimens of slag and of broken
pottery—some of a coarse reddish hue, without any
glaze, and some of a thinner and better make, with a
green glaze—the hones of a rabbit, of a young cat, of a
pig, of a peculiar deerlike sheep, of a small species of ox,
(Bos Longifrons) and of red deer, along with a few traces
of reindeer. Between the upper and lower floors there
were found the bones of horses, and between the middle
and third floors, those of a dog. The bones of a goat were
also discovered. Most of these bones seemed to have
been broken up with a view to getting at the marrow, not
for food, but for purposes of light and fuel. Here then at
different periods when the parish formed as yet but part
of a large hunting-ground, the pious recluse, or the roving
huntsman, or the rude untutored serf, has found a shelter
from the storms of heaven, food for his hungry appetite,
and a resting-place for his wearied frame. There is
another cave at the South end of Ardneil Bank under a
thick bed of quartzite conglomerate with crushed

pebbles, which in so far as known, has never been so thoroughly explored.

The coastline of the parish, of which there is upwards of seven miles, consists for the most part of low and shelving rocks, interspersed, as at Seamill and Ardneil Bay, with a few stretches of sand suitable for sea-bathing. Hence, with the exception of the portion opposite Ardneil Bank, the shore water is shallow and its navigation hampered with rocky islets visible at low water. From Farland Point, near Portincross, which is the most westerly point of Ayrshire, the coast-line, for upwards of a mile to the North, becomes more rugged, and, in the fantastic shape assumed by much of the red conglomerate, shows how true it is that the waters wear the stones. Running parallel to this mile of rugged coast, at a distance of three hundred yards inland, or thereby, there is a precipitous bank, generally known as Ardneil Bank, which at its highest point reaches an elevation of well-nigh three hundred feet. Near its South end is Auld Hill, with its traces of a vitrified fort and an old castle, of which more hereafter. A little to the North, a trap dyke breaks through and runs down to the coast, which would have effectually barred further progress for cart or carriage, had it not been cut through by an opening called the" Nick, or "Throughlet." For a short distance thereafter the bank becomes less precipitous and sweeps round in a grassy, coppice clad slope to the North-East, which slope is known as the "Howgate" or "Windy How." Passing behind North Bank Farm, the Bank again becomes very steep, and has its lower reaches covered with natural wood and coppice; amongst which are strewn large fragments of rock, confusedly hurled under the action of rain and frost from the overhanging cliffs.

The three highest of these cliffs are well-known as "The Three Sisters," (Meg, Jean, and Lizzie,) "The Three Jeans," or "The Three Nuns." They are composed of red

ARDNEIL BANK AND "THE THREE SISTERS"

sandstone, surmounted by brownish porphyry, and separated from each other by deep recesses or scars, up which brushwood and ivy irregularly scramble. The upper half of these precipitous cliffs towers clear above the coppice of ash, oak, plane, hazel and hawthorn, in which the lower half is swathed, and their inaccessible lichen covered recesses are a favourite haunt for a few hawks and a multitude of jackdaws. According to an old tradition, diamonds are said to have been seen by fishermen at sea, sparkling by night in the face of these cliffs, but, unfortunately, none have ever been found. Various. tales of hairbreadth escapes are associated with these precipices.

We find the following in notes left behind by the late Dr. Ritchie:—"One of the innkeepers in the village when fox-hunting once fell over the cliffs towards the North end of the bank, and though bruised, was not seriously injured. On another occasion, J. M'M., whilst engaged in the same sport, lost his footing on the sloped recess between the 'Sisters,' fired off his musket, and was precipitated nearly three hundred feet. His fall, however, was broken by projecting rocks and trees, and though taken up insensible, he ultimately recovered."

But foxes were far from being the sole tenants of the wilder recesses of this bank. In former days neither badgers nor polecats were unknown, while such a name as the "Hawking Craig" given to a a cliff to the North of the "Three Sisters," reminds us of the sparrow and goshawks, which formerly found a safe retreat in larger numbers than now, amongst the inaccessible crannies of the rocks and the labyrinthine mazes of the ivy and copsewood. These goshawks were for long in special demand for hunting purposes, being eagerly sought after by royalty and nobility. Hence so recently as 1822, and as preparatory to the visit of George IV. to Scotland, we find the redoubtable old falconer, Fleming, of Barochan in Renfrewshire, and his trusty old retainer, John Anderson, enjoined to procure eyeses to be trained and presented to his majesty; of which eyeses they were understood to have been successful in obtaining a number from eyries in Ardneil Bank.

The capture of these hawks was far from being unattended with danger, as the following exploit associated with the securing of a nest of "gentle falcons" for the noble family of Kelburn, will shew. The nest being in a recess on the brow of one of the "Sisters," Baldie Malcolm, who was to be its barrier, had a rope fastened to the top of the cliff, by means of which he let himself down to the requisite depth. By swinging himself backward and forward, he gained the recess; but whilst securing his booty he allowed the rope to slip from his grasp. Over the giddy steep it dangled, but beyond his reach. Having tried every other mode of escape in vain, he at length made a desperate leap, caught the rope, swung him. self upward, and reached the top in safety with his spoil. In the crannied shores just off the bank, otters and seals have been rarely seen, whilst the owl still doses in the rocky chambers tapestried with the ever-green ivy, which protects him from the annoyance of his mid-day foes.

To the northern part of this bank, the name "Deil's Elbow" has been assigned,—a relic of those superstitious times when posts of danger and deeds of outlawry were associated with the nether world. This name, however, is more commonly associated with the semi-ruinous cottage standing close by the shore in front of the "Wishing Well," and has hitherto resisted all attempts of former proprietors to give it some more euphemistic title, such as "Lilyburn Cottage," or "Bankend." Here lived with his sister, some forty years ago, a young man who stole out in a bitterly cold January night and drowned himself in a curious recess amongst the rocks; and here, too, about-forty years before that, occurred the romantic escapade of a granddaughter, of the Rev. Arthur Oughterstone, a former minister of this parish. Her father in Greenock had allotted her for the wife of a rich old man there,—but as this was utterly repugnant to her youth and beauty, "she came down," as the late Dr. Ritchie has graphically put it, "to live at a distance from her ancient suitor's importuni-ties, and found a refuge in her grandfather's manse. She associated freely with the people of the district, and is alleged to have fallen violently in love with a young man, then a farm-servant with his uncle at Fences, often walking out to talk with him at his work. This eccentric conduct would doubtless subject her to additional restraint, to the expostulations of her grandfather, to the remonstrances of his housekeeper, and to the gossip of the country. Pressed on every side, she resolved upon a plan of escape. She accordingly left the Manse one day, without returning at eleven p.m., the hour when its inmates were wont to retire to rest. Her anxious grandfather forthwith summoned two well tried, and trustworthy messengers, who at once set out upon a search that proved futile alike that day and the next. Others were then despatched, her family was written to; she was publicly advertised, rewards were offered; they sought her East, they sought her West, no field, no house, they could think of, no ditch, no pit, no moss, no well, no rock, no creek, in the district, was left unexplored. Still, for three weeks no clue nor trace of Ann Oughterstone, could be found, until one day Mary Malcolm, an old fishwife, who was passing Deil's Elbow on her wonted road to the North, called at the door, which she found fastened from within. On looking in at the window, however, she caught a glimpse of a handsome foot, arrayed, it is said, in a white silk stocking, disappearing in a box bed. This made a deep impression on her mind and quickened her curiosity. So graceful a foot could not be Mirn Pock's, the tenant of the house. There was not sic' another foot atween Gourock Burn and the Gogo, but one! Who could solve her doubts and satisfy the desire of her soul but the priest of the parish, and to him she went. The old man, who had at least been equally perplexed, applied to his well-tried messengers, who lost no time in embracing the opportunity to discover the long lost sheep." Here for three weeks she had obtained a safe asylum, although, it is said, the crofter of the day had not been very willing to take her in, as she could neither "milk the kye," nor be of any special service to him. When found, she was only induced by some constraint to return to the Manse, and would only enter it in her own way. When she had been thus secured, she was conveyed, on the arrival of her brother next morning, to Greenock, where, however, she still continued to repel the suit of the rich old bachelor. She afterwards emigrated to the West Indies, and married a man more according to her heart. Another less probable version of the story represents her as eloping with a young boarder from Carlung House, then a boarding school, and having been discovered as above, but able to produce satisfactory evidence of her marriage with the young gentleman.

Musical sands at Ardneil Bay, which emit a peculiar low musical sound when disturbed with the wind or feet, ought to have been mentioned earlier. Proceeding north-ward along the coast, from Bankend we very soon come upon the Black Rocks which form a happy hunting-ground for shell-fish gatherers; and Briguid Point, where used to be a favourite anchorage and ferry for the opposite shores of the Cumbraes.

Still farther North, we reach the Hunterston and Southanen sands, where the tide recedes for nearly a mile to a pillar called the "Perch," erected to warn vessels off a treacherous shore. These sands are very uninviting and dangerous to traverse, being largely composed of the reduced sludge brought down by the Clyde and here thrown aside by the counteracting tide. It often occurs to us, that, had these sands been in Holland, long ere now an earthen or stone wall, or dyke, would have reclaimed them from the sea and transformed them into fertile fields. At various parts along the shore, gravel is found in considerable abundance though in diminishing quantities, and large quantities of seaweed are annually gathered to serve as manure. Of such seaweed upwards of thirty varieties are found. Some of the most common are these,—if we may be allowed to give them in their collo-quial rather than their botanical names, viz:—Bladder-wort, Oar Weed, Ribbon Wreck, Dulce, Tangle, Coralline, Carrageen or Irish Moss, Green Laver, Sea Grasses, etc. The eggs of the Skate and Dog-fish, are occasionally found intermingled. The ordinary shells found off the Scottish coast abound, such as those of the Sea-Urchin, Whelk, Limpet, Cockle, Mussel, Razor, as well as Cat's Cradles, Clams, Silver Willies, etc. Star-Fish, Sea Anemones, and Sticklebacks frequent the pools; whilst Crabs of the spider and other varieties, and Lobsters, find a congenial home in the watery caverns opposite Ardneil Bank. Fish such as Saithe, Lytbe, Ling, Cod, Haddocks, Whitings, Flounders, Herring, Mackerel, Sea Trout, and Salmon in small numbers, are caught off the coast.

The soil of the parish is, generally speaking, fertile, but on the higher ground it is sometimes poor, spongy and moorish. Towards the close of last century, the Old Statistical Account represents it as of three kinds, *first*, a very light dry sandy soil with a mixture of good earth; *second*, mossy; and *third*, a strong tilly clay. Along the sea board it is generally of the first kind, largely inter-mixed with shells, and thus pointing to a time when it probably was submerged beneath the sea. In the interior it is mainly formed of decomposed red sandstone, and in some places of pulverized basaltic rock. The central valley is mossy. The natural fertility of the soil has been greatly improved by cultivation, and not a few of the most productive acres of the parish have been reclaimed from whin, heather, bracken, and moss, within the past 150 years, or less.

The fauna or wild animals of the district are comparatively few and belong to the smaller orders. Foxes preserved for sport, are principally to be found at Ardneil Bank, Boydstone Bank, and amongst the hills. Rabbits are abundant, but Hares and Leverets are gradually disappearing. Had Shakespeare lived in our day and parish, he need not have experienced much difficulty in finding his Land-Rats, and Water-Rats, as well as a galaxy of other vermin such as Hedgehogs, Weasels, Mice, Shrews, Moles, Frogs, Snails, etc.

Many quadrupeds once found, are either, now extinct, or nearly so. Deer, undoubtedly, once roamed over the parish, as is proved by the skeleton of a stag whose antlers had twenty tynes, disinterred in 1573 during the construction of a drain in a small field below Springside House; by the bones of red and reindeer found in the Rockshelter above Deil's Elbow; and by the authentic record of their existence in Little Cumbrae, up to 1594. In that island, too, wild goats were to be found up to the beginning of this present century; and we have already spoken of the Badgers, Polecats and Otters that once frequented Ardneil Bank. Such names as "Wild Cat Road" and "Cat Craigs" also plainly point to the native wild cat as formerly common.

The feathered tribes are of the usual varieties, and include Crows, Jackdaws, Starlings, Pigeons, Magpies, Blackbirds, Thrushes, Sparrows, Redbreasts, Linnets, Larks, Finches, Wagtails, Coots, and many others. In early Summer, the woods and glens are resonant with the

notes of the Cuckoo. Hawks flutter o'er Ardneil Bank
and Little Cumbrae. Owls hoot in Hunterstone Woods,
Herons build their nests in Bawlies Wood. Wild Ducks,
Scarfs and Stockanats frequent Southanen sands and the
mares of Little Cumbrae. Eagles are but rarely seen, and
the Teal, Widgeon, and Capercalzie, mentioned in one of
the old Hunterstone legends, are now extinct. Black Cock
and Grouse, introduced to their heathery haunts about the
beginning of this century, afford good sport in their
season on Crosbie and other hills. Partridges are by no
means abundant, and Pheasants are for the most part
hand-fed.

Insect life of the usual type, Flies, Bees, Butterflies,
Moths, Cockroaches, etc., etc., is abundant. The flora of
the parish is rich and varied. In early Spring, Crosbie glen
is blooming white with Snowdrops; and the Howe at
Ardneil Bank is bespangled with a profusion of
Primroses, Horehound, and Wild Thyme, in early
summer. Then, too, Yellow Daffodils bedeck the braes
by Gourock Burn; whilst the woods of Yonderfield and
Poteath are in June a sheet of living blue with the Wild
Hyacinths which clothe their shades. Daisies, Buttercups,
Kingcups, Blue-Bells, Thistles, Wild Geraniums and a
countless variety, more of the smaller wild flowers,
bespangle Nature's verdant carpet with their rich and
varied hues. Wild Roses and Honeysuckle intersperse the
hedgerows, Whin and Broom bloom on the braes, and the
Ivy with its evergreen mantle climbs fall oft where no
other life is to he seen. Brambles, Rasps, and Sloes await
their gatherers in Autumn, and Hazel Nuts are not
unknown. There are from twenty to thirty varieties of
Ferns to be found in the parish; amongst which may he
mentioned the Hart's Tongue, found in the woods below

the "Three Sisters," where also the Royal Fern was once to be got,—the Buckler's Shield, Lady, and Hay Scented Ferns; the Native, and Black Maiden Hair Ferns, the Oak, the Beech, the Fox or Hard Ferns, and many varieties of Polypods. The district is also peculiarly rich in Cryptogams, Fungi, Mosses, and Lichens. The Sundew, or Drosera, a small flower to be found in the wood near Hopeton, has this peculiarity, that it seems to be insectivorous. It exudes a gum to which the insect adheres, and then, like the spider, sucks its substance into its structure. Bulrushes are to be found in a quarry near the Gill. Upwards of thirty kinds of Grasses grow in the parish, which are capable of a threefold classification into Agricultural, Hill-Pasture, and Sea-Side Grasses. The late Rev. D. Landsborough, of Stevenston, has given the following list of rarer plants to be found in this parish:— "Crow Garlic, Sea-Arrow Grass, Marsh-Arrow Grass, Hare's foot Trefoil, Skull Cap, Wood Melic Grass, Wood-Vetch, Bloody Crane's Bill, Seaside Free Mallow, Bog Pimpernel, Seaside Gromwell, Parsley Water Dropwort, Burnet Saxifrage, Anthriscus, Yellow Horned Poppy, Sea Rocket, Lady's Fingers, Small Upright St. John's Wort, Tutsane St. John's Wort, Pale Butter Wort, Reed, Lovage, Melic Grass, Golden Rod, Black Bog Rush, Sea Radish, Wall Pennywort, Decumbent Heath Crass, Broadleaved Water Parsnips, Whorled Carraway. Enchanter's Night Shade, Common Hart's Tongue, Plumy Crested Feather Moss, Langwort Sticta, Shining Hookina, Broadleaved Bell Flower, Round leaved Sundew, Swine Cress, Sea Holly, Water Pimpernel, Hemp's Agrimony, Wild Carrot."

The woods of the parish, which cover upwards of two hundred acres are partly natural,—as at Crosbie,

Southanen, and Ardneil Bank,—but mostly planted and of no great age. The largest trees are found amongst the Beeches of Crosbie Glen, and the Firs and Ashes of Hunterston; one ash tree near the garden gate. known as the Rest-Tree, having the reputation of being the largest and oldest ash tree in the county. Beneath its shade in bygone days, wearied travellers, exhausted with peat digging, and jaded carriers were wont to rest themselves and their horses, paying by way of toll to the feudal superior, the laird of Hunterston, a "neive-a-fu" of the goods they carried, such as meal, etc. The trees principally grow on sloping ground, and include many varieties besides those already mentioned, such as Plane, Poplar, Elm, Oak, Birch, Chesnut, Lime, Cedar, Willow, Alder, Holly, Hawthorn, Laburnum. The timber produced is largely, though not exclusively used for home purposes, such as fencing.

The mineral productions include Mill-Stones, Free-Stone, Whin-Stone. Coal is reported to have been seen as an outcrop in the bed of the burn above Bawlies; and the late Dr. Ritchie was wont to adduce the authority of one James Paterson, for the existence of coal in small quantities on Hunterston estate; two borings having been taken, one to the South of Campbelton, and another at Holehouse. This attempt seems to have been made towards the close of last century, and there is a tradition that further search was arrested by bribery. The iron impregnations in the streams and sandstone to the Exist of the parish indicate the presence of that mineral at no great distance.

The roads in the district may be generally described as good and well-kept. The turnpike from Glasgow to Ayr traverses the length of the parish, and is a great

favourite with cyclists. Previous to 1750, however, the
parish roads were little better than mere tracks filled up
with field stones, and were far from taking the easiest
gradients—since the avoiding of morasses and the securing of dry ground led the roadmakers of those days to
keep to the ridges. After that date, they began to be
macadamized, the hollows to be filled up and the inclines
to be reduced. Until 1830, the main turnpike road kept
much nearer the sea between Chapelton and Seamill, than
it now does. It passed between pillars still standing
beyond Seamill and Yonderfield, skirted the West and
North of the central morass, and passed Thirdpart,
Campbelton, and the Rest-Tree at Hunterston. In some
parts the whins at the road sides were so high as to
overtop a cart of straw, whilst their roots were as thick as
a man's body. Rights of way, some of them for foot,
passengers, and some for carts and carriages, either
formerly existed or still exist; *first*, from Monfod past
Boydstone, thence below Kirkland, past Meadowhead
and Tarbert Castle to the present Ardrossan road, near
Meadowfoot; *second*, from a point about a quarter of a
mile past Meadowhead, through fields on the farms of
Meadowhead, Yonderton, etc., to Hopeton; *third*, the old
Dairy road wending round the North side of Lawhill past
Hopeton and along the North side of Knockewart Hill to
a point on the present Dalry road between Gill and
Munnock; *fourth*, from the Hunterston to the Kilruskin
road past Milstonford; *fifth*, from the Cemetery road
round Drummilling Hill to Kilruskin road; *sixth*, from
Overton by Bowfield to Seamill; *seventh*, from the foot
of Well Bank near centre of village up a back footpath to
a point of exit on the Portincross road; and *eighth*, from
High Seamill to Glenhead. The western portion of the

present Dalry road was only made in 1820. The Kilruskin road was that chosen by the mail coach from Ayr to Greenock. Halfway Street was for long the main road through the village to the sea, as its name indicates. being derived from the Norwegian "Haaf" (the sea). The western part of Ritchie Street was formed about 1826, the cost being defrayed by money voted by Government to provide work for the unemployed. Before that a road probably led by Alton to the sea. The incline in the middle of the village was long known as "Paton's Brae," from a weaver of that name who dwelt in a house by its tide. The progress of building in the vicinity of the village and Seamill is leading and doubtless will continue to lead to the formation of new roads. Up to 1883, the upkeep of the roads was maintained by dues levied at toll-bars near Kilruskin, Bighthorn, Holmfoot, and Meadowfoot, where junctions, of road occurred. This burden the county rates have now to bear.

Of the older bridges in the parish two may be mentioned, viz., one over Kilbride Burn in Main Street, for which we are probably indebted, as the inscription on a stone in its centre indicates, to Jane, Countess of Crawford, who, in 1623, the date of its erection, was living in Law Castle; and another over the Gourock Burn on the high road to Ardrossan, popularly known as "Tailor Loup Bridge" owing to a somewhat incredible tale of a fatal leap taken in its vicinity by a tailor when pursued by an infuriated bull.

The climate of the parish is moist but salubrious, the temperature being fairly equable, though the sky is seldom altogether cloudless. The prevailing winds are from the South and South-West, and these are not seldom charged with rain. Easterly winds in early Spring are cold and fraught with mist. The Old Statistical Account tells us that the prevalent rains are in Spring and Autumn; and that the more common diseases are:—rheumatics, perip-neumony, palsies, quinsy, and nervous diseases, which are more prevalent in coast than in inland parishes. As illustrative of the salubrity of the climate, it speaks of a man who had recently died in Little Cumbrae at the advanced age of a hundred and one; and it then adds that smallpox, when they are of a virulent kind, carry off a good many; and hitherto all efforts to introduce inocula-tion have failed, as no arguments can overcome the superstitious opinions of the people, or their dread of popular odium.

Thus have we endeavoured to treat of the leading physical features of this parish. In their bold general outline they are today what for centuries past they have been, but we have the record of unwritten story treasured up in Nature's Library,—the testimony of the soil and the rocks—to shew that it has not always been so; that long before the era of written history, the sea overflowed a considerable part of its surface even up to the neigh-bourhood of the village,—as may be seen from the deposits of sand, gravel and shells that lie buried a few feet below the surface; and that under volcanic action not a few hills have obtruded themselves upon the scene, so that the mountains even are not always so everlasting as we are wont to speak of them. But whilst the same bold outlines of hill and dale, of land and sea, have presented themselves to the view of countless generations, the aspect of the surface has greatly altered under the hand of cultivation. Where now the central morass over which the wary pedestrian threaded his way? Where now the whins of. Carlung or Campbelton taller than a man? Where now the stunted scrub of Kilruskin braes or the heath-clad slopes of Hauplands? All gone with the process of the suns and the progress of Agriculture. Thus are we reminded that future generations may very probably gaze upon a landscape similar in its general features to ours, yet, in its details, not a little different, as human science and art continue to operate upon its surface. Still, we may rest assured that the same varied and pleasing prospects, which delight our eyes and enrapture our souls, as we survey the changing view from one or other of the many points of vantage within the district, will continue to be things of beauty and sources of joy to many a generation yet unborn, inspiring renewed energy into many a jaded frame, and new life into many a drooping heart.

# CHAPTER II.
## THE TOPOGRAPHY OF THE PARISH.

WITH regard to the ancient topography of West Kilbride, but little definite or authentic is known, except in so far as present-day names of places point to more ancient forms indicative of early origin. Amongst such names we may mention Poteath, formerly Paltreath (the Hall or the Mansion or the Chief) thought by some to have been the original name of the Hunterston estate—Ardneil, formerly Arnele (Neil's Knope or Rock-Fort)—Yonder-field and Yonderton, (the Field or Town of the Eond or Giant Hero) Goldenberry, formerly Goudenberry, (the Hero's Camp),—Caldrongattel, (the Burying Place of the Celtic Chief),—Carlung (the Place of Defence on a Flat Plain),—Trail Isle, formerly Allinturail, (the Islet of the Noble's Tower). More modern names are to a large extent self explanatory. Many of them are indicative of position, e.g., Bushglen, Law, Lawbill, Lawwoodhead, Meadowhead, Meadowfoot, Glenhead, Glenfoot, Bank, Bankend, Croftfoot, Woodside, Seamill. Others point to previous proprietors, e.g., Hunterstone, Boydstone, Campbelton. Ecclesiastical associations have plainly bestowed their appellations upon not a few places, such as, Kilbride, Kilruskin—formerly Kilronskan—South-anen, Kirkland, Kirktonhall, Kirkstead, Chapelton. The existence of the central morass is embalmed in Bogriggs and Ladybog. Gill tells of the presence of a bickering waterfall, and Blackshaw of a dark moor. Hauplands, which some identify with Hapelands i.e., halfpenny lands, is more probably a corruption of Whauplands, and reminds us of the time when more frequently than now,

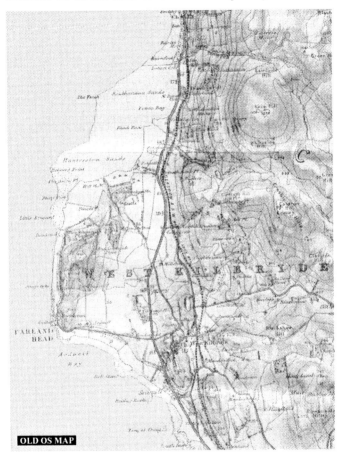

OLD OS MAP

the cry of the curlew broke in upon the solitude of its moorland heaths. Faulds means "Fields." Thirdpart is plainly the third part of an estate or larger farm. Cubrieshaw is Cow-brae-shaw, i.e., the brae and moor grazed by the cow. At Millstonford, the Kaim Hill millstones must at one time have been carried over stream and bog. Diamond Craig points to the fine rock crystal or mica schist still to be found upon it.

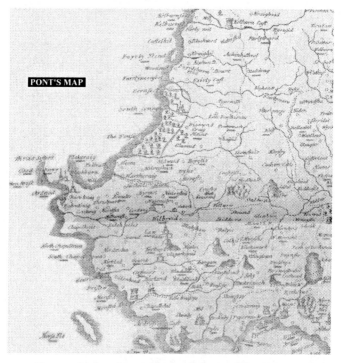

PONT'S MAP

For centuries the surface of the parish was comprehended under seven large estates, or baronies, viz., Southanen, Crosbie, Kilbride, Tarbet, Carlung, Ardneil or Portincross, and Hunterston. Of these, two have been broken up into smaller estates, viz., Kilbride, into Orchard, Springside, Newton Moor, Blackshaw, Gateside, Cubrieshaw, Lower Drummilling or the Stripe,

Coldstream, Nethermiln, Yonderton, Lawhill; and Carlung into Carlung, Drummilling, Millstonford, Woodside, Kirktonhall, and Overton.

The topography of the parish has been considerably influenced by the tendency which has been going on for more than a century to absorb two or more smaller farms into one. This tendency has led either to the obliteration of many names of places, or their retention as mere names of fields. Where, for example, on the estate of Crosbie, shall we find a vestige of Thornescheillis, Quhytside, Meille, Skirricraw, or Glentowne, mentioned, along with other farms still existing, in the last will and testament of Patrick Crawford, of Auchenames, in 1649. The Glentowne, a small fragment of whose ruins still stands by the roadside near Blackshaw, was a comparatively modern erection, built for a Mr. Smellie, a retired farmer of Gill. Where now are Knockhead, Syde, Meikle, and Little Underhill, mentioned in the valuation of the parish in 1640. Netherton and Broomcraig have equally disappeared from the Hunterstone estate; and High Seamill, Knowheid, and Sandilands from the Tarbet Barony; although their former sites may still be known. Glaisterland i.e., Glebeland, and Corsemuir, are now only to be found as names of fields on the farm of Meadowhead. When we look into Bleau's map of the parish, published in 1655, we find not a few names with which we are no longer familiar, e g., Glamud, Hoom, Heathercraig or Harthcraig, Aldwood, Woodhead, Kilburn, Layerksmill, Bristou, Byd, Hirdmelia, Ridshiels, Cordung, Millburnst, Hardsa, Kamelts, Dyrmel, Warmelyn Penruth, Stairns, etc., etc. Some of these have doubtless been modernized, as Hirdmelia into Thirdmailing, Kamelts into Campbelton, Warmelyn into Drummilling;

and others have changed their names, as Ridshiels into Bowfield, but the majority of them have passed into oblivion with the disappearance of the places they represented. Such a fact as this at once reminds us, that in bygone generations the rural part of the parish sustained a much larger population than now. A considerable portion of the morass between Highthorn and Thirdpart would appear at one time to have been common lands, afterwards appropriated by, and apportioned among, the adjoining proprietors. Hence the small fields into which it is still divided. Until a few decades ago, a joiner's shop and smithy stood at Highthorn, the latter of which has been incorporated in the dwelling-house of the proprietrix.

Mills were once much more numerous in the parish than now. Nearly all traces, beyond mere vestiges of their dams and lades, have accordingly disappeared, of a charcoal mill at Nethermill, of a Lintmill at Glenbride, of meal mills at Layerksmill near Tarbet, of Gray's Mill near Crosbie, of Gourock Mill, between Kirkland and Glenhead, to each of which latter meal mills it is probable that some of the neighbouring farms would be thirled by way of being bound to grind a certain proportion of their grain produce at them. Beside Gourock Mill there was also a clachan of whose existence the only reminders now are the daffodils, whose roots were once probably thrown out from the cottars' gardens, and the spindle whorls occasionally found in its neighbourhood as well as at Chapelton. These spindle whorls are small circular polished stones about the size of a penny with a hole in the centre, which were formerly fastened to the thicker end of the spindle, by way of lending weight to it in the twisting of the yarn. They are still used in India. Some have called them "Elf-stones," in which case they would probably be worn as charms against the mischievous tricks of the brownies.

But if the aspect of the rural part of the parish has considerably altered during the bygone centuries, not less has the appearance of the village. A hamlet, there has probably been since 1306 or earlier, for at that date we find Robert the Bruce giving a grant of the lands of the Barony of Kilbride to the Boyds, a branch of the Kilmarnock family, and if, as some think, St. Bride's Chapel was founded not long after the building of Kilwinning Abbey in 1140, as a vicarage dependent thereon, then probably it would not be long until houses gathered round it—if they were not there before it. There is an old tradition that a seafaring man built the first house in the village, in the hollow near the Cross, and that ere long a hamlet sprang up around it, with a smith and wright's shop, a public house, a general store, and a place of worship. But whatever may have been the aspect of the village in those early times, we have abundance of evidence to prove, that since the latter half of last century its aspect has greatly changed. Then there were but few slate-roofed houses in it, but now they are more plentiful than thatched ones then were. Then there was no Ritchie Street, and flax grew where the Horse Shoe now is. Then, there was only one shop in the place; and steps jutted out into the street at nearly every door, with not a few outside stairs. Then a blacksmith's shop stood right opposite the western end of the Church-yard, and until little more than thirty years ago a conglomeration of buildings projected into the street at the Cross, consisting of an old barn and a butcher's dwelling house and shop, thus rendering the street very narrow at that point. Low thatched houses stood, where the Clydesdale Bank and adjoining properties now are. Forty years ago, weavers' shops were to be seen on every hand, now they are rapidly disappearing.

Whilst there are a few houses in the village marked with the initials of their proprietors or builders and the dates of their erection, there is only one which takes us beyond the bounds of last century—but it is the most interesting house in the village, being Kirktonhall House, the birthplace of the eminent mathematician, Professor Robert Simson. It stands about the centre of the village with its back to the street, with the letters R. S. and M. W.—the initials of his grandfather and grandmother carved upon a stone on that side, and the date 1660, which was the date of the original building. It was so greatly altered in 1791 as to be largely rebuilt, and was still further enlarged in 1868 by the addition of the present kitchen and chapel. The room, in which the professor was born, is said to be the second window to the right of the front door entrance.

KIRKTONHALL HOUSE AND PROFESSOR SIMSON'S DIAL

The estate of which it forms the mansion-house contains about one hundred and thirty-five acres, made up of a part of the five pound lands of Overton and the ten pound lands of Carlung. It is generally believed that Robert Simson, the professor's grandfather, purchased it from Alexander Cunningham, the then proprietor. This Robert Simson, or some of his descendants, was also for a time proprietor of Knockewart. Previous to their removal to Kirktonhall, the family are said to have resided at North Thirdpart, and there is a tradition that being of obscure and humble origin, Robert Simson was enabled to make the purchase by means of a deposit of treasure accidentally found in a stone basin by one of the girls in the family, when playing about. There are still some venerable pear trees in the garden or orchard attached to the house, which are said to be coeval with the original building. In front of the house stands the professor's dial, bearing the initials of his father and mother, I. S. and A. S., and at one time, though now obliterated, the date 1717. It has further an armorial shield bearing three crescents, representative of the stages of life. In the old church-yard there used to be a tombstone with the following inscription—"This is the place appointed for the burial of Robert Simson of Kirktonhall, Writer in Kilbride, his wife and children, 1639, R.S., M.W."

Robert Simson, L.L.D., was born at Kirktonhall, October 14th, 1687, O.S. He was one of a family of seventeen sons, only six of whom reached manhood; a brother being Thomas Simson, M.D., Professor of Medicine at St. Andrews. His parents were John Simson and Agnes, daughter of the Rev. Robert Simpson, minister of Renfrew. He was educated at Glasgow University, and was originally destined for the Church; a project which he abandoned owing to his inability to prove to his

satisfaction certain theological doctrines. At an early age
be taught the class of Oriental Languages, during the
Professor's absence through illness, and is said to have
been very proficient in theology and botany, with a
strong predilection from his early years for the analysis
of the ancient geometers. For upwards of fifty years he
was Professor of Mathematics in the University of
Glasgow, and his lectures were marked by perspicuity of
method and language. By his students he was respected
and loved. He translated and edited Euclid, supplying the
lacunae in Book V. Hence he has been called the
Restorer of Euclid. He also published a work on Conic
Sections. His fame as a mathematician, especially in pure
geometry, is world-wide. Lord Brougham, his biogra-
pher, considered him one of the four great philosophers
of the reign of George III.—Black, Priestly, and Cavend-
ish, being the other three. He died at Glasgow University
in 1708, and his remains were interred in Blackfriars'
Burying Ground. From a marble tablet with a Latin
inscription surmounting his grave, we learn that he was a
man of old-fashioned, but honourable, simplicity of
manners as well, as of signal integrity; and that he was
the one man who restored to its pristine splendour the
geometry of the ancient Greeks—after it had lain buried
for nearly 2000 years. His portrait adorns the walls of
Glasgow University. His estate of Kirktonhall he
bequeathed to his nephew; his collection of mathematical
books and manuscripts to his Alma Mater. The use of
these latter, which are of special value because of his
notes, is regulated by special rules.

In personal appearance he was a man of commanding stature, of fine countenance, and of graceful carriage.
Unless in mourning, he dressed largely in white. He was

never married. A vast fund of general information gave a charm to his conversation. He was extremely methodical in his habits; his hours of study, of exercise, and of amusement, being all regulated with unerring precision. Even his walks in the College Square, or garden paths, were measured and limited to so many hundred paces. He had a great fund of humour, was very fond of whist at his club, and usually dined every Saturday at the village of Anderston, then half-a-mile distant from Glasgow. Because of an elongated nose he is said to have been able to drink his toddy only out of a glass of a peculiar shape, which, when accidentally broken by a servant, had to be specially re-made. One or two amusing anecdotes are still current with regard to him. On one occasion an intruder on introducing himself as "Robert Simson, Esq., of Kirktonhall," was greeted with the reply, "Then, God preserve us, I'm an impostor." On the discovery of one of the most important lacunae in Euclid, Book V., over which he had been thinking for a long time, he exclaimed, "I've got it," just at the moment when he accidentally, in his abstraction of thought, came against a tree, and had accordingly the answer returned by one who was present, "Ay, you have nearly brained yourself."

Sir John Moore, the hero of Corunna, was maternally related to him, and Francis Jeffrey, the great critic and reviewer was married to a relative of his. Through the exertions of the late Mr. Fullerton of Overton, and very largely at his expense, there has been erected to his memory a monument in the centre of West Kilbride cemetery, which is a prominent feature in the landscape. This monument which is fifty feet high, takes the form of an octagon of two tiers; the lower of plain ashlar work, with a gateway in the East front; the upper ornamented with a pilaster at each corner, the whole being surmounted by a copula and globe. On a marble tablet within, there is the following inscription:—

TO
## DR. ROBERT SIMSON,
*of the University of Glasgow,*
the Restorer of Grecian Geometry; and by his Works the
Great Promoter of its Study in the Schools.
*A Native of this Parish.*
"And buried learning rose, redeemed to a new morn."

In 1789, the estate of Kirktonhall passed out of the Simsons' hands into those of F. C. Ritchie, shipmaster, Greenock, to whose heirs it still belongs.

Another man, who has given celebrity to West Kilbride as his native place, was General Robert Boyd, who was assistant to General Elliot during the siege of Gibraltar, (1779-1782), when Rodney threw in supplies to the beleaguered garrison. He is said to have been the son of a small farmer, to have begun life as a sailor in a coasting vessel from Irvine; and afterwards to have become a soldier, raising himself to high position by dint of extraordinary perseverance in the exercise of great talents.

In 1829, Robertson in his "Topography of Ayrshire," describes the village, "As a clean, handsome place, with a street of about a quarter of a mile in length, the houses mostly of one storey, with slated roots and fertile gardens." Still, even then, it was so largely a sleepy hollow as to merit the description sometimes given of it as "A land that no stranger came to since the beginning of the world, so shut in by hills." Hence also the familiar saying, "Out of the world, and into Kilbride." Still further evidence of this formerly isolated life, we find in the peculiarly extensive and intricate inter-relationships of the older families in the district, pointing to a no great distant past, when marriages were largely restricted within a limited circle.

Previous to the erection of the old barn at the Cross,

OLD BUILDINGS AT CROSS, WEST KILBRIDE

to which we have already referred, there would seem to have existed a ruinous building on the same site, with a sawpit and well close at hand; whilst the Stripe rivulet meandered past on its way from Drummilling Hill to Kilbride Burn. On the lowermost projecting corbel steps of the old barn itself there were carved the initials J.R. and M. K. which were those of its builders, James Rankine and Margaret King. James Rankine would seem to have been possessor of the "Kirk Croft," which after consultation "with old Hunterston and the rest," he gave in exchange for the "Kirk Lone," which would seem at one time to have been common or public property. Thereon he built what was considered a good house for the time. Margaret or Mary King, his wife, was probably a relative of W. King, then miller in the place.

With regard to churches and schools in the village, we shall have occasion to speak in another chapter. To a few buildings of a semi-public character and of modern erection, we shall little more than refer. Such are, *first*, the Convalescent Home, which is built on an elevated site to the North-West of the village, gifted by the late James Arthur, of Carlung. It affords accommodation for about sixty inmates, with ample sitting-rooms, dining-room, recreation room, etc., and we understand the managers propose adding thereto very soon. It is skilfully managed, and well patronized, especially by convalescent patients from Paisley Infirmary. In its welfare, the late Mr. John Clark, of the Anchor Thread Mills, Paisley, took a warm interest, and to it he bequeathed a legacy of £2000.

*Second*, the Hydropathic and Sanatorium at Seamill,

THE SANATORIUM

which, after several additions, can now accommodate upwards of a hundred visitors. Its dining-room, recently built, can accommodate a hundred and fifty guests. It is fitted up with hot and cold, fresh and sea water baths of various kinds, as well as many labour saving arrangements in kitchen and laundry. It is beautifully situated close by the shores of the Firth, and commands an extensive prospect of Arran and other islands. Under the able management of its present proprietor, it attracts a large number of visitors, especially during summer.

*Third*, the Co-operative Seaside Home, just approaching completion. It is finely situated, just above Seamill, being well sheltered from the North and East, and commanding an extensive view in other directions. It is an imposing building, with accommodation for about fifty inmates. One of its wings has been the gift of Mr. W. Barclay, Glasgow, an enthusiastic supporter of the co-operative system.

*Fourth*, Holland House, Ardneil Bay, now one of the Seaside Homes connected with the Fresh-Air Fortnight Scheme, of the United Evangelistic Association of. Glasgow, and understood to be the gift of some relative of the Allans, of the well-known shipping line. Relays of forty children from the fetid lanes of Glasgow, here enjoy the benefit of a summer holiday, in a house well adapted to its purpose.

For the recreation of the resident and visiting community, there are a Golf Course, beautifully, though a little inconveniently situated at Ardneil Bay; a Bowling Green in Bowfield Road; Curling and Skating Ponds on Crosbie Meadows; and Boats for hire at Seamill.

Of remarkable buildings in the rural parts of the parish, the first place must be assigned to its old castles. Of their historical and antiquarian associations, we shall have occasion to speak in a subsequent chapter. Meanwhile, we merely treat of them from the architectural point of view, acknowledging in this connection, our indebtedness to M'Gibbon and Ross's "Castellated and Domestic Architecture of Scotland from the twelfth to eighteenth centuries," and first, we mention Portincross Castle, situated close by the sea, and founded on solid rock, a little to the North of Farland Point. Its main block measures fifty-eight feet from East to West, and thirty-one feet from North to South. In height it measures thirty-five and a half feet, in addition to which there is a parapet of fifteen feet. It is of four storeys, and has an entrance both on the ground and first floors. The ground floor is vaulted, as also the hall on the first floor. There has apparently been a wall containing an outer gateway, between the castle and the edge of the rock, the checked rybat of the jamb being still visible. A path eight and a half feet wide leads to the entrance door, inside of which, a steep and dark flight of steps in the thickness of the wall leads to the first floor, where it ends. From its landing, a wheel stair in the South wall, leads to the top. The central wall which contains the main staircase divides the castle into two parts. The large apartment on the ground floor, which seems at one time to have been a stable, has the native rock for its pavement. The large window to the North-West, would seem to have been protected by its being opposite deep water, the other windows which are more accessible being mere slits. It had two kitchens, one on the ground floor for retainers and servants, and the other on the first floor, for their master and his guests. By entering at the lower door, servants could reach the upper floors and battlements without passing through the hall. The lower kitchen measured eight feet eight inches, by six feet nine inches, or with its arched fireplace, eleven feet two inches. It had a rough doorway slapped from the outside, because of the awkwardness of the entrance from the stair, with steps both up and down in a dark passage. At the top of the stair on the first floor, a door on the right led into the hall, and another on the left into the upper kitchen. The hall measured twenty-four feet by sixteen and a half feet, by nineteen and a third feet to the top of the vault. There seems to have been an upper room in the vault reached by a doorway from a landing in the wheel stair, but it is now built up. It was lighted by a large window over the fireplace of the hall. The hall itself was lighted by two large windows with stone seats, the one on the South having been enlarged at a later date. A mural chamber at the South-West angle entered off one of these windows. A service window opened from the kitchen into a recess adjoining the entrance passage. At the top of the wheel stair there are two doors, both leading into the main block, one into a chamber in the roof space over the hall, and the other into the parapet walk which went round the building. On passing round this walk, a flight of steps, six feet wide is reached, which leads up to the parapet of the higher wing, whose additional height permits of two floors above the kitchen. By raising the parapet wall on the South side and including the walk in the room, one of the apartments in the attic would seem to have been enlarged at a later date. These rooms in the tower were evidently bed-rooms, being provided with fireplaces and gardrobes.

Cumbrae, Law, and Fairlie Castles were so similar in their structure, that they may be spoken of together. That on Little Cumbrae, which measures forty-one and a quarter feet, by twenty-nine feet, by forty-five and a half feet, resembles Law and Fairlie Castles in having the hall and the kitchen on the first floor—which is reached by a wheel stair from the entrance door on the ground floor; part of the hall in each case being screened off with a stone partition, so as to form a kitchen of small dimensions, four feet by fourteen feet; within which is the fireplace separated from it by an arch, this fireplace being as large as the kitchen either at Law or Fairlie. In Cumbrae Castle, the entrance to the kitchen was through the hall, but at Law Castle from the stair. These kitchens were doubtless rude and imperfect, yet they were a great advance in comfort upon many of the small castles of the period. At Law and Fairlie Castles, a private stair led to the cellar, but at Cumbrae Castle such a stair was not required, as the entrance door—though not now—was originally on the first floor, and led straight into the hall, so that the stair, leading from the entrance door down to the cellars, was entirely under the control of the head of the house, and therefore in a manner private. The two cellars are in all three Castles vaulted, but only at Cumbrae Castle is this the case with the hall. The second floor is in each case divided into two rooms, each with a fireplace, and a gardrobe in the thickness of the walls. At Cumbrae and Fairlie Castles, the corbelling round the top of the walls is of the same design and consists of a continuous course, above which the chequered arrangement of corbels is introduced. At Fairlie Castle there is a round angle-turret at each corner, whilst at Cumbrae Castle these only occur at three corners. Law Castle has no chequered corbelling, but only three continuous courses with circular turrets.

Hunterston Castle formerly stood in the midst of a morass, and had a protecting moat and rampart. The original keep measured twenty-four feet, by twenty-one and a half feet, by thirty-four feet to the top of the parapet. It consists of four storeys, the undermost being vaulted and probably forming the store. It has no fireplace but the usual stone drain, and an opening for a hoist, which would seem to have been the only means of communication with the floor above. The main entrance was on the first floor, whence a wheel stair in the thickness of the wall led to the top. The parapet walk was protected by a battlement which projected on small corbels round three sides, but this corbelling ceases near the end of the North wall; after which the parapet is continued round the East side flush with the wall, an alteration probably made when the wing was added to the East. The walls are nearly five feet thick. This keep has apparently been enlarged in the seventeenth century, so as to convert it into an oblong, with a staircase turret projecting towards the middle of the South side. In this turret is the entrance doorway on the ground floor, and the circular staircase, which gives access to both the old and new parts of the structure. On one of the skew-stones of the staircase turret, are the initials R. D. The new part has been divided by timber partitions into apartments, and probably at the same time, the old hall on the first floor was screened off from the wheeled staircase and gardrobe. It has been fitted up as a library, and is still used as an occasional-room by the present proprietor. The large old stone fireplace has been filled in with a smaller one, but the caps of the old are still in position. Above it is an old painted hatchment containing the Hunter Arms and the motto, "Cursum Perficio." The small court on the South side seems old. Unseen at any great distance, because of the surrounding foliage, this picturesque old Castle takes the visitor by surprise. Until 1803 it formed the family residence of the Hunters of

Hunterstone. Their present mansion-house, considerably enlarged in 1883, is beautifully situated amidst its tall ancestral trees, about a quarter of a mile to the North-West, and not far from the shores of the Firth of Clyde. From its higher windows it commands a fair prospect by land and sea.

Other mansion-houses in the parish worthy of mention are: Auchenames House, the residence of the Craufurd family, nestling amidst its shrubbery of green, like a shooting lodge, beneath the shelter of Ardneil Bank; "Carlung House," the residence of the Arthurs, of the well known commercial firm in Glasgow, by whom it has been greatly enlarged and embellished. Its turret affords an extensive prospect, whilst its well-kept lawns and gardens form a pleasing feature in the landscape; "Overton House," before which Arran with its rugged outline lies outspread in the deep blue sea, once the residence of the Fullertons, a branch of the Kilmichael family in Arran, and now the property of Mr. Adams, Glasgow; "Springside House" and "The Orchard" both lying on the lower slopes of Lawhill, with fine prospects of Great Cumbrae and the adjacent Firth—the former the residence of the Hyndmans of Lunderston in Renfrews-hire, and the latter the property of Mrs. Dr. Robertson, as a member of the Boyd family; "Crosbie Castle" by the side of a romantic glen; in its present state but about 80 years old, but still retaining an air of antiquity in its thick walls, large fireplaces, small windows, oak wainscotting, and iron-studded doors, and probably incorporating a small portion of the previous edifice which was burned down after standing for two hundred and fifty years. This in turn occupied the site of a still older Castle which had been the residence of Wallace's Uncle, Reginald Craufurd, in the thirteenth century.

Nothing has done so much to modernize the aspect of the village and parish, as the introduction of the railway in 1878; an influence, under which it is gradually being transformed from a quiet rural retreat into a popular watering-place and summer resort. Previous to that date, passenger traffic was usually by rail from Ardrossan or Dalry, and earlier still, by the Ayr and Glasgow steamboats, to meet which, small boats put off from Portincross with, or for passengers. Goods were then principally conveyed either by rail to Dalry, and thence carted to West Kilbride, or by carriers to Glasgow, Paisley, etc. The carriers' quarters were at that portion of the Gateside road, where it is causewayed and unusually wide. Stage coaches also ran from Ayr to Greenock and from Saltcoats to Largs. Their arrival at Hawhill Inn, with red-coat driver and sound of horn, was the event of the day, as it broke in upon the quiet monotony of the village life.

Postal communication was for long kept up via Greenock, but is now via Ardrossan. Postal missives, exclusive of parcels, are now delivered to the number of something like three thousand three hundred per week, whilst about two thousand five hundred will be posted in the same time. Parcels will average nearly one hundred per week delivered, and about sixty will be posted in the same time. Telegraphic business has largely developed since the introduction of the sixpenny rate, so that, whereas in 1879 there were scarcely two thousand such messages, there are now nearly ten thousand per annum; and other departments of Post Office business, such as Money Orders, etc., have proportionately developed.

Almost still more remarkable has been the development of railway traffic, as even this one fact shews, that whereas the number of passengers' tickets sold in 1883 was twenty-nine thousand nine hundred and thirteen, and in 1889 thirty-nine thousand nine hundred and eleven, in 1895 they numbered fifty-seven thousand five hundred and twelve and a half. If the outgoing passenger traffic has thus increased, still more has the incoming, especially under the fostering care of cheap Saturday fares, and season tickets. The goods' traffic, though more fluctuating, is, on the whole, on the increase, last year amounting in value to £5,613, whereas in 1889 it was only £3,214. So that now the proverbial donkey-cart, that was wont scoffingly to be named, as sufficient to carry West Kilbride's traffic from Ardrossan, may be considered as laughed out of court. It may here be mentioned that the first proposal was to construct a railway from Dalry, a proposal, which we know was revived a few years ago, notwithstanding the present communication via Ardrossan, only again, however, to fall into abeyance.

Before the days of railways, however, there was another and more objectionable way in which goods of a certain class were brought into the parish, viz., smuggling—a practice for which West Kilbride had acquired great notoriety during the last century, as the following extract from Kirk-Session and other records will shew. On May 25th, 1720, the Session are informed that some one was seen lately carrying off brandy on Sabbath morning; and in 1724, that it had become a practice for young women to carry loads of brandy some twelve to sixteen miles out of the parish; whilst in 1725, there is a report of Sabbath profanation by persons concerned in the brandy trade. In 1757, we find even the schoolmaster of the parish dealing in the running business; and as late as 1802, the Moderator acquaints the Kirk Session that he had received information that David Raeside and others had one Sabbath gone out in a boat, and boarded a ship going to Greenock, from which they brought five casks of rum, etc., which they had put on shore that night betwixt nine and ten o'clock.

From the Irvine custom house books, now in London, we have further evidence of this contraband traffic in the district, *e.g.* in a case of date, January 18th, 1724, which is brought under the notice of the authorities by the collector and comptroller, and tells of a considerable seizure near Fairlie of brandy, rum, a pack of playing cards, etc. Again on November 6th, 1726, we find mention of the frequent running of goods between West Kilbride and Largs. Then on September 27th, 1728, there is the report of the arrival at Saltcoats, on September 6th, of a vessel called "The Prosperity," of Kilbride, with a cargo of brandy, woollens, etc., accompanied by a King's sloop to prevent the cargo being run; the avowed object for coming to Saltcoats being to take in a further load of salt. The master delays sailing on a pretext of having met with damage and of inability to proceed on his voyage. Another letter of October 28th, mentions that a mob had attacked and robbed the above vessel, after having severely beaten the officers in charge; and on November 7th, one of the officers is reported as dangerously ill, with his life quivering in the balance, owing to the bruises he had received on that occasion. November 10th, 1730, shows a troop of dragoons at West Kilbride assisting the custom house officers in the discharge of their duty, but they do not seem to have remained for any length of time.

In 1855, the late Dr. Ritchie tells of an old woman, who remembered the Highlandmen having their casks of whiskey from Skipness hidden amongst the whins, whilst they lay all night at the back of the dykes waiting for carts to take them inland; and the late William Gemmell, senior, could remember many boats, riding in the creek at Baston Craig below Yonderfield, which were engaged in the illicit traffic. This traffic was far from being always unattended with danger, as may be seen from the case of one, Barbour, who lived in the Yonderfields, and had a scar in his face, the result of a bayonet-wound he had received in a scuffle with the military at Kilruskin Wood. When caught amongst the glens, woods, bogs, whins, or coppice, in Braid, Carlung, or Crosbie, the smugglers frequently came to close quarters with the soldiers.

This contraband traffic is generally supposed to have been started by way of revenge upon England for the imaginary prejudicial effects of the Union upon Scotland; but we are also told that the spirit of opposition to the Whig ministry of 1688, led the inhabitants of the West, under the influence of the Boyds who leant to the National Party, to practise smuggling extensively. Doubt-less also, illicit gain had not a little to do with it; and the smaller landlords rather encouraged it, as it enabled their poorer tenants more regularly to pay their rents. Still, it cannot be denied that the irregularities and disorders connected therewith were most demoralizing. Thereby habits of excessive drinking were acquired, rights of property violated, the Sabbath desecrated, profanity fostered, and deceit cultivated. Few of those engaged in it ultimately realized any profit from it, whilst many possessed of considerable property were thereby ruined. Still the smuggler was very often a popular favourite, and the contraband goods in which he traded were harboured and guarded against seizure by the custom house officers.

When captured, they were not seldom released, even sometimes at the cost of breaking into the custom house. When they were brought to court, juries frequently found in their favour, and there were but few places in which the gauger or exciseman was made welcome. Hence Burns' well known song, "The Deil's awa' wi' the Exciseman." But neither had the custom house officers themselves at all times clean hands in the matter, as the following instance will show. On February 23rd, 1765, Robert Thompson, vintner at Fairlie gives his oath that in February, 1763, there came into the Large a wherry from the Isle of Man laden with five or six hundred casks of brandy and rum which were landed there, when Archibald Stewart, officer of excise at Largs was coming and going upon the shore. He further swears that before the goods were landed, the said Archibald Stewart compounded with a farmer in Large and others then present, for eighteen casks of the same; which he, the deponent, delivered to Mr. Stewart with his own hands. He then told him that nine of these were for the King, and the other nine for himself. He still further swears, that Mr. Stewart delivered these eighteen casks to John Craig, cooper, in Largs, who carried them off and lodged them in the excise office; while Mr. Stewart remained and saw the residue of the cargo carried off, and be further said that neither he nor any other excise officer would trouble those, who were concerned in the cargo, for two or three days, etc. This contraband traffic was generally carried on by ships from the Isle of Man, which island formed a convenient *entrepôt* for the French and others to deposit enormous quantities of wines, brandies, rum, tea, coffee, tobacco, drugs, spices, lawns, lace, and other goods, on which high duties were paid in Britain. These were afterwards smuggled in wherries upon the coast of Scotland. Of these wherries not one in a hundred was either taken at sea, or afterwards secured. To the proprietor of the Isle of Man, certain small dues were paid on the goods thus stored. Large vessels, then called "Buckers," lugger rigged and carrying from twenty to thirty guns, were sometimes engaged in this illicit traffic. The contraband goods after being landed, were hid in a great variety of places such as, in ditches, heaps of manure, in drains stuffed with straw, in sand, amongst whins, under sheaves, etc.

As carried on in this parish, the illicit goods were generally landed near the Baston Craig below Yonderfield, where until lately a post was to be seen to which were fastened the small boats used for going out to the larger wherries; and until lately, too, there used to be a stone in one of the Carlung fields, behind which the abettors of this contraband trade lay on the outlook for the appearance in the offing of expected luggers. The kegs were often concealed with such skill amongst the whins of Yonderfield and Carlung, that, though the excise officers might be looking on from the top of Crosshill while they were being secreted, they could not find them when they came down to search for them. Not seldom, too, the revenue officers were either overpowered or outwitted. Thus, on one occasion, some smugglers carrying on horseback some bags of contraband salt, met one or two excisemen near Law farm, whom they warned, if they did not want to be forced, to take the road to Saltcoats, whilst they themselves would hold on by the old Dalry Road. At another time, a smuggler was running off with a cask, closely pursued by the gaugers, when coming to a manure heap, he threw it in—thereupon another man seized an empty cask and made off, thus leading the revenue officers upon a false track. We are also told of another, who, riding along the old Dalry road and seeing a gauger approaching, diverted his attention from a cart with contraband goods a short way ahead, by dismounting from his horse and dancing in the middle of the road until the cart had passed out of sight. He excused his eccentric conduct by saying, that be had just remembered that he was invited to a wedding on the following day, and wished to revive his knowledge of dancing preparatory thereto. Then again we find a gauger treated in a public house at Portincross, until smuggled goods are removed from a house he is on his way to visit, after which it is thrown open to free and unfettered inspection. The late Dr. Ritchie tells of a case in which ready wit, akin to that of Rachel's when hiding her father's images, stood a Mrs. Donaldson in good stead. When the revenue officer came to the door, a cask was standing on the floor. She instantly threw a plaid over it and sat down upon it with her infant in her arms. On his entrance, she civilly and satisfactorily answered all his questions, but never rose until the representative of the law had departed without discovering the fraud. On another occasion, a cask was recaptured in Halfway Street from a gauger who was sitting upon it, by snuff being thrown into his eyes from behind by a woman. Blinded and enraged he rose, and men concealed at no great distance soon made off with the cask, leaving the gauger to vent his impotent wrath upon his numerous foes. Sometimes the kegs were cast into the sea, and when brought to land were taken care of by the people, who received so much for their trouble, until carts arrived to take them inland. Thus the late Dr. Ritchie tells of a case, in which two men took a puncheon of rum from a ship, which being too large for their boat, was towed astern to the shore. They were, however, observed by a government cutter, which gave them chase and landed her balls dangerously near them. On being got ashore it was carried off by a cart in waiting, secreted beneath some sheaves on the farm of Yonderfield, and though searched for, it was not found. Sometimes even, a full cask with the top off, with a spigot and a can beside it, stood on the shore head for free use. Sometimes also, secreted casks were afterwards found and freely used. But dishonourable, though the traffic was, those engaged in it had a code of honour of their own, and hence they would not conceal their goods in any outhouse under lock and key, lest on discovery the proprietor or tenant should become liable to the heavy fine thereby incurred. Those who dealt with the smugglers were not, however, always honourable, as sometimes whole boat-loads would be disposed of without payment. The Tams of Thirdmailing seem to have been noted local smugglers. One of them, we are told, was a strong heavy man who had thrashed many a gauger, but never killed one. The names, Beatson and Moncur, occur amongst those of local resident gaugers. Brandy and rum were by no means the only articles thus surreptitiously trafficked in. Tobacco was taken to the snuff mill near Dalry, whilst salt was smuggled from Larne, and whiskey from Skipness, slates, wall-paper, Indian goods, china-ware, silks, gloves, and many other articles were also included in the contraband list, A curious instance was for long to be seen in Hawhill House of a room, whose walls were covered with small squares of paper, which had been smuggled in this form in order to escape payment of duty.

Neither was smuggling the only way in which an illicit traffic was carried on in the parish. Well nigh a century ago, there might have been seen in the still quietude of a calm summer morn or eve, a thin streak of blue smoke rising from the midst of the tangled copse-wood through which Glenside Burn bickers onward to the sea. Whence came it? From a hut in which in all probability peat-reek was giving a flavour to the product of an illicit still. We know not whether or not the farmers and cotters around were bribed with some of the genuine article in its native purity, but well knowing of its exist-ence in their midst, they breathed not a hush of its presence. Happily for social order and the welfare of the community, these are now the days that are past.

Thus have we wandered through the parish in its ancient and modern topography. We have marked how not a few places have mingled with their kindred dust, whilst others have been greatly altered. We have glanced at some of the architectural features of a few of the older buildings, and turned our attention to some of the more recent associations that have gathered round them—things both honourable and dishonourable—that linger in the memories of a generation now rapidly passing away. Thus have we prepared the way for our thoughts going backward to times more remote, and dwelling upon the topics of historical and antiquarian interest, which will be the theme of our next chapter.

# CHAPTER III.
## ANTIQUITIES OF THE PARISH.

THE earliest history of the parish ante-dates by many centuries the era of written record. It is fossilized in the more ancient names of places in the parish, in its forts, urns, cists, relics, old coins, carvings and castles. It is embalmed in the charter chests of its more ancient families, and has come floating down to these later days in the legends and superstitions that have gathered round persons and places of the olden time. After we have seen what some of the more noteworthy of these are, we shall be in a better position to make use of the historical imagination in conjuring up a probable picture of the life of this parish at a date even anterior to, as well as reaching through; the Roman period, when the eagles of that warlike people fluttered during the earliest Christian centuries in a very fickle and uncertain mood over the hills and dales of Ayrshire, which was then included in the province of Valentia. Of that period, and as evidence of the presence of the Romans in the district, the only probable relic we have heard of is a gold torque or twisted ring found on Crosbie Hill. It was thought by its finder to be a ring connected with a horse's harness, until taken to a jeweller in Dalry, who know better at what value to appraise it. Previous to that period of very partial Roman subjugation, the county had formed a portion of the territory of the Damnii, one of the aboriginal tribes of Scotland, and after them came the Scoto-Irish, who pastured large herds of cattle and burned up the woods for fuel.

Looking first then, at the names of places in the parish, we found in our last chapter that very many of them are of comparatively modern origin and self-explanatory, being derived either from natural position or ecclesiastical associations, or early proprietorship. It is not, of course, by such names that we expect much light to be thrown upon the earlier annals of the district, but rather by such undoubtedly ancient names as Poteath, Ardneil, Yonderfield, Yonderton, Goldenberry, Caldrongattel, which we explained in our last chapter; and to which may now be added "Fairlie," or in its older form, "Fairnelie," which signifies "The Stockade of the Warrior." "Portincross," or, in its more antiquated form, "Portcrosch," meaning the "Castle Port of the Ross, or Hero Chief," and etymologically allied with Ardrossan, the "Castle of the Lord of the Rosses," who were Scandinavian or Danish heroes; and "Kaim," which means "The Camp by the Bay."

Such names as these evidently point to an age in which the parish of West Kilbride was traversed and ruled by a race of warlike heroes, who found it necessary to have forts, and stockades, and camps, wherewith to defend a territory held on precarious tenure, or whence to issue on praedatory raids upon the domains of neighbouring chiefs. But they also shew that intermixed with these were "Clerics in their hospices, and anchorites in their retreats." It was a rude life they doubtless lived, their time and energy largely absorbed in war and the chase; the chiefs lording it over their serfs and menials who dwelt in the conical wattled or wicker-work huts, that clustered around the forts, whilst these chiefs themselves revelled and fought, hunted and fished, lived and died, to have their ashes long centuries afterwards brought to light in the urns exhumed in the district.

Of the *Forts* they tenanted, there are remains of some six in the parish, and one on its borders. These forts have been traditionally assigned to the era of the Danish invasion, or earlier; and are generally formed by the detachment of a portion of a raised bank, so as to leave a rounded, conically-shaped mound, with an enclosure of some thirty or forty feet in diameter on the summit. This enclosure was surrounded by a rampart of six or eight feet in thickness, which was faced on both sides with large undressed stones neatly laid, the space between being filled up with small stones intermixed with soil.

Of the six forts in the parish, the first we mention is the Castle Hill on the North edge of the Glen Burn; on the lands of Glenside. This is a circular mound in a fair state of preservation, about twenty-nine paces in diameter. In his "Prehistoric Man in Ayrshire," Mr. John Smith describes it "as having a low turf rampart, forty-two paces in length on the land side, which rampart rises about five feet above the level of the surrounding ground. This fort is hollow in the centre, with a very steep side towards the Glen, and a low side towards the West."

Proceeding round the coast from North to South, we next come to the site of the vitrified fort on Auld Hill, above Portincross. In these vitrified forts, the stones would seem to have been run into a sort of slag by the application of fire from above. This fort has an esplanade of some forty or fifty paces in length, and a portion of its vitrified stone may still be seen in the Andersonian Institute.

The next fort we reach is at Seamill, beside the villa named from it, "The Fort." (A plan of its internal structure may be seen in the volumes of the Ayrshire and Wigtonshire Archaeological Society's proceedings.) It was of considerable dimensions. When opened and explored about sixteen years ago in presence of Dr. Cochrane Patrick, H. F. Weir of Kirkhall, Dr. Boyd, Seaview, and others, some traces of the life of its inmates were found in an old abandoned entrance, as also in the space between the double ramparts. These included a hammer of quartzite, a stone-ball, seven bits of stone discs and perforated shale, a perforated piece of bone, five bits of deers' horns, a sandstone whetstone, a bronze

RELICS FROM FORT SEAMILL

wheel with attached loop, a bronze disc, five bits of sheet bronze, portions of iron and glass, whelk and limpet shells, etc.; all of which had probably been thrown out into the kitchen refuse heap. It had no well, but water could easily be obtained by dipping a vessel into the stream at its base.

Proceeding still further South along the coast, we next arrive at Glenhead double fort, not far from the Gourock Burn and overlooking the old raised beach. Of these the one towards the land side measures sixteen paces in diameter on the summit, and is defended by a wide ditch thirty-one and a third feet deep from the top of the rampart which is five feet above the level of the fort.

Between this fort and the outer one there is another ditch thirteen and two thirds feet deep from the higher and six feet from the lower fort wall. All the sides of this double fort are very steep, down to the burn on one side and raised beach on another. The part of the wall next the land side is stronger than elsewhere, and both walls and ditches seem to have been constructed in proportional strength to the risk of danger from an outside enemy.

GLENHEAD FORT

A short way South from this double fort we come upon Boydstone fort, which is defended on the land side by a broad ditch thirteen and two-thirds feet below the top of the outer rampart, which is constructed of earth and boulders and rises seven feet above the interior of the fort. It measures twenty paces by fifteen, and though steep, except on the land side, is not in so strong a position as Glenhead fort.

Of the fort or stone circle on Blackshaw Moor, a little beyond Hopeton, the traces are somewhat indistinct; but from its proximity to the famous Cup and Ring

Markings on the other side of the Dalry road, it is probable that Church and State here found a local habitation.

Rather less than a mile to the South-East of this, and
just outside the eastern boundary of the parish, is Knock
Georgan fort with its triple rampart and double ditch and
doorways—a good point of vantage from which to mark
the advance of an approaching foe.

In addition to these, flat spaces on the summits of
Goldenberry and Carlung Hills, as well as mounds South
of Bushglen, are at least suggestive of further fortifications. To what do such forts point, but to an age when the
food of the people was largely fish and flesh, their implements rude, and their occupation war!

From the forts we next turn our attention to "Cup
and Ring Markings," of which there are two noteworthy
specimens in the parish, one on a single outcrop of rock,
forty-five feet in length by nineteen feet in breadth at one
end, and three feet at the other, lying to the North side of

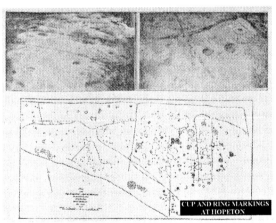

CUP AND RING MARKINGS
AT HOPETON

the old Dalry road, a little beyond Hopeton,—the other

on an outcrop of rock to the South of the wood on Diamond Craig. These cup and ring markings are found in various parts of the island, from Strathspey to Cornwall, as well as in Egypt and India, in earth-houses, in lake-dwellings, on mummy cases, etc., and are generally believed to be of religious significance. Various conjectures have been made as to their uses. Some are of opinion, that the cups were filled with the blood of the sacrifice, which might sometimes even be human, and that it ran in the radial grooves from one cup to another. Others suppose that they were filled four times a year with oil or fat, which was set on fire at the prayer of the priest at one and the same time, wherever in the country the ceremony was performed. Mr. Smith, who is credited with the discovery some sixteen years ago of those on the Blackshaw Rock, tells us that perhaps they are as interesting as any yet found in Scotland. Besides the cup and ring markings there are Hoofs and Spirals. They are disposed with no mathematical regularity, though the conjecture is sometimes ventured that their arrangement may sometimes have some resemblance to certain of the constellations. The cups are sometimes arranged in groups and sometimes alone. Occasionally the groups are enclosed by a ring. Some cups have two or three rings, and some have a shallow gutter or groove running up from them, whilst some have two grooves. Sometimes the grooves cut through the rings, but do not enter the cups. Two cups are some times connected by a groove, and two grooves sometimes meet at a sharp angle, or one runs into the side of another. In one instance the surrounding ring is nearly square. Sometimes a ring is not connected with a groove coming out from a cup, and a groove from a cup may run in between two rings. There is only one instance of a solitary ring without a cup inside it. Some cups have no ring, and where they have, the rings are not always complete. A few of them seem to be about three or four inches in diameter, and are still well defined, but the majority of them have suffered greatly from weather influence, and whilst still visible, are little better than mere finger-tip marks. The hoof markings are often single, sometimes in pairs, or even in groups. Crescent-shaped, they are deepest toward the concave side. In only two instances do grooves run from ringed cups into hoof-markings, and towards the deep side. The spirals are both dextral and sinistral. Mr. Smith has given the following summary of these interesting markings:— Cups, 364; Rings, 63; Hoof-markings, 37; Grooves, 34; Spirals, 3; Spectacle-markings, i.e. two cups joined by a groove, 2.

The cup and ring markings on Diamond Craig are

DIAMOND CRAIG CUT AND RING MARKINGS

not nearly so extensive, there being only about twenty fairly visible, and of these only about one or two with a fairly well-defined ring. They would seem to have been executed with rather too soft a tool, as the hard quartz is occasionally left to mar the perfect rotundity of the circumference.

As we stand by these markings we learn that man is instinctively a religious being, a worshipping animal, but we also learn the twofold truth, that "as is a man so is his god," and "as is his god, so is the man." As we conjure up the blood or the wine of the sacrifice filling these cups and grooves, or the Elijah-like miracle of the oil consumed by fire from heaven, we behold the rude forefathers of this parish in their morning devotions to their Baal, the rising sun, and we thank our God for the rising of a Better Sun with truer healing in His wings.

As relics of a kindred age we may mention an arrow point of flint found at no great distance from the cup and ring rock, as also bits of a gas-coal ring discovered in a joint of the rock. Betwixt it and the stone circle on the other side of the rock there was also found a few years ago by one of the workmen engaged upon the Irvine water works, a fine stone hammer, which had doubtless done yeoman service in the bands of some of the wild and warlike natives, who dwelt in those parts when its population was but a stage in advance of barbarism. Other relics of the stone period are a perforated stone

STONE AXE HAMMER FOUND AT HUNTERSTONE

axe-hammer with concave faces and three parallel grooves, measuring four and a half by two and a half inches, found at Chapelton; a hammer-axe, eight and three quarters by three by two inches, found at Hunter-stone; a greenstone hammer-head found at Carlung, now in the Antiquarian Museum, Edinburgh; a stone hammer found in an urn at Carrick View, Ritchie Street; another at Boydstone; a spindle-whorl one and a half inches in diameter with incised lines, found on Chapleton; a bit of slate from a shell mound, on which an attempt has been made to draw a few incised lines with others crossing them at nearly right angles; and a bit of coal money got in the same mound at a depth of four feet.

Another volume of our unwritten history is to be found in the urns, of which a large number have been found at several places in the parish. In these urns, in addition to calcined human bones and dust, implements of the stone and bronze periods have occasionally been found. They point backward to a pre-Christian era when cremation must have been commonly practised. Of these urns, perhaps the finest are those found at Seamill, and especially those discovered on the making of the present turnpike road in that neighbourhood, in 1830. One of

URN FOUND AT SEAMILL

these, now in the possession of Mrs. Hunter-Weston, is a remarkably perfect specimen. It is of a light brown colour, measuring seven and a half inches in height, six and a half inches in greatest and three and an eighth inches in smallest diameter. The decoration, which consists of ornamental straight lines above and diagonal cross lines below, extends over the concave belt. Similar lines encircle it at the top and bottom of the rim and at the base of the belt. It still enshrines the bones found in it, whilst the human dust is preserved in a bottle by its side. Another found at the same place is now in the museum of the Andersonian College, Glasgow. Yet another in a good state of preservation was found in the same district by Miss M. Boyd. It was covered with a stone slab as is

URN FOUND AT DIAMOND CRAIG

generally the case, unless when the urn is inverted. It is elegantly shaped and skilfully made, narrow at bottom and without ornamentations. The enclosed bones were remarkably dense and heavy, and though thoroughly burned, were beautifully white, those of the spine being spongy and light. Two urns were also found near the Fort gate, of which one, greatly damaged, has been

pieced together by Miss Boyd. Other two were found at
Tarbet Villa, of which one is now in the Antiquarian
Museum, Edinburgh, (see "Anderson's Bronze Age")
and the other in the possession of the owner of the villa.
Some seven or eight have also been found near Highthorn, but not generally in such a good state of preservation as to be capable of removal. They varied in depth
from six to fifteen inches, and were found at a depth of
two or three feet, without mound or cairn to mark their
position. Though unglazed, they bore traces of having
been exposed to the action of fire, being blue within and
red without. Hand made, they were as well proportioned
as if they had been wrought on a potter's wheel. Others
of a similar character have been unearthed at Tarbet Hill,
Yonderfield, and Southanen. One found near the summit
of Diamond Craig has specially fine markings. These
markings are generally believed to have been formed by
the imbedding of straws, grasses, or cords, in the soft
clay, which, when exposed to fire, would, of course, be
burned out and leave their impression behind.

Could the bones preserved in these urns be clothed
anew with flesh and blood, could these tongues arise and
speak, what a strange revelation of human life and affairs
in the parish of West Kilbride some two thousand years
ago would they give. Out of the grey mist that gathers
round the dawn of our national story, ere yet the earliest
gleams of Christian truth had done anything to dispel the
gross darkness that covered the people, they cry with the
voice of struggle, and call up a scene of wild turmoil,
long since hushed to rest in the progress of the centuries.
Deer, wild oxen, and very probably wolves and other
wild animals roam through the morasses and tangled

woods. The smoke of sacrifice rises to the morning sun.
The doughty chief,

> "The shaggy wolfish skin he wore,
> Pinned by a polished bone before,"

goes forth from his rude fort to deeds of daring on the
field of battle, or feats of venture in the chase. The
brawny arm of the toiling serf swings his stone hammer
or axe with a will. The angel of death spreads his wings
on the blast, and the warrior chief lies stolid and still—
his rough work done, his rude life lived. His remains are
cremated and their ashes committed to the urn that, for
well-nigh twenty centuries, is to lie buried beneath a few
feet of earth; until brought to light thus long after, that the
men and women of to-day may gaze with curious eye and
absorbing interest upon the ashes of one who served his
day and generation where now we are serving ours.

A few centuries pass away. The voice of the heralds
of the Cross has been heard in the land. The rude and
primitive churches of the Columban era—rugged structures of logs thatched with reeds begin to dot the land,
one such chapel being possibly at Seamill. Around this
chapel God's Acre is laid out, and heathen cremation
gives place to Christian burial; and hence the skeletons of
fourteen human beings disinterred in 1878, at the formation of the present road to the Sanatorium. They were
found enclosed in rude stone cists in the midst of fine
gravel or coarse sand. One of the cists. which contained
no bones but only a little dark-coloured earth, was much
smaller than the others. It may have been that of an
infant. Moat of the bones were in an advanced state of
decay, and could scarcely bear handling. The position in
which they were laid (East to West) points to early Christian times as the date of sepulture. The late Dr. Ritchie

collected nearly the whole skeleton of a male, and pieced together most of the bones of a female, apparently of great stature (six feet) and stalwart frame. They could not, therefore, as some have conjectured, be the remains of those who had fallen in some ancient battle, or of those recovered from some wrecked Armada vessel. The absence of weapons points in the same direction, though the presence in the neighbourhood of stone axes, etc., has led some to assign to them a pre-historic date of burial. A portion of one of the skulls with well-preserved teeth, is said to be still in possession of Mr. M'Gillivray. The supposed stone of another cist was unearthed a few days ago in the excavating of a track for a gas pipe in the neighbourhood.

About the same time, i.e. sixth century, A.D., the din of war is heard around "The Castle on the Flat Plain" and the moss of Carlounge, as Prince Arthur with his brave and doughty knights there gains the ninth of his twelve battles against Saxon invaders and foes.

In another century, 714, A.D., the walls of a humble sanctuary arise on " 'Wey Kumra," to form a shrine for the pious devotions of Santa Vey in the closing years of her beneficent life.

In about three centuries more, we catch the morning gleams of historic record struggling through the darkness of legend and superstition, but still we must pick our steps with caution, so as not to relegate to the field of fact what largely belongs to the realm of romance and dwells in the airy castles of tradition. Before, however, endeavouring to disentangle fact from fiction, we may be allowed to linger for a little on enchanted ground, so as to mark some of the legendary traditions and superstitions which are still afloat with regard to persons and places of local interest.

Of these, we begin with the immense strides his Satanic Majesty is said to have taken across the parish from Knock Georgan to Tarbert Hill, thence to Campbelton Hill, thence to the "Three Sisters," and thence to Little Cumbrae, as is shown 'by the footprints of the cloven-hoof found on rocks at these several places. On reaching Little Cumbrae he is said to have met a stranger with whom he entered into conversation, when some women whom he had been taking captive, took advantage of his inattention to them, "A' ran" and hence "Arran." In taking such gigantic strides, we can well imagine his wings to have been of some service to him. His presence in the two last places may serve to explain the existence of a "Deil's Elbow" in the vicinity of both.

The second legend we note has reference to the erection of the castles at Portincross and Little Cumbrae, in which giants were engaged, who had only one hammer betwixt them, which they were in the habit of throwing across the two miles or so of intervening water, as occasion required. One day, however, it unfortunately fell into the intervening channel, and hence the castles were left unfinished. There is, however, another version of this legend, which represents old Satan as having the building of the castle at Portincross, whilst young Nick was employed on that in the Little Cumbrae. Young Nick would appear to have been more expeditious than his father, as be completed his work first. Old Nick then threw over his hammer, and desired his son to build a bridge between the Greater Cumbrae and the Ayrshire coast. Young Clootie lost no time in carrying out his father's instructions, and laid the foundations for the great span on both sides of the channel, and was preparing to throw over the arch, when old Nick paid him a visit. The "Big Deil" was much displeased with his son's work, and knocked his heel through part of his erection, which accounts for the hole in the Lion Rock on Great Cumbrae.

A third tradition is the well-known one, that the bodies of the ancient kings of Scotland were brought by the old Dalry road to Portincross to be shipped for interment in Iona. Hence the name Port-in-cross, formerly Pencross (*Portus Crucis*). Boats going thence with bodies for burial, or pilgrims for the presentation of votive offerings at Iona, are said to have called at Loch Ranza in Arran, on the way.

Our fourth tradition is that which locates the birthplace of Sir William Wallace at Crosbie Castle, then tenanted by his uncle, and forming at that time a hiding-place for his mother. A small window in the upmost storey of the castle is still pointed out, whence Wallace is said to have jumped, in his efforts to escape from the English. From Crawford's "History of Renfrewshire" we learn that the Wallaces and Crawfords. had frequent communication, as being connected both by marriage and blood. Wallace's chair is said to have perished in a fire which destroyed the greater part of the Castle about three centuries ago. Blind Harry represents Wallace and his uncle as coming from Crosby on the morning of the Black Parliament, when so many of the leading men of the county were put to death in the "Barns of Ayr." On arriving at Kingcase, near Ayr,

> "With heidfull hast then sperit Wicht Wallace
> At Schyr Ranald for the charter of peese,
> It is lewyt at Corsbe in the kyst";

*i.e.* Wallace and his uncle discover that the bond of peace entered into with the English, has been left at Corsbie in the charter chest. Some, however, are inclined to think that a Corsbie, near Prestwick, which has the ruins of a church and a well, still called Wallace's Well, is the one here referred to. Against this is the fact that this latter Corsbie has never been the property of the Crawfords, Wallace's uncle, but of the Fullertons of Fullerton.

But the great mine of legendary lore for the parish is "The Hunterston Legends," for the perusal of a manuscript poetical version of which, I have been indebted to the courtesy of Mrs. Colonel Hunter-Weston. Of these there are six. The first is entitled "Aylmer the Norman," (1141 A.D.), and has reference to the origin of the family name; which is said to be derived from Aylmer, a Norman knight, who came to Scotland in the train of David I., and on becoming "Hunter Royal," received a grant of the lands of Arnele-Hunter from the King. The Legend opens with the representation of the King amidst his courtiers opposite Hunterston shore watching for sport by sea and land, and cursing the delay of his huntsman who should have met him there ere then. An oath to the following effect is then made by the King

> "Our hunstman the first chiel shall be
> Whose hounds bring quarry to our bow;
> And royal hunter make we he,
> Whose game our arrow shall lay low."

Just then with his bow across his knee, two sleeping greyhounds one on either side, and his casque on a tree, Aylmer, bewailing his desolate estate, happens to be at hand. He laments the fate of his grandfather, slain at Hastings, as also that of his father. He mourns over his distance from his native shore. Spurred, armed, and ready for war, he deems his fate too likely to prove true to his motto, "*Cursum Perficio*," when his cry "Ehew" awake his dogs which start a hare, and catch it. Thereupon he winds his horn in praise of their feat. Its echo is heard by the King. His retinue strain their eyes to catch its winder, when Aylmer makes his appearance, and is roused from his musings by the scene that bursts upon his view. The King forthwith makes himself known to Aylmer, and asks him who he is, to which Aylmer replies that he is a Norman knight and wanderer, brave and true "Ready, aye, ready to fight for you." The King then tells him that it is game, not men they wish to slay; regards him as heaven-sent in default of his tardy, absent huntsman, and exclaims:—

> "There are coverts in yon brae-side wood,
>  Lay on your dogs, and we will make thee,
>  Royal huntsman, by the rood."

Just then a hind speeds by, the greyhounds follow and double; and at length she falls, pierced by arrows from the King and Aylmer, whereupon the King exclaims:—

> "Henceforth our royal hunter be,
>  Yon land thou see'st 'tis called Arnele,
>  And Ardnele now we give to thee
>  Forever, thy sons, if leal.
>  Thy name? Sir Aylmer, then shall we
>  In token, thou art feal,
>  Claim greyhounds two, as tenure fee,
>  Sir Aylmer of Arnele."

The second of the Hunterston legends, is dated 1263, and entitled, "The Spirit of the Well." It is a tale of the battle of Largs, and tells of Haco's coming to Scotland,—of an eclipse of the sun, which the weird sisters regard as ominous of coming woe to the Norse, and of death to Haco—of the laird of Hunterston standing at his castle gate, waiting for the arrival of Alexander III. to whom he is expected to do homage and pay his tenure fee. As thus he stands, an old grey-headed man approaches, salutes him, and introduces himself as a pilgrim, "With news for thee, Arnele." He then calls him to the "Wishing Well" that be may gain knowledge, both as to the present and the future, and overcomes his scruples to going, because of the King's expected arrival, by telling him that *that* day the King is otherwise engaged. At the well, the aged pilgrim asks Arnele what he sees in the water? The reply takes the form of a vision of the past, of the present, and of the future. He first sees a gallant fleet rounding Kintyre, and his gaze is specially fixed upon Haco's ship with its pennon sheathed in gold, and its twenty-seven banks of oars. In its wake, many other ships seem to follow, all "Girt in battle's stern array," and steering for Great Cumbrae. In the second part of his vision, he sees a tempest gathering and break-ing, with many a galley cast on a rocky shore; while some weather the gale and steer for Sudrey-jar. In the third part of his vision, be sees the galleys borne along; the slopes and shores of Largs clad with Gaels awaiting their prey, and some Norse landing on the sands, which are strewn with the dead. He then sees the royal steward slain, the Scottish King wounded, himself taking part in the fray, and the battle fought—a dearly-won victory. He further sees the Norse allowed to land and bury their dead in one sepulchral mound; the vision closes with the burial of Ivar Holm, a comrade cf Haco's at Lamlash,. and of Haco himself in St. Magnus' Cathedral, Orkney.

The title of the third Hunterston legend is "The Hostage Brothers," its date 1332-1338 A.D. After his raids into Scotland in the earlier part of his reign, Edward III. in order to ensure its submission frequently took hostages with him into England and amongst these were two youths of the Hunterston family, who were imprisoned in Chester Castle, managed to escape, and amid difficulties wended their homeward way. The legend begins with a vision of the Lady of Hunterston sitting within her castle walls, forlorn and desolate, her husband, a wanderer o'er the hills, and her sons in prison. She contrasts her present state with what it was when she came as a bride. She wails for a deliverer from Edward's tyranny. The imprisonment of her sons in Chester's Castle, "grim and gray," is then depicted, the dreariness of the scene, and their yearnings for freedom. The two brothers are seen consoling each other by day, and intertwined in sleep by night. They are united in their prayers ere oblivion steeps their eyelids in slumber, as well as in their home-sick longings throughout their wakeful hours. At length they conspire to form a rope from the scanty covering of their beds, and to file their prison bare with a knife. The elder mounts the lattice bars, reaches the garden and the trees beyond, under cover of night, and the younger follows. But their dangers are not past, for they dimly descry two figures approaching in the dark. They crouch in silent terror, but are relieved on overhearing the words, "Fly, dearest, I implore"; for these are fugitives too, only of a different order,—the keeper's only daughter, eloping with her lover. Beyond the postern gate they feel more secure. Through brier and bramble they grope their way, bruised yet fleeing. By day they sleep in the woods or in some crofter's hut, "by rustics kindly kept." By night they wander on. Their food is berries or growing grain, or an occasional charity-given meal. On reaching Gretna and Annan they forget that "they'd prisoners ever been." The great joy at Hunterston on their return is left untold.

The fourth Hunterston legend, of date 1513 A.D., is entitled "The Ghost of Flodden." Led on by their chiefs, the men of Hunterston and Campbelton were with the Scottish army at Flodden, on the fatal September 9th, 1513, when the "Flowers of the forest were a' wede awa." Both Robert Hunter of Hunterston, and Sir Hew of Campbelton were slain; and their combined estates fell to the infant heir at Hunterston. The tale opens with the laird away, and no one left to shield his domains or till his fields, none save women and children. The lady of Hunterston sits in the keep alone, gazing at the castle walls; with her infant son, to whom as her all should his father be slain, she addresses a soliloquy. Then follows a description of the dreariness of the storm heard that night in Hunterston Hall, as there the lady sits and nurses her "all." She thinks of her early days and breathes an ineffectual prayer for her husband's safety. It is then told how Sir Hew with his dying breath bequeathed his estate of Campbelton to her son, whom she reared and inspired with the recital of his father's and uncle's prowess and courage.

"The Hawking Craig," is the title of the fifth Hunterston legend, its date 1547 A.D. Quentigern Hunter succeeded his father in 1540, and seven years after, was slain at the battle of Pinkie, or Fawside, the last battle between English and Scotch as separate nationalities, and one marked by a headlong flight and great carnage at the "Fords of Esk." The legend begins by introducing us to the trysting-place of Quentigern and the Sybil, on the shore near Briguid Point, with the Hawking Craig and

Goldenberry Hill in the background. The picturesqueness of the scene by moonlight is graphically described, with a gloomy cave—a robbers' haunt. As eerie and alone, he stands upon the shore, the laird recalls to mind a former tryst when he had been told that, in seven days he would succeed his father, and be laird of Hunterston for seven years. It is now within a month of these seven years. Still, with a strange infatuation he fain would know his further fate. Soon, at his call, a demon laugh is heard; whilst dancing on the wave by Briguid Point, the fairy light of the Sybil, who has crossed from Cumbrae in her frail wickerwork cobble, is seen. She immediately lands and stands before him—a grizzled hag, with flashing eyes and tangled locks. She reminds him of her previous disclosures, tells him how the Earl of Moray has already set out against the Earl of Somerset, and how the western lairds and knights are repairing to Dunedin's Hill. Quentigern feels be cannot refrain from joining them, and though, suspicious of his fate, he wants to know it more decidedly. He braces up his courage to join the war by memories of his ancestor who had fallen at Flodden. His farewell to wife and children, and his prayer for their weal are then narrated; after which follow descriptions of the march to Pinkie, of the Earl of Warwick and Gray's fell execution, and of Quentigern's death.

The sixth and last of the Hunterston legends is a brief one, entitled " The Old Rest Tree," a tree to which we have referred in a previous chapter. It is hundreds of years old, and may be coeval with the castle itself. The legend tells of the love of a son of Hunterston for a fragile maiden whom be thought be saw, and to whom he breathed out his passion beneath that tree. But not a word did she utter, for she was a "'fairy lass." He sought a kiss, and in the ground she vanished 'neath that tree.

Other later traditions than the previous, may also be included in the legendary lore of the parish. One of these has reference to the sinking of the vessel belonging to the Spanish Armada, off Portincross in 1588, which has been superstitiously ascribed to the spell of Geiles Buchanan—a witch mentioned in the Irvine Presbytery records, (1650), along with others, who, acknowledge the abominable sin of renouncing their baptism and taking a new name. She is said to have been spinning on one of the heights above Portincross, when seeing the vessel approaching, she snapped her thread, and immediately the vessel sank. Another version of the legend is, that the vessel disappeared on her holding up her hands in imprecation. The birr of another witch's wheel at Ardrossan is said to have helped to raise the wind.

Violet Mudie was also the name of a witch at one time well-known in the parish. And then a little to the South of Thirdmailing, there stood, until lately, the Witch's Ash Tree, the passing of which, in twilight or dark, was a source of terror to not a few of the older inhabitants of the parish in childhood's years; its evil associations being traceable either to the supposition that a murder had taken place in its neighbourhood, or that those who had fallen victim; to the Plague of 1665 had been buried close by.

The following lines, in the ballad descriptive of the ride of the last of the Barclays of Ardrossan to the church of St. Mirren's, Paisley, for the Deil's gift of the "Enchanted Bridle," which proved so fatal to his son, have a parochial reference:—

"The thunder brattled wi' eerie thud,

As he rode ower the moor o' Kame;
But when he came to the Baidland Hill
The lichtnin' spelled his name.

O, up and see this eerie nicht!
Cried a shepherd in Crosby Glen;
But as he spak, the swift bay steed
Had passed ayont his ken.

Now saddle me fast, my father's steed,
Put his new bridle on,
For I maun ride to Portincross
Before the licht is gone."

Another romance having some small association with the parish, is that of the "Wandering shepherdess," who, with her docile followers is said to have found a night's shelter in the porch of the old church. In early life she had been a lady of rank, who had fallen in love with her father's shepherd. Out of revenge her father had slain the shepherd, who, with his dying breath, bequeathed to her his thirteen sheep. She forthwith adopted a wandering life, and these sheep followed her withersoever she went. Like the Good Shepherd she knew her own sheep by name. On reaching in her wanderings the neighbourhood of Woodside, she is said to have looked around and exclaimed, "And this is the lowlands of Scotland." Mrs. Boyd of Seaview, to whom I am indebted for the following ballad descriptive of her career, says, that her grandmother had seen this shepherdess at early morn lying nith her sheep around her on the grass which then grew where St. Enoch Square, Glasgow, now is.

"In Exeter's fair city a lady did dwell
For wit and for beauty she much did excel;

She loved a shepherd, below her degree,
Which caused her much pain and sad misery.
When her father came to know it, his anger was hot,
And with a loaded pistol the shepherd he shot;
And as he lay bleeding, the lady came by
which caused her to weep and to sigh bitterly.
O cursed be the gold since my true love's slain,
My joys are transported, my pleasure turned to pain,
O, yes, said the shepherd, none can my life save;
But, a wonder you'll see when I'm laid in my grave.
The flock that I feed now, my share is but small,
They are thirteen in number, they feed on yon hill,
My dear, they'll attend you wherever you go,
They'll be your companions, in the frost, wind, and snow.
She took up his crook, his cloak and his plaid,
Like a faithful young shepherdess to the valley she strayed,
And when she came near them, the sheep to her came
All-bleating, entreating, her love to obtain.
The ram she called Andrew and Sally his dame,
And Charlotte and Godfrey, each knew its own name.
With them she forth wandered, away from earth's strife,
Lamenting her shepherd all the days of her life."

We have lingered long on enchanted ground, and we find at the point, where unwritten story gives place to written, a suitable halting-place to look before and after. Here the day dawns and the shadows flee away. Hitherto they have been phantom forms that have been flitting before us, but it always requires some substance to cast even the faintest shadow. We must not therefore imagine that all upon which we have been dwelling had no reality behind. Rude they may have been, but they were stalwart men and true, who in those far back centuries traversed the glades and marshes of this parish. They loved and hated in their own rough way. They toiled and struggled, they did their work, bore their burdens they lived and died; and yet, their labour and existence have not been all in vain, for they did the rough hewing out of which was to emerge the more polished statue of a later day. They laboured, and succeeding generations entered into their labours, and sometimes for weal, sometimes for woe, reaped the fruits of what they had sown. And so, as from the dawn of written record we look after, as well as before, we see how the stream of time bears all its sons along, each new generation helping to swell the depth and volume of the ever flowing river that winds its way to the eternal sea.

# CHAPTER IV.
## ANTIQUITIES OF THE PARISH.—*(Continued).*

WITH the reign of David I. (1124-1153) gleams of historic light begin to break upon the scene; for then Hugh de Morville became Constable of Scotland and acquired a grant of the bailiwick of Cuningham, large portions of which he divided amongst the "Lesser Barons," who in turn subdivided their territories amongst a numerous class of freemen or tenants, who were the actual possessors. This Hugh de Morville was one of the most opulent and distinguished of the Anglo-Norman chiefs, whose ancestor had come over from Normandy at the time of the Conquest; and he was followed by many from England who settled under him as vassals, and became the progenitors of many ancient and honourable Ayrshire families, such as the Hunters, Cunninghams, Stevens, etc. The Eglinton family is an exception, being of Anglo-Saxon origin. In the reign of Malcolm IV.(1153-1165), De Morville is styled the lord of "Cuningham, Largis and Lauderdaill." As West Kilbride is in the bailiwick of Cuningham, it would be apportioned amongst the followers of De Morville.

Previous to the contest for the Scottish crown in 1292, the lands of the parish seem to have been chiefly in the hands of the Baliols and Rosses, but with the accession of Bruce to the crown (1306) we find a great overturn which particularly affected the district of Coningham, because of its close connection with Baliol, the ultimate heir and successor to the De Morville family; whose own great estates in it as well as those of the De Rosses and other adherents to his cause, formed a rich booty wherewith to reward the Conqueror's friends and followers amongst whom were the Stewarts, Boyds, Cunninghams and Sempils. Hence in 1306 we find the lands of Kilbride gifted to the Boyds, a branch of the Kilmarnock family, and we know that from early times the Cunninghams, or Glencairn family, possessed the estate of Carlung, and the Sempils that of Southanen. It is noteworthy, however, that although Aylmer de la Hunter of Hunterston had been one of the "Magnates Scotiae" who in 1296 submitted to Edward I. in the Baliol-Bruce controversy, yet his estate does not seem to have been forfeited on Bruce's accession to the throne.

Previous to this date, however, there had been fought in 1263, the well-known battle of Largs, in which Haco the Norwegian king, had suffered so signal a defeat at the hands of the army of Alexander III. At that time the defence of the central valley of this parish is said to have devolved upon the Boyds. On the King's enquiring who was acting that part and being told it was Boyd, he is reported to have replied "1 can trust him." Hence their coat of arms, "A clenched fist with two fingers pointing upward" and the motto, Confido, still to he seen on Boyd of Orchard's tombstone in the cemetery.

In connection with this battle of Largs, there would seem to have been a skirmish at the foot of the cliffs near Bank End, the sight of which was for long marked by a cairn, in which skirmish Sir Robert Boyd is said to have gained a victory over a detachment of Haco's army.

Fleeing from that skirmish some Norwegian warrior chief in all probability had dropped at the foot of the

Hawking Craig, a beautiful brooch of exquisite workmanship wherewith his plaid was fastened, and there for more than five centuries it lay in undisturbed repose until James Glass and another labourer, going there to quarry stones in 1826 stumbled upon it. This is the far-famed Hunterston Brooch, sold a few years ago to the Antiquarian Museum, Edinburgh by the late Mrs. C. M. Hunter. Professor Daniel Wilson has pronounced it the most remarkable relic yet discovered of the Scoto-Scandinavian period, and Professor Stephen of Copenhagen says, "It is the finest fibula ever found in Scotland, and the only one known to exist in that country bearing runes." The workmanship has been supposed to be Kelto Northumbrian or Carlovingian, (894 A.D.) and the Runic writing, a specimen of which may be seen in a cave on the Holy Isle, points to the Isle of Man. It is of the usual form of early Celtic brooches;—is of solid silver, gilt and ornamented with gold filigree work and set with amber. Its longer diameter is four and three-quarter inches, its shorter, four and a half inches. The pin, which wants a portion towards the point, is five and a half inches in length. On the blank spaces between the panels at the back, two former possessors have inscribed their names in runes of the Scandinavian alphabet. MALBRI-THA A TALK THAELE I LARI, *i.e., Malbritha oweth* (owneth) *this dalk* (brooch) *Thyle* (Speaker or Lawman) *in Lari* and TO ALK A OLFRITI *i.e.,* This brooch belongs to Olfriti. With less probability Professor Wilson makes the inscription read "Malbritha a Daimibeh I Daeol Maolfride," *i.e., Malbritha* his friend, in recompense to Maolfride. Although in Scandinavian characters, the name of the first owner is Celtic, and both names are such as were common among the Gallgael or mixed population of the Norwegian kingdom of the Western

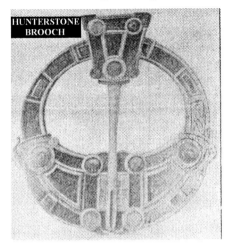

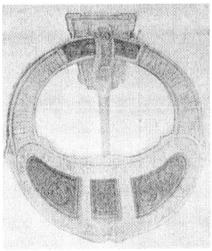

Isles. The forms of the runes are said to indicate a date for the inscription not later than the tenth century; and

this corresponds with the period when Celtic workmanship in Scotland was rising to its highest expression.
Whilst there may be variety of opinion as to the date and
other details of this brooch, there is practical unanimity
as to its great value. It found a place in the Paris Exhibition of 1862.

In addition to the brooch, there have been found in
the same locality some graves formed with rough stones,
several ancient coins, some cinerary urns, and a quantity
of partially calcined human bones. To the same period
may also belong the circular building now in ruins on
Auld Hill, Portincross, which is supposed to have been
used as a watch-tower during the Danish invasions; when
signalling stations were also established on the summits
of Tarbert, Law, and Kaim Hills.

From the accession of the Stuart dynasty, the
historic light becomes much clearer and principally plays
around the castles of the parish and the families associated with them. Of these the more remarkable are
Crosbie, Portincross, Cumbrae, Hunterston, Law, and
Tarbert Castles, for the most part keeps or towers of great
similarity of aspect. With their architectural structure we
have already dealt, and we now confine ourselves to their
historical associations.

The present Crosbie Castle, once nearly burned,
occupies the identical site of a former tower taken down
in the seventeenth century, although some portions of the
ancient walls have been retained. In the thirteenth century
it formed the residence of Sir Ranald Craufurd, the uncle
and friend of Wallace; and here, tradition has it, the
patriot passed many of his early days, and found at times
a refuge from his merciless oppressors. The ruins of a

sort of barbican or gate-tower by the side of the present approach to this mansion, seem to point to an early date.

Portincross Castle must date at latest from the reign of Robert II. (1370-1390), as there are still in existence some seven charters of his, and the following reign dated "Apud Arnele," which, of course, means Portincross Castle. In one of these deeds, "Adam More de Rowallan" is a witness to a charter granted by Robert IL to "Fergusio de Fullartone de arane terra de Orquo honyne etc.," and the deed is dated "Apud Arnel 26 to die Novembris Anno regni nostri Secundo," (1372). This charter is in the possession of Captain John Fullarton, of Kilmichael, Arran, the lineal representative of Fergus. Another of these deeds, of date 1374, conveyed the lands of Sir Andrew Campbel to the Hunterstone family. And yet another of date, 1390, the mills, multure etc., of Kilwinning and Beith to Kilwinning Abbey. But we have highly probable evidence that a castle was standing at Portincross in the days of Robert the Bruce; since we find that monarch granting to Fergus Fullarton a charter of the lands of Kilmichael, and the hereditary office of coroner of the bailiedom of Arran—which latter office entitles the lairds of Kilmichael to the perquisites of a firlot of oats and a lamb from every village in the island, still said to be punctually paid at the ordinary terms—and this charter is dated at Alderneil Castle in Cuningham on December 29th, 1307; but Mr. Weir of Kirkhall is of opinion that this castle more probably stood on the height

PORTINCROSS AND CASTLE

above Portincross, known as Auld Hill, where the foundation walls of a castle similar in dimensions to the present Portincross Castle are still traceable—the present one not being erected until the reign of Robert II. But wherever this castle may have been, we can boast of the great hero of Scottish independence holding court within our borders in the second year of his reign. Portincross Castle formed the chief messuage of the ancient barony of Ardneil, which in 1306 passed from the De Rosses, high sheriffs of Ayr, to the Boyds of Kilmarnock. As the Boyds, through their supposed descent from Simon, the brother of Walter, the steward, would thus be cousins to the King, what more naturally than that in passing from Dundonald Castle where he frequently lived and ultimately died, to his domains in Bute, Robert II. should halt for a few days at Portincross on a visit to his relatives?

The style of the building with its solid walls, arched roof and scanty light, points to the twelfth or thirteenth centuries as the date of its erection—before the introduc-

PORTINCROSS CASTLE TODAY

tion of gunpowder into warfare. In more modern times a larger window has been inserted to give light to some store-rooms to which a portion of it was adapted. As a mansion-house for the proprietor, the castle was abandoned shortly after the restoration of Charles II. but continued to be inhabited by fishermen and other tenants, until unroofed by the "windy January" of 1739. Since then, its walls have been slowly succumbing to the action of wind and tide.

This castle remained in the possession of the Boyds until 1737, when along with Drummilling Mill acquired from Carlung in 1725, it was alienated through their attachment to the failing Stuart cause, and passed into the hands of the Craufurds of Auchenames, who still possess it.

On the green beside this castle, there is an old iron cannon greatly rusted, one of five fished up in 1740, from one of the vessels of the Armada, which had been wrecked a few yards off in ten fathoms of water. This cannon is eight and two thirds feet in length, eighteen inches in diameter at the top, and twelve inches at the mouth. Up to 1837 the Spanish crown and coat of arms are said to have been visible near the touch-hole. The following extract from "Defoe's Tour," Volume IV. pages 257-58 has a bearing upon this subject. "Now," says he, "we are upon the western coasts, I shall mention that in the month of August, 1740, an attempt was made by diving to come at one of the largest ships of the Spanish Armada stranded in 1588 on these coasts. Another was dived for some years ago, but the sand being loose it turned to little or no account. This, which was lost near Portincross, was begun to be searched after by Sir Archibald Grant, and Captain Rae in August, 1740; and the following was the account that was transmitted to us, which we the rather insert, as it gives some notion of the operation by the diving engines. The country people had preserved by tradition the spot pretty near where she sank, and gave them all the information they were able. Immediately the divers went to work and swept for her, which they do thus.—They have a long line which they sink with leads; one end of the rope is fixed to one boat and the other to another; they row and whatever interrupts them, the divers go down to make a discovery. They soon happened on the place where the ship lay, which is scarce a quarter of a mile from the shore, in ten fathoms and a foot of water. Captain Rae immediately went down and found the vessel to be very entire, to have a great number of guns on board, but to be full of sand. The first thing he fixed upon was a cannon, which lay upon the sand at the heel of the ship. To this he fixed his tongs, which are made of strong bars of iron. They are open, when they are let down, and have teeth, which join into one another, as soon as they are fixed upon anything, he gives the signal, when they are made to shut, and the heavier the subject, the closer they hold. The cannon was drawn up with a good deal of difficulty; it measures full nine feet, is of brass, greenish coloured, but nothing the worse. On the breech there is a rose with an E. on the one side and a R. on the other side with this inscription— 'Richard and John Philips, brethren, made this piece, anno 1584.' But we may observe that by the E.R. on the cannon, which denoted Elizabeth Regina, and the Rose, as also the English inscription of the makers, it should seem to us that it could not belong to the Armada, but rather to some English ship that might have been cast away there. Ten of these brass cannons, and ten iron ones have been since carried into Dublin, and they hope to recover sixty." He further tells us, that when found the guns were charged; and that much of the iron scrap and rust brought up, was very warm to the touch, until exposed for some time to the air, when it cooled and crumbled away. The captain of this vessel and sixteen of its crew are reported to have been saved, and to have settled among the former inhabitants with whom they intermarried, thus giving rise to such names as Fairie (from the admiral Ferrara), Ravie, and Latta, long common in the district. Traces of Spanish extraction are still discernible in the features of the fishermen's children in the place.

A company was afterwards formed to recover the treasure supposed to be in the vessel, but, as its chief promoter died, it came to nothing. Of Cumbrae Castle and its historical associations we shall speak in our next chapter.

Hunterston Castle—"Tower, Fortalice, and Manor Place"—has been described by Fullarton as "a very perfect and interesting exemplification of an old Scottish

HUNTERSTON CASTLE

baronial dwelling, sadly mutilated and metamorphosed by being converted into a farm-steading, with, of course, its necessary, but most incongruous range of farm-buildings." This unsightly incongruity has been almost entirely removed by improvements recently carried out by Lieutenant Colonel G. Hunter-Weston. As to the date of erection of this castle nothing certain is known, but, as the Hunterston family have resided continuously on their estate since 1374, or even earlier, and as there is no discernible vestige of any older mansion or tower on the estate, either it, or one occupying the same site, may have been erected about that time; some, however, think the style of the present one points to the sixteenth century. In the historical memoir of the Eglinton family it is described as a small moated tower or keep, situated on the verge of what had originally been an inaccessible morass. The finding, in 1894, about two feet below the surface of its courtyard, of an iron ball such as used to be fired from a falconet or culverin,—a wall piece moving on a swivel—would seem to indicate that the din of warfare had not been unknown within its walls.

Law Castle, which Pont describes as a "Stronge grate Dounijon" is situated on an eminence at the base of Lawhill, and is of somewhat more recent date than the previous castles, having been erected by the Kilmarnock

LAW CASTLE

family. It was the principal messuage of the ancient barony of Kilbride, and seems to have formed a sort of guard-house to the village. It is a well-proportioned oblong tower of four storeys, measuring forty feet by thirty feet, by forty-six feet to the top of the bastions. The walls are six feet in thickness and of solid masonry. It is well lighted, having no fewer than eight windows on one side. There are four or five gun ports in its lower storey

LAW CASTLE TODAY

and a low doorway. A spring of water arose within. From its parapets an extensive view is obtained to the North-West and South. Its walls are still wonderfully entire although it has been for long unroofed, some of its parapet stones and flags having been used by "Prophet Boyd" in the early part of this century, to repair some of the orchard outhouses. The battered condition of some of the old stone-work about the door would seem to point to its having been stormed and pillaged at one time. As there is extant a charter of date October, 14th, 1482, conferring the lands of Kilbride, Dalry, etc. upon the Princess Mary, Sister of James III. and wife of Thomas, the Master of Boyd and afterwards Earl of Arran, in life-rent, and upon James, her son, in fee; and this Law Tower was the only house on the property suitable to form a residence for a lady of her rank, it is quite probably that this Castle was her abode for a time and that her royal brother may have occasionally graced its halls with his presence. Towards the beginning of the seventeenth century, it appears to have been tenanted by the Countess of Crawford, widow of David, Earl of Crawford, who was her second husband, her first husband being Robert, Master of Boyd. In this tower she probably spent the sunset of life, and as there is a tradition long current, that the bridge over Kilbride Burn was built by a lady who lived in Law Castle, it is conjectured that the inscription on the stone in the centre of the north parapet wall of that

REBUILT 1730.

I C.

MAII 1623.

bridge refers to this Jane, Countess of Crawford, as its builder. Shortly after her day, the estate was alienated and the castle allowed to fall into ruins. It was purchased in 1670, by Major Hugh Buntine, of Kilwinning, who had distinguished himself at the battle of Philiphaugh, and been appointed by Cromwell, Master of the Horse in Scotland. In 1711, it passed into the hands of William Baillie of Monkton, in whose family it remained until 1759, when his grand-nephew, through losses sustained by investments in the ill-starred Darien Scheme, was compelled to part with it by judicial sale. It was then broken up into ten sections—the Law portion being purchased by Thomas Boyd, of Dykehead, Dalry.

Tarbert Castle, which stood at the back of Tarbert Hill, immediately to the North-West of Meadowhead, was originally the Mansion House of Ross of Tarbert, an estate in which were included Blackdykes and North and South Chapelton. In 1450, it was alienated to Ross of Hawkhead, and afterwards passed through the Dundonald family into the possession of the Eglinton family. Its ruins stood until 1790, after which its stones were largely used in the building of Meadowhead farm-steading. A Mr. Baillie who died in 1856, aged 81, and who was familiar with the South end of the parish, well remembered Tarbert Castle as an old ruinous keep, with narrow, thick walls and small slits for windows. Castle, plantation, and mill, are now all alike extinct.

Just outside the northern boundary of the Parish are the ruins of Fairlie Castle, which the "Origines Parochiales Scotiae" describe as "a strong tour and very ancient, beautiful with orchards and gardens." It is a keep or tower very similar in appearance to Law Castle. Up to the middle of the seventeenth century, it belonged to the Fairlies, descendants of the De Rosses, who took their name from their estate; and one of whom, William de Fairlie received letters of pardon from Edward III. in 1535 for crimes committed in war with England. Its walls, long roofless, are still entire, but its once famous gardens are now no more.

Up to 1770 there existed near the site of the present mansion house at Carlung, an old castellated ruinous building, which doubtless had been, in its day, the scene of war and revelry, since a skeleton in armour was found in a field at no great distance.

A primitive fortlet or castle-hill, supposed by some to be a tumulus, also once stood about two hundred yards to the West of North Kilruskin. It measured thirty-seven paces in diameter at the base, seven and a half feet high on the one side, and thirteen and two third feet on the other. "It stands," says Fullarton in his notes upon Pont's Cuningham, "on the edge of a little ravine; is about forty feet across the top, perfectly circular, and detached from the adjoining surface behind by a broad and deep foss. A few years ago, the stones which had formed the rampart being carried off, a cavity or cell was discovered to have existed in the centre of the hill. It was of an oblong form, extended across its entire breadth within the wall, and was about six or eight feet in width and depth. Its walls were very neatly constructed, but entirely without mortar or any kind of cement. Nothing appeared to indicate in what manner it had been roofed; the place being filled solidly with stones and earth which had fallen in from above." Querns are said to have been found in its neighbourhood. A raised mound in the field, with a tree on its slope is all that now marks the site of this ancient fortlet.

The ruins of Southanen House, sometimes erroneously spoken of as the ruins of Southanen Abbey or Chapel which undoubtedly stood somewhere near, stand

RUINS OF SOUTHANEN HOUSE

close by the railway, about a third of a mile to the South of Fairlie station. This mansion-house was erected by Robert, the fourth Lord Sempill, who brought its model from Italy, probably when he was ambassador to that court in 1596. Its form was that of a square internal court surrounded with a piazza, and the spring of one of the internal arches, as well as the built up external arches of the piazza on the North side are still visible. The West or sea-front was only closed by a high screen wall, and had a spacious arched gateway in the middle surmounted by a moulded niche, designed for the armorial bearings of the builder with their chivalrous motto "Keep Tryst." A great part of this wall still stands. The ivy-mantled gables with a window in each are rather narrow, and there are the remains of six large windows on the North side. At the entrance-gate there is a stone seat on the one side, and a small recess on the other. The wine-cellar, and a small stone arched room, now used as a laundry, still exist on the East side, as also a ruined recess traditionally reported to have had at one time a subway connection with Fairlie Castle. Much of this side, inclusive of the dungeon, has been cut away by the railway. A very old yew tree stands by the gate, and a large number of fruit trees were uprooted in an adjoining field some years ago, by the present tenant. Of the South side there are no remains. The Sempills, who were noted for their obstinate adherence to the Roman Catholic faith, continued to inhabit this house till the beginning of last century, when the estates were alienated. It then passed to Lord Dundonald, who let it to humbler tenants, one part of it being used as a school, and papered with Dutch leather-paper. Some years ago, during drainage operations on Southanen farm to the North-East of this house, two cannon-balls were found, which point to a tale of battle in the neighbourhood.

Of the fort said by Pont to be near the village, the only possible reminder may be the name "Ward Road," sometimes given to Gateside road; but Mr. Weir is inclined to regard this fort as the one at Seamill, the chapel to which it was near being at Chapelhouse, as is shewn in Bleau's map.

Of the ancient families connected with the parish, whose history can be traced, the most ancient is undoubtedly the Hunterston family, variously known in old documents as Huntr, Huntar, Huntare, or Hunter. It is not our intention to enter into such genealogical details with regard to this or any other of the families of the parish as may be found with greatfulness in such works as Robertson's "Ayrshire Families" or Paterson's "History of Ayrshire," but merely to record very briefly a few of the more interesting incidents connected with them. From these and other sources we learn that the Hunter family was of Norman origin, Norman and William Venator or Hunter having probably come from England in the train of David I. in 1141. An ancestor of his crossed the channel as a follower of William the Conqueror. As evidence of this we find William Hunter appearing along with De Morville as a witness in an inquisition in 1116, by David of Cumbria, regarding church-lands at Glasgow. For some time there was a contest between the Hunters of Hunterston and a now extinct family, the Hunters of Polmood in Peebleshire, as to the origin of the family name; the latter adducing in favour of its priority an apocryphal rhyming charter of the reign of Malcolm Canmore (1057.) As this charter is a curiosity in its way, we may here reproduce it. "I Malcolm Canmore, king,

the first of my reign, give to thee, Norman Hunter of
Polmood, the Hope up and down, above the earth to
heaven, and below the earth to hell, as free to thee and
thine, as ever God gave it to me and mine, and that for a
bow and broad arrow, when I come to hunt in Yarrow

                    And for the mair Suith
The year         I byte the white wax with my tooth
of God.          Before thir witnesses three,
                    May, Maud, and Marjorie."

Unfortunately for the genuineness of this document,
Norman Hunter could not be born until some years after
the death of Malcolm Canmore, and royal charters were
not granted to laymen before the time of David I. The
Hunter family name appears to be allied to that of
Grosvenor (Le Gros Veneur, the great Hunter). Such
surnames descriptive of occupations or personal features
were not common in Scotland until the thirteenth century.
The next notice we have of this family is in a charter of
the reign of Alexander III. (1271) conferring the estate of
"Manners" upon William Baddebie "Excepta terra
quondam Normanxi Venatoris quod Rex Malcolmis
frater Regis Wilmi avi nostri ei dedit." We certainly
reach firm ground in 1296, when, between Robert De
Boyd and Rauff de Eglinton, we find the name of Aylmer
de la Hunter signing the Deed of Submission to Edward
I. in the Baliol-Bruce controversy as to the Scottish
Crown. (See Ragman's Roll.) The traditional origin of
the family name noticed in last chapter, derives some
support from their armorial bearings, viz, "Three Hunting
Horns," as also from their being for long the hereditary
keepers of the royal forestry of Little Cumbrae, and
holding their estate on condition of supplying so many
Kestrel Hawks per annum to the royal hunting establish-

ment. The oldest representation of their armorial bearings is to be seen on Melrose Abbey, being those of Abbot Andrew Hunter, who was Confessor to James II. and Lord High Treasurer of Scotland from 1449 to 1453. It was probably pride in the antiquity of their family lineage that prompted the mother of the late Mr. Hunter to reply to the then Earl of Eglinton, who had made a remark as to the length of time the family had been in the district, "Ay, langer than yersel' mair than aucht hunner years."

There are at least eight well-known families in Scotland and England who claim descent from the parent stock. The name of the ancestral estate, whose rental in full of all duties and services would seem to have been a silver penny per day, seems to have been changed from Ardneil or Arnele-Huntar to Hunterstoune, somewhere between 1462 and 1511. In addition to this estate, they also at one time possessed other lands in Ayrshire, Great Cumbrae, Holy Isle, Arran, Lanarkshire, and Forfarshire. Craufurd in his "Peerage" thinks from charters that they must have owned at least part of their Cuningham estates from the time of Alexander II. (1214-1249).

The earliest original document in the charter-chest of the family is a Crown-Charter from Robert II. conferring the lands of Arnele, resigned by "Andre Cambell Miles and Sheriff of Ayr," for faithful services rendered to that monarch. It is dated at Stirling, May 2nd, 1374. In 1513 John Hunter is slain at the battle of Flodden. From 1527-1536 his grandson Robert sells various of their estates, and in 1527 obtains a royal charter, making him sole proprietor under the Crown of Little Cumbrae. In 1547 his son Quentigern is killed at the battle of Pinkie.

From a younger branch of his family were afterwards descended the Hunters of Abbotshill, and two ministers of the Tron Church, Edinburgh; the Rev. Andrew Hunter, D.D., (1784) and the Rev. John Hunter, (1832). In 1562 Quentigern's eldest son Robert, signed, as one of the Ayrshire gentlemen, the "Band" in defence of the Reformed religion. In 1609 there is a serious dispute between William Stewart, the governor of Dumbarton Castle as representing King James VI. and the laird of Hunterston, as to the right to the falcons on Red Farland Craig. Meikle Cumray, which Robert Hunter claims as his, because on his estate of South Kames. He refuses to give up his right, or to appear when summoned before the King, at Edinburgh. The governor is ordered to go with a force to seize him, but helped by his neighbours, the refractory laird repulses the governor with loss; we are not told how the matter ended.

During the troublous times of 1647 Patrick Hunter is a member of the Committee of War for Ayrshire, and in 1662 he is fined £600 by one of the arbitrary acts of the Earl of Middleton. In 1665 he dies, and has the following epitaph inscribed to his memory.

"Lee heir a cedar lye that seventie-four years stood,
 By Neptune's strand spreading his blossoms fair,
 Feeding and sheltering Hunters in the wood,
 Bravely out-daring the cold winter air.
 Yea in dispyt your (*i.e.* Times) long continued chase
 He saw his children's children's children's face,
 But can we cease to sigh when we do mynd
 How thou repaired our Huntar's ancient towne,
 How Judgement, Witt, and Righteousness combined
 To make thy great old age a glorious croone."

From his third son Francis, were descended the Hunters of Long Calderwood, Lanarkshire, to which family belonged the celebrated physicians and anato-mists, Dr. Wm. Hunter (1718-1783), and Dr. John Hunter

(1728-1793). The former bequeathed the whole of his extensive Museum to the University of Glasgow, along with £8,000 for the erection of a suitable building for its preservation,—once the pillared hall to the rear of the Old College, and now the Hunterian Museum in the West End Park. Glasgow. The latter was as eminent as his brother as surgeon, anatomist, and physiologist, and some interesting memorials of him have but last year been presented to the Royal College of Surgeons, England, consisting of his portrait, and that of his father, his clock, Family Bible, and five volumes of interesting autographs containing letters from the time of Queen Anne to the present day. Their sister Jane was married to the Rev. James Baillie, minister of Kirk of Shotts, and afterwards Professor of Divinity. in Glasgow University, and thus the mother of the celebrated royal physician Dr. Baillie, and of Joanna Baillie, the well known authoress, and personal friend of Sir Walter Scott. Reverting to the main line of descent, we find in 1689 Patrick Hunter narrowly saved from the disastrous consequences of too pronounced a leaning to the Stuart cause;—his brother Robert becoming laird of Kirkland in 1686, and another brother James, the father of General Robert Hunter, Governor of Jamaica in 1734,—and yet another brother David, ancestor of Captain Charles F. Hunter of the 72nd. Highlanders, who served in the Crimean War at Kertch and at the fall of Sebastopol as well as in Central India. Patrick's grandson, Robert died in 1796 aged eighty-six, he was commander of a merchant vessel in early life, and afterwards by dint of economy and prudence succeeded in clearing off the encumbrances with which he found the estate burdened on his acces-sion; be left a comparative fortune to his successor. He is described as a regular Baron of Brodwardine, who wouldn't displace the hereditary tenants on his estate, but lived in their midst a plain and simple life, passing his leisure in hunting and fishing, and cherishing strongly Jacobite sympathies. Of his two daughters, the elder, Eleanora, married her cousin Robert Caldwell, who assumed the name of Hunter, and built the present mansion house. His grand-daughter, Jane, is married to Lieutenant Colonel Gould Hunter-Weston, a member of a Dorsetshire, and, previously a Staffordshire family. He entered the Indian army in 1840, and was engaged in diplomatic service at Oude under Sir W. Sleeman, and Sir J. Outram. From 1849-1857 he was in sole charge of operations against the Thugs and Dacoits, professional stranglers, poisoners and gang-robbers in Oude, except for a short time in 1854 when he was in Northern Burnish. He was present at the annexation of Oude, being then in command of the Military Police. He overawed three thousand fanatics at Mullebad, commanded an outpost at the siege of Lucknow and was present at the whole of the engagements at Alum Bagh up to the capture of Lucknow. Next in antiquity to the Hunters come the Rosses, who are associated as vassals of De Morville with the estates of Portincross, Kilbride and Tarbert; but as most of these estates were alienated in 1306 because of their devotion to Baliol, it is needless to dwell upon them further than to remark that for a considerable time they seem to have held the hereditary office of "High Sheriff of Ayr."

The Baliol family had also for a short time a footing in the parish at Southanen, of which John Baliol, afterwards King of Scots, is known to have been proprietor.

Of nearly equal antiquity with these are the Craufurds of Auchenames, whose title is derived from a small estate in Renfrewshire feued out in 1764 by Patrick Craufurd, with the retention of the feudal superiority over it. This family is descended from the Crawfords of Crawford through the Second or Crawford-John branch, and its first connection with the parish is through the estate of Corsby, where we have already seen Wallace's uncle Sir Ranald or Reginald Craufurd residing. This Sir Reginald had two sons, Reginald, who succeeded him in Loudon, and Hugh, generally reckoned the first of Auchenames. Some however hold that, Hugh was rather a nephew than a son of Sir Reginald. There is some evidence that Craufurds held Crosby as early as 1220.

In his "History of Renfrew" Crawford in 1710, says that the Craufurds had been in possession of Auchenames for well nigh four hundred years. In 1401 we find Thomas, the fourth of the line, receiving a charter of confirmation from Robert III. dated at Ardneil. In the same year we further find the same Thomas, making a "Mortification" for the health of his soul, and of his wife, and for the soul of Sir Reginald Craufurd, his grandfather etc. Then in 1498 James Craufurd receives a charter for the lands of Corsbie and Munnock. Amongst the more famous of this family were Robert, slain at Flodden (1513), and John, killed at Pinkie (1547). Three of its members have served their country as Members of Parliament *viz*; Patrick for Ayr in 1741 and 1747, and for Renfrew in 1761;—John for Old Sarum in 1768, and Renfrew in 1774;—and Edward for the Ayr burghs in 1866. About the end of last century, John Craufurd of Auchenames was an intimate associate of Charles Fox, and another John, the grandfather of the present Hugh, was an intimate friend of Gibbon, the historian, being with him, a few hours before his death. His uncle William was for some time Paymaster General of the Forces, and a brother of this latter, Donald, was a captain in the Royal Artillery, distinguished in the Peninsular War, and wounded at Waterloo. The family crest is a phoenix rising from the flames, with the motto, "God Shaw the Right," and "Tutum to Robore reddam" for Drumsoy.

The Crosbie estate has just passed by sale into the hands of J. Graham, LL.D., Largs.

The Boyds, Known as the Kilmarnock family— Kilmarnock crest, being still underwritten with the legend "Golden Berry"—have associations with the parish from 1306, when they received as royal gifts the estates of Kilbride and Portincross. According to Crawford's history of Renfrewshire the first found of the Boyds of Ardneil is a "Dominus Robertus Boyd, Miles," as witness in a contract between Bryce de Eglinton and the village of Irvine, (1205). There is a tradition that fifteen of this family of the name of Robert have been interred within one tomb in the parish churchyard of West Kilbride. Sir Thomas, successor to Sir Robert, who got the grant from Bruce, was present with David II. at the battle of Durham, (1346). The first of the house of Portincross is the Robert Boyd to whom Crawford refers in his peerage of Scotland "as mentioned in a charter of 1444, per Thomas Boyd de Kilmarnock, dilecto avunculo Roberto Boyd terrarum de Arneil." We have already referred to Thomas, afterwards Earl of Arran as probably once residing in Law Castle. In 1470 most of his estates were forfeited for behoof of the eldest sons of the Kings of Scotland, but most of them were restored in 1482 to

James his successor. Robert Boyd of Portincross and his eldest son Archibald obtained remission for fighting on Queen Mary's side at the battle of Langside (1567). Heirs (male) having failed, about 1680, Grizel Boyd married Alexander Fullarton of Kilmichael in Arran, and their son William Fullarton Boyd, who assumed the family name, succeeded his grandfather in 1712 and in 1737 alienated the ancient family estate to Craufurd of Auchenames. His grandson was Robert Fullarton, afterwards of Overton. Boydstone, formerly known as Little Monfode, is said to have come into the possession of the Boyds as a solatium for the murder of one of the Boyds by one of the lairds of Monfode; the spot where the untoward event occurred being known as "Cuffholm." The Boyds of Kilbride were patrons of the parish previous to the Earl of Eglinton.

The Glencairn family have their connection with the parish through Hugh Cunningham, the third son of William, fourth Earl of Glencairn, being the first of Carlung. In 1403 along with the adjoining lands of Drummilling, the estate of Carlung formed part of the endowments of the Collegiate Kirk of Kilmaurs, of which Sir William Cunningham a member of the Glencairn family was patron. Drummilling probably at one time belonged to the monastery of Kilwinning, and, at the Reformation, was gifted to Lord Boyd. Carlung came into the possession of Hugh Cunningham through his brother Alexander, the good Earl of Glencairn (as he has been called), and zealous co-adjutor of Knox. Alexander had received it from the Crown, to which it was alienated at the Reformation. Hugh's successor, Archibald, was killed in the feud which so long prevailed between the Cuninghams and Montgomeries. In the earlier part of last century through failure of heirs (male), the estate passed to John Boyd of the Pitcon family through his marriage with Marion Cuninghame of Carlung. Their son John built the nucleus of the present mansion-house; and in 1799, his daughters alienated the lands of Carlung and Corse to Archibald Alexander of Boydstone. From him they passed to Mr. Anderson, Banker, Glasgow, a relative of the founders of the Andersonian Institute, and thence about twenty years ago to James Arthur of the well-known commercial firm, Glasgow.

The Sempill family had its association with the parish through Southanen, which remained in their possession until about the beginning of last century. John the first Lord Sempill perished at Flodden. One of them built the Abbey or chapel in the reign of James IV. and another of them, the house in the time of James VI. Because of their strong attachment to the Roman Catholic faith, they were for long excluded from having any representative in the Scottish parliament.

The ancient house of Eglinton, surnamed Bryce, of Anglo-Saxon lineage, and probably dating from the reign of Malcolm Canmore (1057-1093), first acquired a footing in this parish on Little Cumbrae, first as protector of it in 1515, and then as proprietor in 1535. Any interest the House of Eglinton has in the baronies of Tarbet or Southanen only dates from last century, when these estates passed from the house of Dundonald into their possession.

With regard to families whose interest in the parish is of more modern date, we would simply mention, that Monfode of Monfode,—a small portion of whose ruined castle still stands to the east of the railway—a family dating from 1417 and one of whose members fell at Flodden;—held Boydstone as Little Monfode until the fatal feud to which we have already alluded;—that the family of Hyndman of Springside was originally of Lunderstone near Inverkip in Renfrewshire, which they possessed as far back as the reign of James V. and that they acquired the property of Springside by purchase in 1790, from Alexander Fairie, whose daughter Miss E. Fairie continued to reside in West Kilbride village until 1820;—that the Boyds of Orchard inherit that property from Mr. Robert Boyd of Dykehead who in 1759, acquired it from the Baillies. As the present representative of this family is Mrs. Doctor Robertson of Ardrossan, the name of Boyd, once so powerful in the district, may now be said to have passed out of its list of landed proprietors.

The last topic of antiquarian interest we would briefly deal with is, that of the ancient coins found in the sh, as shewing there were "bien folks" in West bride then as now. Of these the more remarkable known to us are *first*, those in the collection of Mr. M'Gillivray, Main Street, West Kilbride. They include (1) two silver pennies of the reign of Alexander Ill. (1249-1286) with the following inscription, xALExANDER DEI GRA REX SCOTORVMx, and were found near Portincross.

(2) Two silver pennies of James I. of Scotland.

(3) Two shillings of James I. of England, one found at Glenhead, and the other at Seaview, Seamill, with this inscription on the one side, JACOBVS DG ANG SCO FRA ET RIB REX, and on the reverse side:—EXSVRGAT DEVS DISSIPENTVR INIMICI.

(4) A gold Demi or sovereign of same reign found at Campbelton.

(5) A shilling of Elizabeth's reign found near Chapelton.

(6) A halfpenny of Charles I. time, found on Kaim Hill.

(7) A crown of William III. (1696) time, found near Meadowhead.

(8) A guinea of George III. reign, found in Church-yard.

*Second.* Coins in possession of P. M'Conchie, Schoolmaster.

(1) A shilling of Charles II. with the concluded words of the XII. Tables of Roman Law as superscription, *viz.* "Lex Suprema Salus Republicae." This coin was found in a drain near Biglees.

(2) A Gold Jacobus of James I. value twenty-five shillings found near Chapelton.

(3) A copper coin of date 1171.

III. The well-known Chapelton Find of three hundred and sixty coins ranging from the reign of Edward VI, (1547) to that of Charles II, (1660), and including a considerable admixture of foreign coins, especially German and Austrian. They were discovered more than twenty years ago by J. M'Pherson, ploughman, when working on a hill-face in front of Chapelton Cottages. They had probably been enclosed in a canvas bag which had mouldered away. For some years there had been a tradition current in the parish that there was a fortune, buried in that bank, but no one knew where, until these coins were accidentally discovered. Some of them are still in possession of Mr. David Cunningham, Clydeview; Mrs. Gemmell, Well Bank; Miss Boyd, Seaview and others in the parish, whilst others are scattered further afield. On very many of these coins, the image and superscription are well-nigh obliterated but specimens are such as, coins of 1571 and 1573, shewing figure of Queen Elizabeth with decoration of the "Garter;" others of James I reign, with such inscriptions as "Faciam Eos in unam Gentem," or "Qum Deus Conjunait, Nemo Separet," with plain allusion to the union of the Crowns; another of Charles' reign with the superscription "Auspice Regno, O Christe," etc. etc.

Having thus endeavoured to trace the historic annals of the parish from the dawn of written record through some seven centuries, we have seen that its bounds have not always been too obscure to be passed over even by royalty. We have noted the patriotism of its sons on such fields as Largs and Flodden and Pinkie. We have trod its ancient castles and companied with its ancient families. We have tried to read the tale of its old coins and other relics, and we leave its past story with the halo of enchantment around it, wherewith distance in time, and manners, and sentiment, encircle it; thinking of the days when a future generation shall read the story of the present in the same enchanted light.

# CHAPTER V.
## LITTLE CUMBRAE

"In night the fairest prospects sink,
Where Cumbrae's isles with verdant link
Close the fair entrance of the Clyde."

SO wrote Sir Walter Scott in his "Lord of the Isles" and in these lines he accurately describes the position of the island which is to form the theme of this chapter, for just where the Firth of Clyde is opening out to mingle its waters with the Atlantic lies Wey Cumra or Little Cumbrae "Grand Island, guardian of the Clyde. If thou wert only fortified" keeping sentry by the entrance to the great commercial waterway of the West of Scotland;—its most secluded recesses ever within sound of the ocean's

moan and the swish of the vessels that by night and day
are speeding past it. Far from, yet near to, the busy haunts
of men, it is an emerald gem in the midst of the azure
deep, well worthy of a visit; because of its picturesque

scenery, its wide prospects, its rugged cliffs and skerries,
its retired nooks, "its breezy bracken-clad slopes, its trap-
terraced heights, its marshy meres, its lonely caves, as
well as for its ecclesiastical and historical associations. It
is not a large island, being only one and three-quarter
miles in greatest length, one mile in greatest breadth, and
yet, there are spots in it so retired that one feels quite shut
out from the noisy world that lies so near;—alone with
Nature and with Nature's God;—spots in which the poet
might have erected his lodge in a wilderness, as St. Vey,
long centuries ago, did her simple chapel, where rumours
of oppression and deceit, of unsuccessful or successful
wars would never have reached him more.

The prospect from its highest point on Barr-Hoy,
four hundred and nine feet above sea level is at once
extensive and attractive. In a clear summer day, there lie
at our feet the smiling waters of the ocean, stretching
south-ward, far as the eye can reach, with. Ailsa Craig, or
Paddy's Milestone as it is humorously called, boldly
outlined in the offing. Eastward the eye ranges from the

northern confines of Wigtonshire along the whole sweep of the Ayrshire coast, inclusive of Carrick with memories of the patriotic doings of a Bruce, Kyle with the fond recollection of the poetic fire of a Burns, and Cuningham with the remembrance of a Scottish king's victorious arms. As the eye still sweeps on to Renfrew, hills and dales and sylvan scenes are ever continuing to greet the gaze. Northward, and nearly thirty miles away, the view is bounded by the hills of Dumbarton and Argyleshire, and embraces not a few of the watering places on the upper reaches of the Clyde Estuary. Westward we scan the undulating hills of Cowal and Cantyre, backed in the distant horizon by the Paps of Jura, whilst close at hand we survey the rural beauties of Bute and the Larger Cumbrae. The eye then sweeps along the jagged peaks of Arran, inclusive of Goatfell, past the Holy Isle and down to the neighbourhood of Pladda, after which Neptune resumes his reign,—the whole, a panorama, which, when seen amid bright sunshine and under a cloudless sky, it would be difficult to match in any land, or to equal amongst the many fair prospects with which our native land abounds. And if there is one period of the day at which it is lovelier than another, it is, when the sun is setting in a bath of mingled purple and gold, reflected from the heather wherewith the western hills are clad.

Cumbrae is probably derived from "Cum," as in *Cum*-berland, a steppe, and the ordinary Scotch word "brae," so that it means, "The Stepped Height." Lytteil however regards "Cumra" as a contraction of Keil Maura, the Church or cell of Maura or Mary, a pious virgin, who, after a life of active beneficence amongst the wives and daughters of the ancient chieftains from St. Bees to the Cumbraes, settled down on the Meikle

Cumra. Here she devoted herself to the godly training of a company of young maidens; occasionally visiting her like-minded sister Beya on the Little Isle, and at length gave name to the church she loved to frequent near Kirktown of Cumbrae, as she also probably did to that of Kilmaurs. The epithet Little is generally thought of as a distinguishing prefix, but as in olden time the island was known as "Wey or Vey Cumra," *i.e.*, the Cumbrae of St. Vey, Lytteil thinks "Little" is but the Anglificatioh of the Scotch "Wee."

Little Cumbrae can be conveniently reached by small boat either from Millport in Great Cumbrae or Portincross on the Ayrshire coast, the distance of the landing-place oh the East side near the castle being about two miles. Its most northern promontory, Sheanawally Point, will not however be half that distance from Porta-han Point, the southern extremity of Great Cumbrae. Between these two points there runs a strong current, called the Tann, which in stormy weather, has oftener than once claimed its tribute of human sacrifice.

The coast line is, generally speaking, rugged and precipitous, especially towards the south and west, small patches of sandy beach being few and far between. Basaltic columns, known as the "King's Chair," lying about a quarter of a mile to the south of the present light-house, are well worthy of attention. Small rocky islets, such as David Allen's Stane, Trail Isle, and Boll's Rock, lie close to the East coast.

The surface is rugged and covered for the most part with coarse grass, foggage and bracken, through which ever and anon the naked rock makes its appearance. Marshes, such as Gurag Mere, Lang Mere, Tammis Loch, etc., make their presence known more by their verdant vesture of reeds and rushes than by the amount of water visible from any great distance. A few tiny rills drain their waters to the sea.

The geological conformation of the island may be described as four or five trap terraces resting on a basis of old red sandstone, and sloping upward from South to North at an angle of about thirty degrees. The fauna of the island may now be said to be nearly confined to rabbits and a few wild birds. Wild goats were found upon it up to the beginning of this century, and three hundred years ago deer scoured its wind-swept heights and dreary solitudes, as the following extract from Mr. Donald Monro's description of the Western Isles in 1594 will shew:—"Besides this (*i.e.* Greater Cumbrae) lyes ane iyle callit Cumbray of the Dais, because there is many Dayis (*i.e.* deer) intil it." The Rev. D. Landsborough, however, is of opinion that "Dayis" is rather an old name for its trap terraces, because of which it was callit "Cumbray Dayis." The catching of its numerous rabbits is the main occupation of the tenant during the winter season, and forms a source of considerable revenue, though not to the extent it was in the earlier decades of the century, when as many as four hundred and fifty dozen have been known to be captured annually. The stock is kept up by the occasional transportation of a hundred rabbits or so from other parts of the Eglinton estate, and on one occasion at least we find an infusion of new blood by the introduction of three hundred from Ireland.

In addition to the familiar sea fowl, such as seagulls and divers, wild ducks, scarfs stockanats, and snipes, visit its meres, hawks flutter over its southern end, and

the cry of the plover frequently breaks in upon the still-
ness of its solitudes.

Lobsters are caught off its craggy shores, and saithe,
ling, whitings etc. abound in the surrounding waters.

There are few trees on the island, but ashes are
found towards the North-East, and a few patches of elder
and ivy are scattered here and there.

Natural bay is gathered from a meadow to the North
of the farm, whilst the brackens are cut, dried and stored
for bedding purposes. Furrow marks on the higher part of
the island indicate unremunerative attempts at cultivation. The only portions now under tillage are the garden
attached to the Light-House, and a few plots near the
farm-house where very early potatoes are grown. Cows
and sheep roam at their sweet will over the island and
browse upon the natural herbage.

Four families at present reside upon the island, two
on the East side, (farmer and a tenant), and two on the
West, (Light-House Keepers), but in the ruined circular
stone walls scattered over the island, there are signs of
enclosures which probably at one time included dwellings and gardens of some eight or ten other crofters who
all shared in its occupancy, tilling small portions of its
surface, and eking out a scanty livelihood with abundant
fishing. One of these circular rows of stones about fifteen
feet in diameter, and lying about two hundred yards to
the S.S.W. of the old Light-house, is supposed by some
to have been one of those bee-hive shaped houses which
were once so common in the North of Scotland. In 1818
we find the population of the island twenty. During the
summer season, it is considerably augmented both by
resident visitors and frequent tourists. The superficial

area is about eight hundred imperial acres or one and a quarter square miles.

In 1715 we find the island equally divided betwixt three tenants, Robert Montgomery, William Harper, and Robert Muir, with a total rental of, £200 Scots. It is however doubtful if the latter two resided on the island. According to the Eglinton Rent Roll, the yearly rental in 1847 was £105, and £6 from the Clyde Trust for lighthouse and grounds. Since then, however, the annual rental has been as high as £280. From the governmental point of view, the position of this island is somewhat anomalous, since politically it is connected with Bute, civilly with Ardrossan, and ecclesiastically with West Kilbride.

Small though its bounds be, this island contains many a spot that is fraught with antiquarian and historical interest, the nature of which may be partly gathered from the still surviving names of places, and their significance, *e.g.*, "Sheanawally," the Headland of the ancient Cairns; "Magga Clagh," the Burying Place of the Pechts or Picts; "Banclan Toyo," Holy Woman's Hillock; "Gurag Meyre," Lady Lakelet; "Santa Beya's Chapel"; "Belstane," Feast or Play Stone; "Cravie's Hole," Creek of the Devout Folk. "Allanturail," (corrupted into Trail Isle) Islet of the Nobles' Tower; "Steedhaum," Harbour of the Church Establishment; "Ryssel's Cave," Cave of the Champions; "Ocregman's Cave," Cave of the Bedesmam" Monks Cave, &c., &c.

Such names as these suggest many a scene of the olden times of which this little Isle was called to be the theatre. We have seen in a former chapter its association with a superstitious age, in the mark of the Deil's footstep, the existence of a Deil's Elbow, and Young Clootie's assistance in the erection of its Castle.

But, as we emerge from such gross darkness and peer through the mist of a distant past, through such names as those mentioned above, we can do something more than merely conjecture its bygone story, when we find our horizon bounded by the "Heroes Cairns" at Magga Clagh, close by Sheannawally Point, and we stand by, whilst the Yeats, or Picts—the old Gadeni of the Romans—bury their dead in their kistvanes of rude stone slabs, beneath the cairns fast by the sounding sea.

This takes us back to an early century of our Christian era, either before, or shortly after the light of Christianity had begun to dawn upon our Island, ere yet, the Scoti had dispossessed the Picts of their territory. It is a rude and barbarous age of war and bloodshed, and of these the Cumbraes have their share. The possibility of relics being found beneath these cairns was first suggested to the late Mr. Weir of Kirkhall, by variations in the compass, when brought near the spot. When the largest of them was opened in 1813, Lytteil tells us that there was first found a sword of great length and weight, with a guard for the welder's hand, and then a hauberk of scale armour with an iron byrnie, or breastplate; iron guards for the wrist and back; an iron Casque or helmet, very similar to the Roman "Galea," which consisted of pieces of wood connected with thin plates on each side, rivetted through and through with clenched nails,—a second sword so corroded by rust as to fall to pieces as soon as touched; and then at a greater depth, a short kistvane with an urn containing some brown dust and a few fine white teeth. The present Mr. Weir of Kirkhall, thinks that the nails found, were boat rivets, and that the mode of sepulture had been the mere upturning of an old boat over the remains, with stones heaped upon it. Whilst the cinerary urn may be referable to some ancient chief of the Firbolgs or Picts, who may have lived in the fort, of which there are vestiges on the cliff-top a short way to the South, the armour may very probably belong to some Norwegians, who had fled from the battle of Largs, and been buried by the sounding sea. The following poem of unknown authorship, sent to me, embodies this conjecture:—

> How beautiful Little Cumbrae lies
> Beneath the laughing summer skies,
> A gem upon the ocean's brow,
> It sparkles in the sunshine now.
> Come, let us seek its northern shore,
> And every cliff and crag explore,
> Climbing to where the sea pink waves
> Above the brave Norwegian graves,
> For—here, when on Largs' bloody field
> Their bravest chiefs were forced to yield,
> They fled from foes they dreaded more,
> Than fiercest surge that sweeps yon shore.
> Perchance, as each sad morning rose,
> Starting from their disturbed repose,
> They hastened to this very spot,
> And half their wretched fate forgot,
> As some white sail far out at sea,
> Gave hopes that they might soon be free.
> Then busy fancy's roving eye,
> Piercing the future mystery,
> Would place them on their own loved shore,
> And they would hear the cascade's roar,
> Or, 'neath the pines when evening fell,
> Of their heroic actions tell.
> Ah, no, the sail has passed from view,

> And with it passed those bright hopes too,
> And day by day, the less'ning band,
> Showed well that death's relentless hand
> Was busy there; his work sped well,
> Till none remained the tale to tell.
> And many centuries had passed,
> When bleached by every wintry blast,
> Upon this very spot of ground
> Their whitened bones at length were found,
> Then generous pity laced them here,
> And rained these cairns above the bier.

Here then, by the restless sea, there slumber in peace, the remains of our painted ancestors in their urns, and of our feudal heroes in their armour, awaiting the day when all the dead shall be raised to give in their account of the part they played on the stage of time. These relics were taken to Eglinton Castle, but appear to have been lost about 1819, or soon thereafter; possibly by dispersion, on the death of one of the Earls.

The echoes of the battle field die away upon the ear, contending Picts and Scots are laid to rest, the ambassadors of peace, the heralds of the cross, make their progress through the land, and amongst them, two ladies of distinguished piety, consecrated life and far-reaching philanthropy; Sancta Maura, and Sancta Beya, whose praises are in all the land from St. Bees to the Cumbraes, because of their missionary zeal. These ladies are supposed to have belonged to families of princely rank. In the heigh-day of life they had devoted their energies to the religious instruction of the maidens taught in their schools, and to the zenana-like work of bringing gospel truth to bear upon the matrons of the West. Wearied out with their labours more abundant, they at length sought to husband out life's taper at its close by retiring to the

Cumbraes, where each had a church or shrine consecrated to her memory: Sancta Maura's being on Great
Cumbrae, and Sancta Vey's on Little. By mutual visits
they solaced each other's solitude and sustained the fire
of each other's religious fervour, and in "the green
bracken-clad hollow of the rocky amphitheatre," in
which her chapel was planted, it is probable that St. Beya
breathed her last, and was buried in one of the graves
about a dozen yards to the South-East of her chapel.

It is a pleasing and soothing picture that rises before
the mind's eye, as we stand by her chapel's lonely site.
The matins and vespers of well nigh twelve centuries ago
float upon the breeze, and we think on the saintly woman
who there spent the sunset of life in meditation and
prayer, leaving behind her a shrine to which in after days,
many pilgrims repaired, landing on their pious errand
either at Cravies Hole on the East side, or Steedhaum on
the West.

We conjure up her image as she stands on the "Holy
Woman's Hillock" and surveys the scenery around,
whilst the walls of her modest chapel are reflected in the
"Lady Lakelet." We mark the pilgrims who believe in
combining a holiday with a holy-day, as they leave the
little fane after their devotions, and gather round the
Belstane to share in the sports and festivities of the
Saint's Day. And then, there come stormier times, when
the Peapars or Clerical fathers of St. Beya have to seek
refuge from their persecutors in the dim seclusion of the
Monks, or the Bedesman's cave, and then the old church
life vanishes from the scene.

The scanty ruins of Sancta Beya's chapel, which
was probably a dependency on Iona, are now no more
than the merest fragments of its foundation walls. These

ruins lie about half a-mile to the North-West of the Castle, in a spot so secluded, that little else than the immediately surrounding grassy and bracken-clad slopes, and the blue sky above can be seen; verily a meet abode for a hermit soul, "just such a place," as Lytteil remarks, "as meets the requirements of the legend of St. Vey."

This chapel is probably the "Ailan-na-ingen," *i.e.*, "The Islet of the Virgins," the church of Tighernac referred to in the Annals of Ulster, who states that it was built in 714 A.D. The Scoto-Irish called it "Chaibal Bhay." It appears to have been a chapel of mean construction, some forty-two feet in length, by twenty feet in breath, outside measurement. Of its length, twenty feet was occupied by the choir, which was divided internally into two sections, so as to allow one of them to be used as a chamber for the priest in charge. With regard to this chapel, "The New Statistical Account" supplies us with the additional information, that its walls were three feet thick, and, that in their construction, bad mortar had been sparingly used; that in the tomb, a little to the North, are two flat stones, on one of which, now broken in two, are sculptured some ornamental tracery, such as is usually to be seen on those ancient monuments called "Danish Stones," but without a vestige of inscription; that there was originally a a surrounding stone wall, whose foundations only now exist; and that there was a tradition, that this chapel, another at Ardrossan, and a third on the Garroch Head in Bute, were all served by one and the same priest, who journeyed "per vices" among them.

A few paces to the West of these ruins lies Gurag Meyer, or the Lady Lakelet, and about twelve yards to the South-East, two rifled grave kists, composed of rude slabs, after the manner of ancient pre-christian burial. To one of these we have already alluded, as the possible burying place of St. Vey, and Reid, in his history of Bute, tells us that on its being opened some years previously, a cist was found lying near the surface. The larger of the two graves is about seven feet in length, lies East and West, and has a large block of porphyry at its West end. The other grave, some few feet off, lies North and South, with a slab at its Southern end. There is a tradition that one of the priests connected with St. Vey's chapel was buried, with his gold chain, somewhere near. The keenest efforts of avarice to recover the gold chain, have as yet been unavailing, owing to the water and mire from the adjacent marsh rushing in to take the place of whatever excavations are made.

About eighty yards South by West, from the site of the chapel, and not far from an ivy-clad crag overhanging the Langmere, are the foundation walls of an old house twenty-two feet square, which may have been the residence of the priests serving at the chapel. About fifty yards to the South-east of this, we mark the site of another ruin some thirty feet in length, at the Eastern end of which, are the foundations of a round tower, probably used as a belfry. Some of these buildings may have been used as a hospice for the reception of pilgrims visiting St. Beya's shrine. About ninety yards North-East from the last mentioned tower, and fifty-five yards or thereby South from the South-east corner of a wall-crowned cliff known as Priest Hoy, there may still be seen the site of another chapel of later date very similar in dimensions to the former, whose place it may have taken. It has good lime cement in its walls; of which, the northern one, three feet thick, is still visible. The priest in charge had apparently a chamber, eighteen feet by ten feet, to the North of the choir. A cairn to the North of this marks the site of an ancient homestead.

Nearly a hundred yards to the South of the last mentioned chapel, is the Belstane, whence were viewed the games attendant upon St. Vey's festival day—which would be conducted on the plain stretch away to the North and East. This Belstane is a finely-pointed pyramid about five feet high, resting upon a bare patch of rock surrounded with grass and bracken.

Seven yards to the West is the Cup-stane, so named from a cup-like hollow in the centre of its South face, four inches in diameter, by one and a half inches in depth. In appearance like a mill stone, its purpose is shrouded in mystery. Other places associated with St. Vey's name and fame are Banclan Toye, or Holy Woman's Hillock, about a third of a mile to the North of the Belstane; Cravie's Hole, or the Creek of the Devout Folk, immediately to the North of the castle; and Steedhaum, or the Haven of the Church Establishment, a short way to the South of the lighthouse.

The caves of the island are enumerated in the old Statistical Account as seven. One of them is a square room of thirty-two feet; another has damp and mephitic air, the recesses of which have never been penetrated. The most famous of them is perhaps the Monk's Cave, which lies on the slope of the Storrills, about two-thirds of a mile to the South of the castle, with a tree at its entrance. The glen to the East is known as the Cosey glen, or Glen of the Caves. According to Lytteil, the Monks' Cave is over a hundred feet in length, and quite dry. Its entrance through a deep rift in the cliff, is somewhat difficult to discover. Secure within its recesses, there are high ledges, where clerical refugees might soundly sleep. The polished smoothness of its sides seems to indicate the frequent habitation of this cave. Ryssel's cave lies to the South-West of the island, and not far off is Ocregman's Cave.

Many of the caves are more fissures in the rocks. In some of them split marrow, bones and quantities of reddish-brown dust have been found—pointing to an age when the caves of the earth were men's dwelling-places, and the beasts of the field, their food. With the Monks' Cave there was traditionally said to be a means of submarine communication with Bute; and there is another tradition of much more recent date, that secreted stores of liquor, used by some tourist fond of picnicking on the island, are still stowed away in the recesses of some cave.

Ere leaving the earlier story of the island, we may mention "Miller's Fort, or Craig, *i.e.*, the Maiden Camp, or Lady Fort," whose scattered stones lie on a hill to the West of the castle and on the north margin of Tammis Loch; where, tradition has it, there was also at one time a chapel. This fort may have been the island's means of defence before the erection of the castle.

In the earliest Christian centuries, this island formed part of the kingdom of Strathclyde, and was inhabited by the Damnii, with an admixture of Dalriad Scots. During the reign of Alexander III. the island was held by a person of the name of Gilavearn, whose son was held as a hostage by the Earl of Menteath, the sheriff of Ayr; and then we hear nothing more definite about it until 1366, when it appears as one of the possessions of the "High Steward." It must, therefore, by this time have passed out of the hands of the Norwegians, who appear to have held it for some time, along with the Western Isles.

The chastened voices of devotion are drowned by the sound of the hunting horn and the excitement of the chase. Little Cumbrae now forms part of the royal forestry in which it is the king's delight to engage in the exhilarating sport of driving the deer with hound and horn; and if he may not, like those of modem times, have his sbooting lodge, he must at least have his hunting tower. This tower must be strong enough to afford protection and safety to the crowned head, and ample enough to provide accommodation, during the king's absence, for a body of retainers to act as guardians to his deer preserves against poaching intruders. Such a hunting tower, with rampart, fosse, and drawbridge, he finds in the "Auld Castle" on Allinturail, where in the Spring of 1375, we find Robert II. residing for a season—as is shewn by a charter, which he there and then sealed and authenticated with his sign-manual, as he did another from the same place in 1384.

We hear little more historically of Little Cumbrae until 1404, when Robert III. grants by charter to his son, James, *inter alia*, "Totas et integral terras insularum de Bute, Arran, Comrey, Majors et Minore." It has been conjectured that the castle may have been built by Walter, the Steward, who married Marjory, daughter of Robert the Bruce, and thus became the founder of the Stewart dynasty. In this case he would be the noble referred to in the name, "Allinturail."

Of this castle, and the whole island as a royal hunting-ground, the Hunters, of Hunterston, were for long hereditary custodiers—at least from the time of James II.—since the name of William Hunter is entered as keeper in the Chamberlain's accounts in 1454-56. The Hunters are said to have held their estates in Ayrshire on condition of supplying so many kestrel hawks per annum, to the royal hunting establishment. As "Hereditary Foresters of Little Cumbrae," their emoluments would seem to have been at first twenty shillings per annum, and afterwards two chalders of oats from the king's lands in Bute, rights of pasturage on the island, and other perquisites. In 1515, however, the Earl of Eglinton would seem to have obtained the authoritative protection of the island, as is shown by the following entry on the "Register of the Privy Seal," (October 28th, 1515)—"Lettre to Hew, Erle of Eglintoune, makand him and his assignaris,

LITTLE CUMBRAE CASTLE

keeparis, oversearis, correkaris, and supplearis, of the Isle of Littel Comeray, the dere, the cunyngis, and wild besties, being thairin, quhill the kingis perfite age of xv. yere; becaus Robert Huntare, of Huntarestoune, forrestar of heritage of said isle, is nocht of power to resist the personis that waistis the saymin, with supplie and help, etc." This state of matters would appear to have continued until 1527, when the good "forester of the heritage Robert Hunter, of Hunterston, and Jonate Montgomery, his spouse," obtained by royal charter a grant of the island, and thus became sole proprietor under the crown. Notwithstanding this charter, Robert, son and heir of William, Lord Sempill, appears to have obtained a grant of it in 1532, which is revoked, in 1534, in favour of Robert Hunter, It was sold in the following year to the Earl of Eglinton, to whom it was confirmed by Royal Charter, of dates, March 16th, 1535, and June 11th, 1537.

Since that time, Reid in his "History of Bute," tells us, that it has been possessed by his heirs, and was occupied for a time by the Sherriff of Bute. In the testament of Hugh, second Earl of Eglinton, (1546) he leaves to his heir "All and hail the Ile of Litel Cumrays, with the tour and fortilage of the samen, and pertinents thereof, etc." "Upon the occasion, however," says Reid, "of the marriage of Sir John Sempill of Beltrees, at Holyrood, on 5th March, 1565, Mary, Queen of Scots, before her marriage. with Darnley, among other grants to the young couple preparatory to their espousals, conveyed to them the Little Cumray in the shire of Bute, which grant passed the Great Seal. This matter was brought forward afterwards by the Regent Morton, who urged that the gift was null and void, as Crown lands could not be alienated. Beltrees answered that it was a plain deed of gift under the Great Seal, and could not be recalled. Unfortunately, in arguing his point, he lost his temper and expressed himself in a manner that was held to be treasonable. He was accordingly put to torture; but Reid tells us be could not discover how the matter ended.

One thing, however, is clear from the burgh records of Glasgow, that in 1568 it was in the possession of the Earl of Eglinton—for in them there is a register contract entered into by "Hew, Erle of Eglintoune, and George Elphinstoun, glassin wricht, burgess of Glasgow, that the said George suld upheld and mentene the places of Ardrossan, Polnone, Glasgow, and Cumray, in glassin wark, as also the place of Irvin"; for which he was to receive yearly, "Twa bollis meil, and ane stane cheis. Ane gif it happinis the said Erle to hald house in ony of thir foir saidis places when it sal happin the said George to wirk, the said George sall have his meit the time that he wirks; and also when the said George turses creillis of glas and leid to Irvin, Cumray, etc., the said Erle sal caus ane carrage hors to turs the samyn out of Glasgow."

"The tide of time flows on, and the thoughts of men grow greater with the process of the suns." The dark ages come to an end, and the dawn of Protestantism dispels the mists of Papacy. Still, for many long years after the Reformation of 1560, the old faith continues by intrigue and diplomacy to endeavour to gain the ascendancy. And in these dark doings our little island has its share, for off its coast in 1592, there might have been seen cruising a suspicious looking craft, awaiting the embarkation of one, who, from amongst his solitudes as a refugee in the Cumbraes, was seeking to gain the shores of Spain, as the emissary of a dire and disastrous design. In his description of this incident in his "Church History of Scotland," Cunningham tells us that the Cumbraes had swarmed with Danes in Haco's days; that their creeks had often sheltered pirates, who skulked securely there, and landed upon the coast at their leisure; and then he adds, "With no population in 1592 but a few miserable fishermen, and completely cut off from the rest of the country, one should imagine no hiding-place could be more adapted for concealment and escape. But the Church possessed a kind of omnipresence, and no detective police was ever more effective than were its ministers in capturing

Papists. Then, as an illustration thereof, he goes on to narrate how the Rev. Andrew Knox, minister of Paisley, got information that George Ker, a Doctor of Laws, and brother of the abbot of Newbattle, and one who had been excommunicated for Popery by the Presbytery of Haddington, was in the Cumbraes; whilst a vessel was lying in Fairlie roads awaiting a favourable wind to set sail for Spain. Ere, however, he managed to get away, he was seized by Knox and a company of Glasgow students. On the vessel being searched, papers of a suspicious character were found in his trunk. He was imprisoned in Edinburgh, and, under torture, confessed that he was to negotiate the descent of a Spanish force upon the coast, which would be joined by such of the Scottish nobles as were still staunch adherents of the old Faith, and then Roman Catholicism would be again established, or at least tolerated.

The dispute in 1609, between Captain Stewart of Dumbarton Castle, and Robert Hunter, of Hunterston, and others, about the latter's taking away the hawks on Cumbrae, has a more probable reference to the falcons got near Red Farland Point on Greater Cumbrae, and therefore we pass it by with a mere mention.

The years roll on. Charles I. has fallen a martyr to the "Divine right of Kings," and Cromwell is planting his iron heel on every part of the realm, if so be, be may crush to the ground the Royalist tendencies that smoulder in many a breast; and nowhere more strongly than in the hearts of some of the Scottish nobles, amongst whom is Lord Montgomery, who stands charged in Balfour's Annals in 1657 with "six barrells of that pouder which belong to the publicke which was carried to the Isle of Bute (or rather Cumbrae) for defence of his house, for which the said Lord Montgomerie is to be comptable to the publicke." In anticipation of my lord Protector's visit to Scotland and with a view to the safety of wife and family he has his father's fortlet on Little Cumbrae strengthened and garrisoned with forty men. Thither Lady Montgomery and her children have betaken themselves, whilst her lord has joined the war and been taken prisoner at the battle of Worcestor, in 1657. In alarm at her perilous position, Lady Montgomery thus writes to the Marquis of Argyle, "Before my lord marched with the King to Ingland, be had an order under his majestie's band, for allowing of fourtie men of this new leavie out of his father's lands and his own, for the men he has raised (whom he) maintains in this place, it being also weil for the publick good, as the safety of me and my children in these tymes." The object of the application is, that these forty men should be recognised by the Committee of Estates as part of the Eglinton contingent.

Again in September, 1657, Lady Montgomery writes an imploring letter to the same Marquis, in which she says;—"I could be at no quaet till I despatched this bearer with those (tidings) back to your lordship, humbly and earnestly entreating your lordships to let me have your full and free advice quhat you think fitting for me to doe, first in reference to my lord for his relief or supply in such straits as he by his imprisonment will undoubtedly be in, next concerning myself and children's safetie and subsistence and this place quhich my lord by his care and charges has made a considerable strength, and in regard of the situation of it might prove very useful, as weil for the publick as my particular owne (and other friends) good, and has by God's blessing been so this tyme past.

But now I am affrayed for many reasons, not fit to trouble your lordship with at this tyme, that without other helps than I, in my lord's absence, can afford, I shall not be able to maintaine it in such a posture as is neceessary to oppose an enemy; and my fears are, that less than that may rather invite than keep off an enemy etc." To this the Marquis replies:—"For your fort in the Cumbray, I fear the cost of it will outgo the profit; for in my judgement your ladyship must not now in the conditon that (your) family is in retier yourself, but rather ask leave both from the Committee of Estates and Monk, to leive whare you please with your ordinar family . . . so after you have offered the fort to the Committee of the Shyr, if they will be at the charge, if not, you and they both may offer it to be disposed of as the Committee thinks fit; but in my judgement, it will be better for you, that it were demolished and these things in it, I mean guns and ammunition secured, for if you get a protection, it will secour your other stuff."

In this fortlet, too, about the same time, Principal Baillie found a refuge for ten months from the advance of the victorious Cromwell upon Glasgow. Of his retreat, he thus writes in his well-known letters: "Cromwell with the whole body of his army and cannon come peaceably by the way of Kilsyth to Glasgow. The magistrates and ministers fled all away. I got to the Isle of Cumbray with my Lady Montgomerie, but left all my family and goods to Cromwell's courtesy, which indeed was great, for he took such a course with his soldiers that they did less displeasure in Glasgow than if they had been in London, though Mr. Zachary Boyd railed on them all, to their faces, in the High Church."

From the old Statistical Account we learn, that Cromwell's soldiers surprised the Castle, destroyed the fortifications, and burned its woodwork in 1653, leaving it the roofless ruin it still is; an act of revenge probably due to Archie Hamilton, one of the Protector's chief correspondents, having been confined in its dungeon and afterwards hanged.

Ardrossan Castle, about the same time, shared a similar fate, because of the enmity of the House of Eglinton to the Protector. The Protector's Council in Scotland seem to have allowed Lady Montgomery one fifth of her husband's forfeited estates.

Fast by the blue waters of the Firth, Cumbrae's Castle walls, so bare and gaunt, still stand to remind us of scenes of royal mirth and quaking fear enacted within its halls. The sigh of the wind and the moan of the sea are now the only sounds to be heard, where, of yore, song and revelry abounded and the clash of arms resounded. Its glory is departed, leaving behind "the touch of a vanished hand, and the sound of a voice that is still."

The stream of the ages runs on, and feudal pomp and the strife of contending factions give place to commercial enterprize. The products of foreign lands must be brought to feed the industry, and minister to the gratification of the advancing civilization of Glasgow and the West,—a watery highway for the vessels that pass to and fro must be available by night as well as by day, if their voyage is to be unimpeded and the dangers of shipwreck avoided. So in 1750 a beacon fire is kindled, first in a chauffer, and afterwards on the top of a tower thirty feet in height, and twelve feet in internal diameter, on the summit of the isle. This light-house tower, whose ruins still stand, though its staircase is broken down, is said to have been the second structure of the kind ever erected in Scotland, the other being on the Isle of May in the Firth of Forth. At its top was kept burning throughout the livelong night, a coal fire which, for upwards of forty years, continued to guide the mariner on his destined course. An Act of Parliament of 1756 says "that after the lighthouse on Little Cumbrae shall be finished as to have the proper lights and signals put therein, it shall be lawful for the trustees, to levy certain rates from ships passing or

LIGHT HOUSE AND FOG HORN, LITTLE CUMBRAE

repassing, whether by the middle channel or between the Island of Little Cumbrae and Bute, or by the East side of Little Cumbrae, or between the island of Bute and Arran, etc.; also to erect a breast or wharf upon the Island for landing coals for burning in such lighthouse or any other material necessary for building the lighthouse, or other powers connected etc." Powers are also given to the then Earl of Eglinton to feu two acres for said lighthouse, as also to make a road from the shore, feu duty to be £2. Reid says the lighthouse was first lighted with a coal fire in December 1757, and a proposal made in 1785 to light it with candles, was abandoned in favour of its removal to a new site. The earth around, still saturated with ashes, testifies to the large quantity of coal consumed. To bring such a quantity of coals to the summit over a rugged path, must have entailed no small labour; and then, as the old Statistical Account remarks:—"From its too lofty position it was often so involved in clouds as not to be perceptible or only dimly seen." Its light too, must at all times have have been flickering and unsteady. It was doubtless this experience, along with improvements made in the use of lighthouse apparatus, which led to the erection in 1794 of a new lighthouse, at a height of eighty feet above sea level, on a precipitous ledge about the middle of the Nest side of the island. Quoting from the "Gentleman's Magazine" of September, 1793, Reid says that the new erection, whose lantern is 120 feet above sea-level, would be lighted for the first time on 1st October, but that the old light on the top of the island would be continued, until it would be seen how the new one succeeded. It was lighted with thirty-two oil lamps, having reflectors made of silvered glass. In 1826 a new principle was adopted with fifteen oil lamps and silver reflectors, each costing £60, so that its light could be seen like a star of the first magnitude thirty miles out to sea. In 1836 further improvements were made, and prior to 1864 the system of illumination by dioptric lenses which throw out a most brilliant light, was adopted. These lenses regularly keep pace with the march of modern improvements. The oil is raised from the well to the wicks by a species of clock-work, which sounds a warning bell, as the oil approaches exhaustion. At midwinter, about four gallons of oil are consumed in a night. The light is a steady white one. Attached to the light tower by a covered way is the dwelling-house of the principal keeper, and close at hand is that of the assistant keeper, with enclosed and well stocked garden stretching north-ward. A stretch of level pasture-land lies to the South, whilst a boat rides by its fastenings in a little cove or harbour below. In spells of four hours at a time, from sunset to sunrise, each keeps alternate watch by the light to see that all goes right, realizing his responsibility for the safe conduct of many a vessel, whose watch is strain-ing his eye to catch the guiding ray. It is almost needless to say that everything is kept with the most scrupulous cleanness and regularity. A few yards to the South of the lighthouse is the fog horn, which emits blasts of five seconds duration, at intervals of from eighteen to twenty seconds, whenever by day or night, the scene is shrouded in mist.

But, though the erection of the first lighthouse may mark the dawn of a utilitarian age, the star of romance was still shining o'er the isle when it was sending heavenward its tongues of flame, for then there was living in retirement on this lonely isle of the sea, John or Jonete Woodrow, a daughter or grand-daughter of a brother of the great church historian. Robert Woodrow, her father succeeded his father as minister of Eastwood, a charge which he demitted on the ground of ill health, November 26th, 1757. He was twice married, and Jonete was his daughter by his second wife, Ann Ruthven. Scott in his "Fasti" tells us that Robert Woodrow died in Little Cumbrae, May 13th, 1784, in the seventy third year of his age, and fiftieth of his ministry, and may have been buried there. In the "Memoirs of the House of Seton," we are told that Woodrow the author of the "History of the Sufferings of the Church of Scotland," wrote a memoir of Alexander Seton, Commentator on the Epistles of James, first and second Peter, and Acts xviii, and that the M.S. of this work of Woodrow's was found by the Rev. Mr. Leitch of Largs, in the island of Little Cumbrae, where some of the author's descendants resided and died. Around the head of this Jonete Woodrow, there has gathered a halo of romance, which has given birth to two tales, the former of which, to the following effect, is more credible than the latter. As a loving and dutiful daughter, she is said to have sacrificed her social enjoyment and isolated herself with her father in this solitude, with a view to restrain him from habits of intemperance, to which he had become addicted; and to have carefully tended a bower on the spot which she had selected for her grave, and where, afterwards, she was actually buried. The less probable version of the romance is, that, having fallen in love with the young captain of a vessel bound for a foreign shore, she ascended to the spot which was afterwards to be marked by her tomb, to watch his vessel depart; and thither again she repaired about the time of his expected return, to mark the first signal of his vessel's approach. For weary days and months she strained her eyes and scanned the horizon, but neither speck nor sail of the longed for ship could she descry. She then faded away like a flower at early dawn, and was buried on the spot whither she had gone, so oft, with aching heart and longing gaze. This spot, twelve feet square, is situated on the edge of a cliff near a dell on the West of the Bennets, and towards the South end of the island. It contains two tombstones o'ershadowed by a small plane tree, and enclosed within a stone wall. The inscription upon Jonete Woodrow's stone, whose baptismal name was John, is as follows:

"This ston is erected to perpetuate the memory of John Wodrow, daughter of Mr. Robert Woodrow and

Anne his wife. She died on the 17th of April, 1774, in the fourteenth year of her age, and was interred heir at her own desire.

Death is the crown of life, was death denyed, pour mortle live in vain."

JONETE WOODROW'S GRAVE, LITTLE CUMBRAE

This, however, does not appear to have been the original stone, as James Brown, of the Andersonian University, in 1860, speaks in his "Sketches on the Clyde" of the stone being then in ruins, and having this motto:

"Behold the emblem of thy state
In flowers that bloom and die,
Or in the shadow's fleeting form
That mocks the gazer's eye."

The inscription on the other stone is as follows:—

A. W. Archibald, born, 28th June; died the 4th July, 1790.

"Tis God that lifts our comforts high,
Or sinks them in the grave,
He gives, and blessed be His name,
He takes but what He gives."

Ere closing this chapter, we would mention as other spots worthy of a visit, the rugged scenery towards the South end of the island, including Pipers' Loch, the Storills, the Needle's Eye, and Boll's or Buller's Rock— also upright stones, probably monumental, about four hundred yards S.S.W. from the Old Lighthouse—the "Whistling Stane," about one hundred yards to the N.W. of the same Lighthouse, which probably derives its name from the wind, in a certain direction making a whistling noise when passing through a hole in it—and the Lady Rock, so named from its resemblance to a lady in walking costume, on a cliff to the West of the farmhouse etc., etc.

Thus have we wandered, for an hour or more, over the trap terraces and the bracken-clad solitudes of Little Cumbrae. We have traversed its caves and wended our way around its coasts. We have scaled its heights, and stood with fond delight by its spots of historic and antiquarian interest, and now as we leave it, we leave it as something more than a worthless waste, a mere rabbit warren, or a huge rock guarding the entrance to the Firth of Clyde. We leave it with fond memories of its present spots of beauty, and of its past record of historic interest. We commend it to general notice as a place well worthy of a visit, which should not be of less duration than a summer day, if, even hurriedly, one would see its places of interest, and come away with an intelligent conception of their relative positions.

# CHAPTER VI.
## ECCLESIASTICAL LIFE OF THE PARISH.

NOTWITHSTANDING Mr. Weir's opinion that saints rather derived their names from places than gave names to them, the name Kilbride is generally supposed to indicate ecclesiastical life as a not unimportant factor in the early story of places known by that name. The prefix "Kil" or "Cyl" originally signified a cover, or retreat, and was applied to the groves of the Druids, and then to the caves, cells, or chapels of Christian missionaries, as also to the consecrated cemeteries attached to them.

St. Bride, Bridget, or Bridgid was an Irish virgin of the fifth century, distinguished for her piety. She was born at Feughart, near Dundalk. Dr. Waller tells us that her father was a man of rank, probably a prince or noble-man of Leinster—that, whilst yet an infant, she was committed to the care of a bard, who watched over her with paternal interest, and instructed her in all the learn-ing of the age. She soon became distinguished for her extraordinary wisdom and piety, and having voluntarily embraced a life of celibacy, she was admitted to the veil by a bishop in West Meath, in the sixteenth or seven-teenth year of her age. According to the "Golden Legend," a work held in high repute in the Roman Catho-lic Church, the wood of the altar to which she was then led put forth shoots. It also tells us, that, although she gave most of the butter to the poor, of the revenue deriva-ble from which she had to give an account to her mother, in accordance with the custom of the times, she was able so to multiply the remainder, as to present a better account than any of the neighbouring maidens. About 480 she is said to have erected the famous nunnery of Kildare, (The Church of the oak) near a great oak tree, an institution which was largely endowed by the kings of Leinster. She travelled all over Ireland, founding numerous long-celebrated establishments of Brigidine nuns. By her numerous biographers truth is hopelessly mixed with fiction, but she was beyond doubt a very wise and holy person. She was so highly esteemed by the bishops and clergy of the British Isles, that they frequently consulted her on the regulation of religious matters, and on one occasion her counsel was held authoritative in a Synod of Dublin. After a life of piety and charity, interspersed with not a few reputed miracles, such as the healing of the blind, and the curing of lepers, she died in 525, aged nearly seventy, and was buried near the great altar at Kildare. Her monument was ornamented with gold, silver, and precious stones, but both body and shrine were afterwards removed to Downpatrick, to escape the ravages of the Danes. Her memory has ever been held in great veneration, especially in Scotland and Ireland, as may be seen from the many churches and places known by her name.

Thus is our ecclesiastical story associated with a distant past and a barbaric age, when the light of Christianity was but slowly dispelling the darkness of heathenism in our land, and her church fabrics were little better than Columba's cell at Iona,—rude structures of logs, thatched with reeds. Is it too great a stretch of imagination, or too severe a demand upon a pardonable credulity, to suppose that one of those primitive structures may have found a local habitation in West Kilbride, whilst yet the memory of her patron saint was green. Throughout the Dark Ages, whose obscuring cloud still broods over most of the parishes of Scotland, the ecclesiastical story of West Kilbride shares the common fate.

As cemeteries have generally, however, been contiguous to churches or altars, and ancient urns, containing human ashes, have, as we have seen in a previous chapter, been found in sufficient numbers at Seamill to indicate the presence there, even in pre-Christian times, of a burying place, we may reasonably conjecture that a heathen altar, and afterwards a Christian church may have stood in that neighbourhood in pre-historic times. This conjecture is still further strengthened by the rude stone cists containing skeletons, found about twenty years ago near the Sanatorium. The existence of such a church or chapel is also preserved in such names as "Chapelhouse" and "Chapelton" close at hand.

As the vicarage of Kilbride was in Roman Catholic times subordinate to, and dependent upon, the Abbey of Kilwinning—a Benedictine establishment, whose Abbot for long centuries was the ecclesiastical Superior of the surrounding district—the conjecture is far from unreasonable, that chapels at Kilbride and Chapelhouse, etc., may have been erected not long after 1140, the date of the building of Kilwinning Abbey. Another name in the parish with an ecclesiastical bearing is Kirkland—both farm and house—pointing to these, in pre-Reformation times, as church property, and forming part of the spoil that afterwards fell into the hands of greedy and grasping barons; and especially in this parish the Earl of Glencairn and Lord Boyd. The comparatively higher value of the tiends on the estate of Kirkland seems to corroborate this presumption. "Kirktonhall" also suggests the presence of a Kirk somewhere near—if not on the actual site of the present one—in days long past. To the same conclusion points the fact, that a portion of ground, at one time largely waste and unenclosed, but now, owing to its central position amongst the most valuable feuing ground in the parish, (extending from the Cross to the Cemetery Road), was known as the Kirk Croft, whilst the Kirk Loan was close by. Here in the days of yore, St. Bride's Day Fair was held, a fair to which the farmers were wont to bring their horses for sale, the farmers' wives their homespun lint made from home-grown flax; and the fishermen of Portincross and Hunterston their salted herrings. Such fairs were generally on the day set apart in the Calendar for the special honour of the saint, and hence though now held on the second Tuesday of February, O.S., St. Bride's Day was originally on February 1st, her special festival day. These fairs or festival days originated with the clergy, who derived emoluments from them, and were generally celebrated within the church and its precincts. Even up to the beginning of this century, the travelling packmen, who frequented these fairs, continued to exhibit their wares within the church-yard.

Other surviving indications of the earlier ecclesiastical story of the parish are to be found in such names as "Kirkstead," given to the supposed site of an old church at the foot of the hills to the East of Kilruskin. This may have been the cell or church of St. Ruskin, or Ronskan. "Glaisterland" which means "Glebeland" is the name still given to a field on the farm of Meadowhead adjoining Kirkland, though formerly it was a separate croft,—

"Corse, Corsehill, Corseby" are also said to have ecclesiastical associations.

From the "Origines Parochiales Scotiae" we learn that David I. bestowed upon the church of St. Kentigern in Glasgow, tithe of his Kain of Strathgonie, Cunegan, Chul, and Karric, and that West Kilbride was then included in the parish of Largs.

During Covenanting times, West Kilbride seems to have made no great figure; the moderate views of the leaders of the district preventing those zealous outbursts so common at that time in other parts of Scotland.

Of the churches or ecclesiastical fabrics previous to 1732, when that, preceding the present parish church was so greatly repaired and enlarged as to be practically a new church, we know but little definitely. On the strength of these words in Pont's Cuningham (1608)—"Kilbryde Kirke, a Perochiall church seatted in a fertille soyle neir to wich anciently wee ther a stronge forte." Mr. Weir thinks that the earliest church or chapel in the parish was situated at Seamill, where there was a fort; whereas there is no reliable evidence of a fort ever having existed near the site of the present church. This church, which would be a Popish Chapel, would, he thinks, be laid hold of at the Reformation by some powerful baron, and allowed to fall into decay. This opinion Mr. W— supports by the fact, that we find no house of older date than 1660 now standing in the village, as well as by Ridsheelis (Shielings or huts of fishermen) indicating a considerable population near Seamill. On the other hand, there is considerable evidence that the parish church stood on its present site in 1649, as no mention is made of it in the Presbytery Records, as requiring to be transported, when the perambulators visited the parish in that year, under powers conferred upon them for the transportation of Kirks and dismemberment of parishes. The dilapidated condition of the Church on the present site in 1732, when the Presbytery enforces its repair, would also seem to point to its having then stood for a considerable time. It was a very incommodious and mean-looking edifice. The following extract from the Kirk Session Records will shew the necessity for the improvements made a few years later.—"July 29th, 1729, this day reported, that the minister at the desire of Mountain elder, had called for Alexander Cunningham, Wright in Kilwinning, to take a look of the Kirk, who accordingly came, and to the best of his judgement told, that it was in the most ruinous condition of any Kick he had seen of this long time: For which reason (they) thought the sacrament could not be conveniently given till the rest of the gentlemen concerned be acquainted in order to a speedy reparation of it;—ordered further that the minister speak to them about this affair."

That a church had existed in the parish long before the beginning of last century is further well established by the fact that the names of ministers serving the Cure from 1567, have been handed down, and from its having been previously served by a Vicar subordinate to Kilwinning Abbey, whose monks enjoyed its rectorial tithes and other revenues. The patronage of the parish passed from the Boyds to the Earl of Eglinton in 1503. In James V. time the vicarage was taxed at £2 10s 4d of estimated value, and at the Reformation it produced £40 per annum, so that the minister of West Kilbride was then like the rector of "Sweet Auburn" passing rich on £40 a year, and like him too in that, remote from towns, he ran his godly race. But the rectorial tithes further produced to the monks of Kilwinning, seventy-nine bolls, two firlots of meal, fifty-three bolls of beir, and £8 of money.—In addition to the Chapel of St. Bride, Chalmers in his "Caledonia," tells us that previous to the Reformation, there were other chapels in the parish, one, as we have already seen, at Seamill,—another, at Southanen, said to have been dedicated to St. Enan or Inan, a confessor at Irvine who died 839, and was commemorated annually on August 18th. This chapel was built by Lord Sempill in the reign of James 1V, although,. there was probably an earlier one on the same site. Its revenues consisted of ten merks annually from the lands of Meikle and Little Kilruskin; two sowmes of pasture grass in Mains of Southanen,—a sowme being as much grass as would pasture a cow or five sheep—and an acre of land to the North of the cemetery-wall, as a site for the Chaplain's Manse and garden. The ruins of this chapel were to be seen up to 1824.

We have also already spoken of St. Vey's chapel on Little Cumbrae. She died 896 and was annually commemorated on November 7th. Chalmers' remark as to the Parish Church before the present one is this:--"The parish church of West Kilbride is a long, narrow mean-looking edifice, low in the walls, deep roofed, and upon the whole, is of a very bad construction." That it was long and narrow will be seen from the fact that its external measurements were seventy-five feet by twenty-four feet. Its walls were so low as to belittle over ten feet high. These low walls were perforated with small windows, protected by outside shutters, three of which were in the North wall, and two in the South. The roof was deeply pitched and had four sky-lights on the North side, and two on the South. A small belfry, (the pillars of which way still be seen by a fountain behind Springside House), surmounted the East gable, and the bell was rung by means of a rope passing through the ceiling, whilst the ringer stood on the floor of the gallery, close to the door.

OLD PARISH CHURCH, WEST KILBRIDE

Latterly this church had galleries at each end. The Eastern one, erected in 1817, was twelve and a half feet deep, and had six rows of pews. To these galleries access was obtained by outside stairs, at the East and West gables, of which the Western one was latterly surmounted by a covered porch; access to the area of the church was gained by doors beneath the gallery entrances. There were also private entrances in the North or front wall to the Hunterston and Auchenames family pews. In 1834, an important addition was made to the church at a cost of £238. It was known as the "Feuars' Gallery," because erected for their own use by the subscriptions of feuars. The need at that time for such an addition is plainly discernible from the following excerpt from the Kirk Session records:—"July 24th, 1833. The meeting resolved to provide every possible accommodation in the church for people who can procure no seats, by having forms set along the passages." This addition projected backwards from the central portion of the South wall to a depth of eighteen feet, and was forty feet in breadth. The entrance to its seats in the area was by a door in the centre of the South wall, and to its gallery by an outside stair on its East side. This gallery was as large as the East and West galleries of the old part of the church combined. This addition had four windows in each of the East and West walls, two above and two below. Its walls were considerably higher than those of the old portion. Its roof was pavilioned. The church, as a whole was heated by means of two stoves, one near each of the Eastern and Western area doors. The area of either part had no floor, except a foot board to each seat. The Feuars' Gallery was the only gallery floored throughout. A paved passage ran through the older part, from the East to the West door. To the South of this central passage there were square seats, and ordinary pews running North and South, whilst to the North of it, there was a long Communion or Table Seat, running East and West. The pulpit, was transferred at the building of the Feuars' Gallery from the centre of the South to the centre of the North wall. It was surmounted by an "Eye" as the symbol of the Divine Omniscience. Between it and the Table Seat there was a small folding board, designed to serve as a Table for the Communion elements. To the left of the pulpit there was a slightly raised seat for fathers with children to be baptized. The Baptismal basin was inserted in an iron bracket fixed to the side of the pulpit. In the

Feuars' Gallery the seats ran East and West, with a passage down the centre.

The "Jougs," now affixed to the wall behind the church, were then fastened to the West gable. Culprits placed in them stood halfway up the West stair, and are reported to have been pelted with rotten eggs, especially by the women. The late Dr. Ritchie was wont to maintain that they were brought to the parish by his grand uncle on the paternal side.

A high wall separated the surrounding burying-ground from the narrow street, and at the gate which was near its East end, there was a covered burial vault, the property of the Springside and Orchard families. Two enclosed burial places;—one of them with three large altar-stones, belonging to the Hunterston family—were situated near the middle of the North wall of the church. A narrow gateway and stair at the North-West corner afforded another access to the burying ground and church.

Of the tomb-stones in the churchyard, there are none of very ancient date. In so far as we can see there are only three, more than two centuries old. The oldest is a very small one in memory of "Robert Miller, Sailer in Hunter-stown, who deied the year 1671." Next to it in antiquity is a large flat stone, now in the space betwixt the Mission Hall and the Churchyard wall, around whose edge may be deciphered these words:—"Here lyes the corps of Janet Mountfod, Spouse of Archibald Stiel in Newton, who departed this lyfe, the 17th, of March, 1691," within this surrounding inscription there are commemorated other relatives who died at a later date. The only other one of the seventeenth century, bears this inscription: "W.F.—A.M.; here Lyes the Deisied Annie Miller, spouse To William Fareie, Carponder, Who Departed This Lyfe Upon The 24th, of September, 1695."

The epitaphs are for the most part nothing more than a record of the names, dates of birth and death, place of residence and occupation of those buried beneath. Occasionally, however, we get a glimpse of the personal history of those commemorated, as when we are told that Robert Starret Esq., son of Mr. Robert Starret, School-master, in the beginning of this century, resided thirty-six years in the island of Carriacou, West Indies, and that Daniel Love, Esq., grandson of the above Robert Starret, resided a few years in the island of Grenada, West Indies.

Now and again too, we have a eulogium passed upon their character, as when it is said of Mary Jane Love, wife of captain D. Grahame of Glenny, that "to the poor she was charitable and benevolent without ostenta-tion; her irreparable loss as a pious and affectionate mother will ever be regretted by her family"—or of John Boyd Esq. of Carlung, that "he was a gentleman of untainted honour and integrity, liberal in his sentiments, warm in his affections, and amiable in his manners,"—or of James Galbraith, steward, Crosbie, that he "was upright in all his conduct, honourable and amiable in every feeling," that he "lived to the age of eighty, happy in the love of all around him, in the full and cheerful enjoyment of all his faculties," that his "death was the result of a melancholy accident," and that none more sincerely than the family whom he served, lament his loss and revere his memory.

The usual headings are—"Erected to the memory of—; or. "Here lies the corpse of—or. "This is the place appointed or ordained for the burying or interring of.— Verses of scripture are frequently subscribed, *e.g.* "This mortal must put on immortality"—"For I know that my Redeemer liveth, and that He shall stand at the latter day upon the earth."—Blessed and holy is he that hath part in the first resurrection, on such the second death hath no power."—"The Lord gave and the Lord hath taken away, blessed be the name of the Lord."

Still more frequently verses of poetry are found subscribed :—*e.g.*

"How loved, how valued once avails thee not,
   To whom related or by whom begot,
   A heap of dust alone remains of thee,
   Tis all THOU art, and all the PROUD shall be,"

Pope's well-known "Address to the Dying Soul" supplies two inscriptions, one on the tombstone of Mary Smith, spouse to Hugh Parker, Kilmarnock,

"Cease, fond Spirit, cease thy strife
   And let me languish into life,
   Hark, they whisper, Angels say,
   Sister Spirit, come away."

the other on the tombstone of Mary, daughter of the Rev. John Adam, once minister of the parish:—

Vital spark of heavenly flame,
   Quit, oh quit, this mortal frame,
   Trembling, hoping, lingering, flying,
   O the pain, the bliss of dying.

On the tombstone of Allan Spiers, farmer in Kilruskin we find these lines:—

You that pass by, pray lend an eye,
   Think on this and behold;
   You see the grave all sorts do crave,
   The young as well as old.

"Submit to death, no wealth, or strength,
   Will save that fatal hour,

> For you, like I, must yield and die
> By unconquerable power."

On the tombstone of Robert Miller, Farmer, in Sandiland, there are the following lines:—

> "Remember thou that passeth by,
> Thou must return to dust as I,
> Tho' in youth's bloom and vigour brave,
> Thou must descend into the ave,
> Let precious time now be well spent,
> For it will give thy mind content,
> When thy last moments do appear,
> For there is no repentance here."

Another poetic inscription runs thus:—

> "God was pleased me home to call,
> And made my time of sickness small,
> My soul to God I did resign,
> Since I by faith am wholly Thine."

Yet another is to the following effect:—

> "Remember, man as thou go'st by,
> As thou art now, so once was I,
> As I am now, so must thou be,
> Remember, man, that thou must die,"

In another poetic effusion, Agnes Farrie is described as:—

> "A loving Christian spouse and friend,
> Pleasant in life and in her end,
> In humble Dust the Body lies,
> Till all the Sleeping Dead shall rise,
> Rous'd by the great Archangel's voice,
> When saints assembled shall rejoice,
> And like the Stars in Glory shine,
> And sing forever Love Divine."

One need have little difficulty in perceiving that the following lines are inscribed over a sailor's grave:—

> "Tho' winds and waves and Raging Seas,

> Have tossed us to and fro,
> Yet by the hand of Providence,
> We harbour here below,
> Safe from the dangers of all,
> And rest as in a sleep,
> Till He who calleth us, do call
> To join the vocal fleet."

Norman Hunter is bewailed in these lines:—

> "Forgive, blest shade, the tributary tear,
> That mourns thine exit from a world like this,
> Forgive the wish that would have kept thee here
> And stayed thy progress to the seats of bliss,
> No more confined to grovelling scenes of night,
> No more a tenant pent in mortal clay,
> Now should we rather hail thy glorious flight,
> And trace thy journey to the realms of day."

Yet another tombstone bears these lines:—

> "Feeble mortal, why so strain
> To lengthen out thy destined line,
> This world affords but grief and pain.
> Strive in virtuous deeds to shine,
> To heaven at death, thy soul shall fly,
> Whilst low in earth, thy flesh doth lie."

To the far-famed poetical epitaph over the grave of Thomas Tyre, the Pedlar, we shall have occasion afterwards to refer.

The symbolism used, which is often carved on the reverse side of the Stone, is of a very limited range, being almost entirely confined either to emblems of trade, such as a plough with a double team for a farmer; a ship for a sailor; adze and compass for a cooper; crown, hammer, and compasses, for John Robieson, Hammerman in North Thirdpart; or to mementoes of the brevity and mortality of this present life, such as sandglass, coffin, skull and cross bones. There is little to suggest the higher

Christian hope of a resurrection morn, unless it be a rare
cherub or angelic figure, surmounting the emblems of
mortality. In such symbolism combined with the poetic
inscriptions we have recently quoted, we have a clue to
the prevalent aspect of death cherished in bygone centuries by the inhabitants of West Kilbride. Plainly, the
frailty of our mortal being, and the solemn lessons that
the brevity of man's life on earth is well fitted to teach,
were the more prominent features of their conception of
departure from this world, though rays of Christian hope
were not altogether awanting as a relief to the sombre
gloom.

A flat stone to the East of the Church, contains the
epitaphs of four ministers of the parish, viz, the Rev.
John Adam, (senior and junior), the Rev. Arthur Oughterstone, and the Rev. William Vassie. Thus economically
have the parishioners of West Kilbride commemorated
the names of their departed ministers.

The old Churchyard has been disused as a place of
interment since 1858. Still under its sad repose the ashes
of not a few whose memory is dear to the older inhabitants of the parish, and to our minds there is something
more hallowing in God's Acre around God's House, than
is to be found even in our best kept cemeteries. It may be
sentiment, but it is sentiment hallowed by the sanctity of
sacred associations that draw the mind heavenward, and
link a living generation of worshippers with those who
have worshipped in the same sanctuary before them.

In the old church, the collection was taken in plates
placed outside at the foot of the stairs, and some still
alive can remember the incident of the tame jackdaw
once appropriating a shilling of it, and flying off with it
to the top of a house nearly opposite. This coin, and a

small diamond scarf-pin, stolen through an open window
from the Rev. Mr. Findlay's dressing table, were afterwards found in its nest. The collection would also appear
to have been at one time taken by a ladle, as there is still
in the possession of Mrs. Boyd of Highthorn an old
collection-ladle with a brass body and iron handle, which
was purchased at Mrs. Vassie's Sale. But however
gathered, the collections in this old church were by no
means large, as the following specimens of a month's
ordinary collections at different dates will show:

| 1770, | August 5th, Sabbath, | £0 6 4$\frac{1}{2}$ |
|---|---|---|
| ,, | ,, 12th, No Sermon | |
| ,, | ,, 19th, Sabbath, | 0 5 4$\frac{1}{2}$ |
| ,, | ,, 26th, No Sermon | |
| ,, | ,, 29th, Wednesday, | 0 3 8 |
| 1784, | February, 6th, Sabbath, | 0 4 2$\frac{1}{2}$ |
| ,, | ,, 13th, Sabbath, | 0 9 3 |
| ,, | ,, 16th, Weekday Sermon, | 0 7 3 |
| ,, | ,, 20th, Sabbath, | 0 3 11 |
| ,, | ,, 27th, Sabbath, | 0 5 0 |
| 1809, | March, 5th, Sabbath, | 0 11 5 |
| ,, | ,, 12th, Sabbath, | 0 9 5 |
| ,, | ,, 19th, Sabbath, | 0 11 10 |
| ,, | ,, 26th, Sabbath, | 0 2 4$\frac{1}{2}$ |
| 1834, | September, 7th, Sabbath, | 0 12 5$\frac{1}{2}$ |
| ,, | ,, 14th, Sabbath, | 0 12 9 |
| ,, | ,, 21st, Sabbath, | 0 11 11 |
| ,, | ,, 28th, Sabbath, | 0 12 8 |
| 1843, | June, 4th, Sabbath, | 0 5 4 |
| ,, | ,, 11th, Sabbath, | 1 6 4 |
| ,, | ,, 18th, Sabbath, | 0 14 9 |
| ,, | ,, 21st, Fast day, | 0 5 4 |
| ,, | ,, 24th, Saturday, | 0 4 7$\frac{1}{2}$ |

„                       „     25th, Sabbath,        1 14 10
„                       „     26th, Monday,        0   5   4

On September 10th, 1844, we find one as low as
1/10, and about that period they generally ran from 3/- to
8/-

The following extracts from Presbytery and Kirk
Session Records will show for what purposes church
collections were sometimes made in bygone days:—
"August 14th, 1649. A contribution to be gathered from
all the parishes within the bounds of the presbiterie for
reparation of the Houses in Irvine that were burnt."

"October, 24th 1688. 6 lib. Scots, West Kilbride's
share out of the 200 lib. ordered by the Synod of
Glasgow and Ayr, to be given to the Rev. Alexander
Seymour, Junr., on isle of Cumrae, because of his small
maintenance, on condition that he abide fixed on the isle,
except when Presbrie does allow thereof."

March 19th, 1718. Synod's Voluntary Collection for
ministers in Pennsylvania, £28, Scots.

About same date. "For French and Irish Protestants,
24 lib. Scots 3/-"

May 28th, 1729. "This day, Hugh Hill, in Glenhead,
having represented to the Session his bodily affliction by
reason of the King's Evil in his thighs, and that he was
advised to go for Moffat Wells for cure, but had nothing
to bear his charge, ordered that there be a publick collection made for him, and that the minister make intimation
of it from the pulpit, &c."

November 5th, 1788. Collection on the Fast-day
appointed by the General Assembly for the glorious era
of the Revolution, being this day a hundred years, 8/0$_{1/4}$.

September 27th, 1795. Special Collection for
Glasgow Hospital, £2 5s. 0d.

May 17th, 1800. Collection for the poor sufferers by fire at Kilmarnock, £1 10s. 0d.

February 26th, 1807. Collection for Foreign and British Bible Society, £12 4s. 5½d,

The ordinary church-door collections were devoted to general Church objects and the maintenance of the poor. The following extracts from the Kirk-Session Records will illustrate what was understood by general Church objects:

1771, February 14th. To J. Workman, his salary as Kirk Officer, 10/-.

1771, February 26th. To J. & W. King, for mending the School windows, dressing the minister's Kirk door and painting it, 4/11d..

1772, February 19th. To Mr. Dow, for Presbytery Clerk, 6/8d.

1772, June, 2nd. To John Workman, for a Bell String and latch for the tongue, 1/1d.

1773, January. To Robert Starret for Session Clerk, £1 0s. 0d.

1773, July 6th. To James Baillie for going to Troon for the Communion Elements, 2/-.

1774, To Robert Rayside for making a lock and two bars to Kirkyard Yeat, 4/2d.

1781, November 26th. To Alexander Ritchie for laying some flags to the school floor, repairing some of the tables and making a little desk, the most part of the timber belonging to the school, with workmanship and nails, also nails, glass, and a Coffin's poket at the Kirk. 14/1d.

1781, November 27th. To Thomas Robertson for casting Davit and leading same davits to the Session House, per receipt, 2/4d.

1783, April 21st. To the Session for a basket for carrying the Element Bread, 1/6d.

1785, March 16th. To Alexander Ritchie in part for repairing the School-house, which was in a very dangerous condition, and would have fallen of itself, had it not been taken in time, £1 0s. 0d.

1786, March 6th. To John Workman for making Janet Bone's grave, it seems her friends would not pay it, 1/-.

1790, March 5th. To Adam Jack for thatching the Session's House, 1 day, 1/2d.

1792, November 24th. To paper for engrossing the different articles of the Session's Affairs, being the first for past time, 1/-.

1805, October 20th. (Note the illiterate entries), pied for a Lock to the Laft door, 2/6d.

1805, November 10th. A pin of glass for the Kirk laft windo, 1/2d.

1812, July 24th. Paid Robert Dickie for washing the Table finning and all preceding, 6/-.

From such entries as these, we learn that "General Purposes" included such objects as the repair and upkeep of Church, School, and Session's House; the payment of Synod and Presbytery Dues, the salaries of Session Clerk, Kirk Treasurer, Beadle, Sexton, &c., and Communion Expenses.

The present Church bell seems to have supplanted one purchased from Caird and Co. in 1833 for the sum of £7 1s. 0d. whilst the taking down of the old and the putting up of the new bell cost £1 18s 11d. This bell was supplied by the Heritors, after considerable controversy with the Kirk Session as to their liability to provide it;

since they maintained the old one to have been cracked by the church officer—a servant of the session.

With regard to the Communion Plate, which consists of two large pewter plates—apparently also used as collection plates—two old pewter cups, one pewter flagon, two Britannia metal cups, and two flagons of the same metal, two silver cups, two electro-plate flagons, and two electroplate patens; the date of the pewter vessels is unknown. It has, however, been ascertained from the "Old Glasgow" Exhibition of 1894—to which one of the silver cups was sent—that the Hall Mark inscribed upon them, viz., the City of Glasgow Arms (Tree, Bird, Bible, Bell, and Fish), together with the initials I.L., point to 1701 as their date, and to John Luke as their maker. The following extract from the Kirk Session Records will shew when the Britannia metal plate was procured: "July 24th, 1833. The Session resolved to provide two new communion cups, Britannia metal, as near the silver ones in shape as can be procured, and two new flagons of the same metal as the former; and to dispose of the old pewter cups and flagons. Their cost would appear to have been £1 7s 6d. The electro-plate flagons and patens, of which the patens were in memoriam of Mrs. Agnes Lamb, were purchased in 1891, at a cost of upwards of £12.

Up to the incumbency of Rev. W. Vassie, shortbread was used in the dispensation of the Lord's Supper, a practice which still prevails in some parishes—e.g., Inch in Wigtonshire. Admission to the Communion table continued to be by tokens, until about twenty years ago, when a change was made to the present mode of admission by card. As now existing these tokens bear on one

## KILBRYD
### K
### 1720.

side the superscription—the other side being blank. In the old church the communicants sat on both sides of one long table-seat, which ran nearly the whole length of the church. At this table there were generally three successive services. Up to 1823, or thereby, the Communion seems to have been celebrated only once a year, generally in the month of July, and on the Sabbath in that month on which the minister could most conveniently obtain assistance. The Winter celebration then begun was soon discontinued on the grounds of its unpopularity, and the injurious effect upon the revenue available for the support of the poor, owing to that day's collection being devoted to Communion expenses. It was, however, revived in December, 1825, on the minister's undertaking that only the surplus, after the deduction of the ordinary collection, should be devoted to Sacramental expenses. Specimens of the special collections at Communion seasons, which were generally given to the poor, are these: September, 1779, £3 16s 7d; October, 1787, £4 7s; July, 1811, £4 10s 7d; July, 1835, £4 16s 6d; June, 1843, £2 10s 10$_{1/2}$d. From these dates it will be seen that the month adopted for the celebration of the Holy Communion in the parish varied, and sometimes the convenience of the community regulated it, as the following extracts from the Kirk Session Records will shew:—"June 18th, 1718. The said day, the minister acquainted the Session that he designed to dispense the Sacrament of the Lord's Supper to the congregation and desired them to think on the most proper time. The Session having deliberate on this matter, told that it behoved to be before the middle of July, because of the herring fishers." An extract of date, July 15th, 1718, points to an abuse in connection with the communion tables; which the Kirk Session deemed it expedient to remedy by enacting as follows "This day appointed, that none of the Communion tables be lent out at fairs or such times." Occasional entries of expenditure for the bringing of the Communion Elements from such places as Saltcoats, and Troon, show that during last century, they could not be obtained in the village.

The Services then held at a Communion Season, were those with which a bygone generation were in most places familiar, viz.—A Fast-day Service (generally on a Wednesday), a Preparatory Service on Saturday afternoon, Communion and Evening Services on Sabbath, and a Post-communion Service on Monday.

A sanctity almost approaching to that of the Sabbath, was attached to the Fast-day; and how the Session dealt with defaulters in that matter may be learned from the following extracts from their records. — —"July 21st, 1723. This day the minister enquired at the elders how the Fast-day was kept through their several quarters. John Orr told it was very ill observed in the low part of the Tarbert; that immediately after their going home from the sermon, they went and pilched (saddled) their horses, and went down to the Sandilands to get them loaded. Informed also that James Robison with his boat's crew went off late on Tuesday night before the Fast, in the expectation of a loadening of prohibit goods, and did not stay to observe the Fast; ordered to be summoned before the Session." "July 25th, 1802. The Moderator informed the Session that Robert Fleck, farmer in Faulds, had been guilty of a trespass on the late fast before the sacrament, by yoking his plough on that day and working in the fields. The Moderator considering this a gross insult upon decency, and public order, and the established religion of the country, had ordered the officer to summon the said Robert Fleck to the meeting of session. The officer being called in and asked if he had summoned him, said he had. The said R. Fleck being called, compeared. The Session agreed that the Moderator draw up a representation of this matter, and transmit it the Lord Advocate for Scotland."

At the evening services on the Communion Sabbath, the old church would seemed to have been lighted with candles; for which, in 1835, we find a charge of one shilling and seven pence halfpenny.

A century ago, the Sacrament of Baptism was, with rare exceptions dispensed in church—a practice great ly preferable to the now too prevalent private baptism, which has never been sanctioned by the General Assembly of the Church; and for which, the late Dr. Edgar tells us, fines were exacted in some parts of the country, up to the middle of last century. Water was, of course, the only element used—all Popish fragments such as wax, oil, spittle, conjuration, and crossing, being carefully avoided. Still, abuse was not unknown in connection with the customs attendant on baptism in this parish. This, the following extract from the Session Records, will shew.— "May 17th, 1725. This day the session taking to their serious consideration the abuse that's like to creep in all bankets on the Lord's Day by inviting excessive numbers of people to their feast—sometimes two dozen and upwards—the entertainment of whom cannot be without a great deal of unnecessary work on the Sabbath, the session unanimously agree that these excessive numbers be discharged, and that, when baptism happens on the Sabbath, there be not above six persons present, besides the family, and that intimation of this be given from the pulpit next Sabbath."

To the position of the Baptismal Font and Seat in the old church we have already referred. The present Baptismal Font, with its pitch pine stand, was the gift of Mrs. Hyndman of Springside, at the opening of the present church in 1872. For some time a fee seems to have been charged at baptism, viz., eightpence to the clerk and fourpence to the beadle. Since 1693, at least, a register of baptisms has been kept. The nature of the entries therein may be seen from the following specimens:—"June 24th, 1709. Elizabeth Hunter, daughter to Patrick Hunter of that Ilk and Marion Crawford was baptised, June 14th, 1709." "Alexander and Rebekah, twins to William King, and Cunninghame were baptised, August 8th, 1708."

With regard to marriages, Dr. Edgar in his "Old Church Life in Scotland," tells us that they were considered regular, when performed according to Church laws, but irregular, when either banns were awanting, or the marriage was solemnised in a private house. Banns (derived from "Banns," *proclamation*) were quite a different thing from "bands," which were the contract of marriage ratified and concluding with its solemnisation. He further tells us that marriage was often preceded by the formality of betrothal in presence of authorised witnesses;—that parties about to be married were examined as to their knowledge of the Lord's Prayer, the Creed, and the Decalogue;—that the banns required to be proclaimed on three separate Sabbaths, which, in the event of there being no regular service on any special Sabbath, might be done by the Session Clerk at the church door in presence of witnesses—that a pledge, *e.g.*, a ring or a plaid, that parties would proceed to marriage, was often exacted, and in cases of default, was forfeited to the poor;—that the refusal to marry after proclamation was known as "Scorning the Kirk";—that, with a view to the suppression of riot and lasciviousness, especially at "penny weddings," acts were passed securing the purveyance at marriages to certain privileged persons;—that Church law required marriages to be in church on Sabbath, or (1645) at the Week-Day Lecture, with a special pew reserved for the bride and bridegroom;—and that for long private marriages were discountenanced by the exaction of a fine.

We are not aware that illustrations of many of there points can be found in our old parochial records. The benefit, however, which the poor derived from collections both at public and private marriages, as also from fines paid for irregular marriage, may be seen from the following extracts.—"December 26th, 1773. To a private marriage, 2s. March 2nd, 1786. To a publick marriage, 3s 7½d. September 18th, 1810. Collected at Willim Scot's and Mary Galbraith's marage, 3s 6d. July 17th, 1783. Received from Mr. F— M— and spous for their irregular marriage, £2. June, 1825. £5 from M— G—'s marriage with Miss M— L— (*i.e.*, before a magistrate, though afterwards in church.) The revenue derived from collections at public and private marriages in 1776, is 10s 3½d; in 1780, 5s 10½d; in 1786, 0s; in 1787, 5s 4½d."

The first entry in our old kirk treasurer's books showing a proclamation of banns, is of date November 16th, 1777. One in 1778 yields a revenue of 10s 6d, and three in 1780, a revenue of 15s. In 1806, the entry for proclamation fee is called "Crying money," *e.g.*, "June

15th, 1806. Craying Money of Robert Miller in hay semmill and Elizabeth Ralston, 5s."

Public marriages, which may either have been marriages in church or penny weddings, disappear from the records in 1810. Towards the close of last century, the fees charged for proclamation of banns, were for one day, ten shillings; for two days, five shillings, but they appear to have been raised about 1817, for then they stand:—

For one day   6/- to Clerk; 2/- to Beadle; 10/6 to Poor.

„   two days   6/-          „   2/-     „          5/-     „
„   three days 6/-          „   2/-     „          0/-     „

The riotous scenes too common at penny weddings, may be gathered from the following extract. January 3rd, 1722, "This day, the Session, taking to consideration that the Schoolhouse, which was built upon the glyb, and at the expense of the Session, had been much abused of late at bookings and penny weddings, and that the Kirk furms, which was borrowed on these occasions, were also abused, they do hereby discharge the same in time coming."

Registers of proclamation of banns seem to have been kept from, at least, the beginning of last century. The following may be taken as specimens of the entries therein. "September 26th, 1702, Alexander Cunninghame, in the parish of Clocher, in the county of Tyroon, in the kingdom of Ireland, and Anna Hunter, lawful daughter to the deceast Patrick Hunter of that Ilk in this parish, gave up their names to le proclaimed in order to marriage."

"May 5th, 1704. The said day, Patrick Hunter of Hunterston, in this parish, and Marion Crawford, lawful daughter of Thomas Crawford of Crawfordsburn, in the parish of Greenock, gave up their names to be proclaimed in order to marriage."

"1716. Mr. John Adam, Minister of the gospel in this parish, and Janet Campbol. Daughter lawful of the deceast Mr. John Campbol, (late minister of the gospel in the parish of Craigie) in the parish of Kilmarnock, were booked in order to marriage, this twentieth day of October, 1716 years. Married at Galston by Mr. Andrew Rodger, Minister there, November, 8th 1716."

With regard to the burial of the dead, the practices prevalent in the county seem to have found their illustration in this parish. What is now familiarly known as the chesting or coffining, a practice especially prevalent in the West of Scotland, has been long observed in this parish. According to Dr. Edgar, this custom finds its explanation in an Act of 1686, requiring the use of home-made Scotch linen as a shroud, and afterwards in 1709 of home-made woollen for the same purpose, with a view to the certification of which an elder with a neighbour or two gave attendance—when doubtless a religious service would be held, and refreshments distributed. Whilst the Act has become obsolete, the religious service still survives. The services at the funeral itself were considered more of the nature of a grace before and after the refreshments handed round, than anything else, and we are told they sometimes occupied from fifteen to thirty minutes. Near relatives and friends were sometimes invited five or six hours before the lifting of the corpse. Neither were relics of the Wakes or watchings altogether unknown in this parish up to the early decades of the present century. Throughout the eerie hours, the women are said to have primed the pipes of the men. Happily, the orgies previously common enough at chestings and funerals are now almost unknown. Still, so late as 1824, such unnecessary expenditure would seem to have prevailed in our midst, as on March 1st of that year we find a motion made at a joint-meeting of Heritors and Kirk-Session, "to discountenance expensive and unnecessary mode of entertainment common at funerals in this parish." It was then agreed that a meeting of the inhabitants should be called to consider the matter. Until a few years ago, anything of the nature of a hearse was unknown in the parish, the coffin being generally carried on handspokes. Mortcloths were used in the earlier part of the century. The tolling of the Church bell to assemble the mourners, as well as during the march to the grave, was also then common.

We have not been able to discover in the Parish Records any reference to the use of Lawrie's fumigator, pipes, vials and bellows, for the resuscitation of the drowned; nor of any precautionary measures adopted against the lifting of corpses for anatomical purposes, unless the "Coffin's poket," previously mentioned, be of that nature. It is not probable that the elders' wooden house, sold to Mr. Howie in 1842 for £1, had ever served the purpose of a watch-house further than to form a shelter from which to keep an observant eye upon the collection plate.

The services in church would seem to have embraced one service on Sunday, and that, sometimes intermittently, as in 1771, *e.g.*, we find the entry "No Sermon," occurring no fewer than ten times. Some of these occasions are doubtless accounted for by the Minister's absence, assisting at a neighbouring Communion, as such entries occur pretty regularly about the same time in successive years. In addition to the Sunday service, a

Week-day service, generally on a Wednesday, was occasionally held. These Week-day services, however, begin to die away about the close of last century. There were further the usual services at Communion time, and an occasional Fast-day of special appointment, *e.g.*, 1719, October 29th. "A Thanksgiving Day appointed by the Synod for deliverance from the Spanish Invasion, and for the late good harvest."

1733, November 8th. "A Fast appointed by the Synod on account of the extraordinary hail that fell out in June last, whereby many within the bounds of this presbytery suffered great loss in their corn, and in many other places within the bounds of this Synod."

This great hail is also taken notice of in the Session Records of Irvine, as well as in the Records of the Court of Session, from the latter of which it appears that the tenants of Lord Eglinton in three parishes refused to pay their rents because of it. After a lengthened Process decision was given in their favour in 1740.

The various Church services would appear at times to have been rather protracted for the soporific tendencies of at least a portion of the congregation—as the beadle is traditionally reported to have had occasionally to go round with his pitcher of tar to tar the sleepers.

The building so frequently referred to as the Session House, would seem not to have been a Session House in the modern acceptation of the term; but rather a house belonging to the Session, and tenanted in 1772 by the Schoolmaster. After the transference of the School in 1805 to the old Manse, it was occupied by others. No vestry was attached to the old church, but Ministers robed in the Manse.

In bygone centuries the Manse has occupied various sites. In the seventeenth century it is said to have stood towards the North-west corner of the present church yard, and it is probably to this Manse that reference is made on September 11th, 1649, when "Ducathill, a ruling elder, along with the minister, is to visit the Manse of Kilbride, along with the gentlemen of the paroch, before the admission of William Rodger, whose edict had been returned indorsed, and none had any objections against him." The result of this visitation is given on September 24th, when it is ordered to be repaired, the Heritors having agreed to give a considerable sum, and Hunterston, his bond to the presbytery for the amount, This Manse is said to have been a one-storey house, built of red sandstone, and possessing a highly ornamented doorway. It was probably here that the "Rabbling of the Curate" occurred, an incident with regard to which we glean the following information from notes left behind by the late Dr. Ritchie. He tells us that a Mr. Anderson, who lived at Cupplefields on the high road above Springside,—a very peaceable man,—rose up in an assembly of those who were opposed to the presence of an Episcopal Curate in the parish, when they were discussing how they should oust him, and, under a mighty inspiration, as it was thought, exclaimed, "Let us go and put him down the glebe." They accordingly proceeded towards this old Manse, which the Curate evacuated. After being buffeted and stoned from the Church Sanctuary, he was chased down by Coldstream and Nethermiln, and fled to the South. For his decision and boldness as a leader, John Anderson was forthwith dubbed Captain Anderson. W. Malcolm, the old bellman, used to repeat some lines of a

local poet's effusion on the incident, but all of it that has
survived the corroding tooth of time is this:—

"Mr. Snuffs did get his cuffs
And they chased him dowe the glebe."

It was probably either the Rev. Mr. Crawford, or the
Rev. Mr. Boyd, who thus fared at the hands of his
opponents. He is said to have afterwards met the Rev.
Mr. Littlejohn, curate in Largs, who had also been
rabbled out by some covenanters from the South, and
both were for a time separated from their families, their
whereabouts unknown. This old Manse was afterwards
tenanted by a midwife, and gave place to one situated
where the Parish Church Mission Hall at present is. It is
thus described in 1794 in the "Old Statistical
Account":—"An indifferent, smoky, inconvenient house,
standing hard by the village, and projecting into the
churchyard." At the beginning of this present century, it
was transformed into the parish school below, and the
schoolmaster's house above. The present Manse was
built in 1805, Gavin Burns architect, and W. Auld,
Wright, in Saltcoats, contractor. Its erection cost £478
19s.0d. It was enlarged in 1864 at a cost of £238.

Up to 1811, when it was closed by order of Quarter
Sessions, a road ran along the Western boundary of the
Churchyard, past the old Manse, and joined the Mill or
Glebe road.

In 1821, the glebe was enlarged by the addition of
three roods, thirteen falls, from Kirktonhall grounds, at a
cost of £99 9s. 7d., and now measures inclusive of manse
site, etc., 5 acres, 2 roods 25.45 poles, imperial. An old
return called for by the General Assembly in 1750,
shewed that in 1650 the parish minister's stipend was
£400 Scots, three chalders of meal, (Linlithgow measure,

which is three bolls less than the ordinary measure), and one chalder of bere; that there were then, 'thirty-four Heritors, and that the glebe, measuring, at that time, three acres, (probably Scots), was worth 24/- per annum. In 1792 there was an augmentation of three chalders, and the stipend was then worth about £126 sterling, £20 Scots, being the allowance for Communion expenses.

# CHAPTER VII.
## ECCLESIASTICAL LIFE OF THE PARISH.
### (*Continued.*)

OF those who served the Cure of this Parish in pre-Reformation times nothing is known. But thanks to Scott's "Fasti Ecclesiae," we have a complete list of the ministers of the parish from the Reformation to the present day, viz.:

John Maxwell, 1567-1580. Gabriel Cunningham, 1585-1586. Hew Boyd, 1588-1591; John Harper, A.M., 1594-1631; George Crawford, 1632-1648; William Rodger, A.M., 1648-1657; William Cunningham, 1658-1669; Alexander Irvine, A.M., 1670-1672; Robert Boyd, A.M., 1672; Gilbert H. Crawford; Robert Hunter, A.M., 1688-1698; George Rennie, A.M, 1699-1713; John Adam, Senr., 1716-1763; John Adam, Junr., 1751-1769; Arthur Oughterston, 1770-1822; John S. Oughterston, 1805-1812; William Vassie, A.M., 1823-1834; Thomas Findlay, 1832-1843; Alexander King, 1843-1882; John Lamb, B.D., 1881.

With regard to the majority of these we know little more than their mere names and dates of ministry; but from the above list we may gather that the Cure was somewhat irregularly served until the close of the sixteenth century; this was doubtless owing to the difficulty of finding a sufficient number of Protestant licentiates to fill the numerous parishes vacant for some years after the Reformation. In the absence of licensed probationers, laymen, called "Exporters or Readers," were employed. They would appear to have made a house to house Visitation, reading the Scriptures. John Maxwell, the first on the above list, belonged to that class, and his salary as such was forty merks per annum. During his tenure of office, Alexander Callender, Minister at Largs, had the Kirklands of Kilbride as part of his emoluments.

The next on the list of whom we know anything further, than name and date is John Harper, whose name subscribed to old wills still extant, points to the days when the ministers were the makers of the people's last wills and testaments. He obtained his degree, (M.A.), at Glasgow University in 1594, was presented to the vicar-age of Kilbride by James VI. in 1601, and was summoned along with others before the Privy Council in 1610 and 1630 for intercommuning with a trafficking Popish priest.

From the Presbytery Records and other sources we know something more about the next on the list. George Crawford, the son of Crawford of Thirdpart in Renfrew, and remotely connected with the Craufurds of Auchen-ames. He was deposed in the strict days of the Covenant for his worldly-mindedness and Sabbath desecration in the selling of a horse on that day. The story goes, that on coming out of church, the purchasing farmer said, "If it was na the Sawbath I wud gie ye sae meikle for that horne," to which Mr. George replied, "If it wasn't the Sabbath, I would take your offer," and early the follow-ing morning the horse was transferred from the premises of the seller to those of the purchaser. Robert Boyd of Portincross who died in 1722 at the advanced age of nearly a hundred, used to say that he was one of the witnesses against the Rev. G. Crawford before the Presbytery of Irvine. The following extracts from the

Records of that Presbytery will help to throw light on his deposition:

"November 24th, 1647. At a visitation of the Kirk of Kilbride, Mr. George Crawford, the minister, was exercised upon fourteenth chapter of Hosea, and preached on fourth chapter of John, and being removed, the brethren declared themselves satisfied with neither. The elders and also the whole parish were called on to say if they had anything to say against their minister. Ane libel was given in against him. At Kilbride 26th January 1648. The Presbytery met to hear witnesses on the charges against George Crawford, the minister. He offers to make certain confessions, viz. (1) That he did administer the sacrament thrice without ordinary preaching—one time at a marriage read only a piece of a chapter and expounded it—at another time, did baptize two bairns and did expound only a piece of a psalm—and a third time had nothing but prayer. (2) That he did read the Assembly's Acts upon a forenoon and made it serve for a preaching. (3) That he did not enjoin Alexander Cuningham, younger, to make his repentance for fornication, but knew it not until long after he was married. (4) He confesses that no worldly affairs should have drawn him away so often from his charge. (5) He confesses that sometimes in a passion he said, "In faith" and "In conscience," but it was only in his own house. (6) He confesses that he received money for making of testaments. (7) That he rode from Glasgow to Kilbarchan one Sunday morning before sermon. (8) That he desired the people of Newton upon the Lord's Day, to come and till his glehe upon the Monday, but it was twelve or thirteen years since, and (9) That upon one Sabbath day at ten hours of evening he went to ane Cordoner, and desired him to have his boots ready against the Monday morning early.

The confessions being heard, the Presbytery, according to the desire of the said Mr. George, did condescend upon some more points of the libel to he proven, sic as his carriage to his wife and family—his fearful cursing—his profaning the Lord's Day etc.

The following witnesses deponed (1) A. Cuningham, younger, of Carlung, that the minister knew that he was guilty of fornication, and he had confessed it to him after marriage, and he did not call him to account for it. Further, that the minister frequently made use of oaths, and that he is a common curser in sic words as D——l take him etc. . . that the minister had drawn up a certain Act at a meeting of the parish, which he denied having in his possession, although he was afterwards obliged to admit he had the document—that upon a Sabbath day he went from Kilbride to Hunterston about a marriage and afterwards went to an alehouse and there drank healths till midnight to the parties good luck . . . . . . The article being read and Alexander Cuningham examined upon the same, he attests the whole except his vomiting, and this was about eleven years since. Further, that about ten years ago he paid the minister his tiends upon Sabbath day after preaching and got a discharge from him—that upon another Sabbath he and the bellman came to Carlung and prigged about some kyne, but did not buy any.

Robert Gray deponed that the minister reproved some of his people who followed ministers who were teachers of novelties and left the old way, and said, that meikle preaching makes people worse and that homeliness spoils courtesy, for to be over homely with God's

Word, says he, makes the people count the less of it— that the minister railed upon those who went from his preaching to others, calling them brainsick, giddy headed, and given to the itch of the ear—and also some other charges as to his homeliness in preaching—that he passed delinquents too easily—that he seldom uses any spiritual communication—and that he flatly denied, with a protestation to God, having the document above referred to, but afterwards did produce it.

Hunterston, younger, a witness was objected to by the minister, that he, and also Cuningham, younger, as witnesses, were contrivers of the charge against him, and had enmity to him, but was allowed to give evidence. He confirmed the statement of Gray as to his slackness in discipline. Farther, that the minister mixed the communion wine with water to the common people, but kept it unmixed to the gentry. Farther, that there was not a week almost in all the year but Mr. George raged, and that his wife regretted to him how very heavily her husband struck her—that he heard Mr. George say often "Ex fide;" "Bona fide;" and "As I shall answer to God;" and farther he heard him say "By the firmament," and "Coram Deo"—farther, that there was a man in an alehouse with him that both cursed and used unchaste language, which Mr. George did not reprove—that Mr. George denied with a protestation to God that there was such an Act as the one referred to above, and that after he desired it, he produced it to the grief of sundry who beheld it,—that he came down to witness's father's house on a Sabbath day seeking his counsel about the feuing some rooms (ground) in Monkton.

Ann Stevenson depones, that being his servant four years ago, she saw Mr. George strike his wife with his hands and his feet, and that she had heard him swear.

Isobel Fairie, a former servant, about three years ago, gave similar evidence to the last witness.

Margaret Wilson, a former servant, also deponed that she heard, about a year since, Mr. George swear horribly—that she never heard ane swear like him, and that very often, and that she never served the like of him.

Three other witnesses depone as to his applying to them on Sabbath days about tilling of the ground, purchasing a horse etc.—that some of the matters deponed happened seven years ago.

The Presbytery in the meantime find as much proven as to merit the censure of suspension, and accordingly do so during their pleasure.

March let 1648, Mr. George Crawford appeared, and prayed, that if the points already proven did not merit deposition, he earnestly desired they would surcease the suspension. He also admitted the truth of several of the minor charges against him. The Presbytery agreed to hear some further points in debate.

March 14th 1648, Mr. George Crawford this day deposed.

August 1649, Mr. George Crawford, late minister of Kilbride, having applied for church privileges, and made a full confession of his guiltiness with tears, is to go to Kilbride and there satisfy the first Lord's Day. At next meeting it was reported that Mr. George Crawford had done as directed, and it was agreed that he be admitted to church fellowship, without any relation to the opening of his mouth towards the ministry.

In 1632, this Mr. George Crawford had given xx merks towards the erection of Glasgow University Library. One of his sons became Town Clerk of Irvine, and founder of the family of Newfield near Kilmarnock. A daughter was married to Dr. Robert Crawford of Nethermains.

These were the days when all the faithful were expected to subscribe the Covenant. Hence this entry in the Presbytery Records:—"January 2nd, 1649, Largs and Kilbride to be taken into the Covenant. Concerning the Kirk of Kilbride, because the laird of Hunterston, younger, did shew that the people of the parish was presentlie to go to the fishing at Balantrae, and if the Covenant were not tendret to them, this next Lord's Day, it was likely that the paroch would lye out long eneuch."

Of Mr. Crawford's successor, William Rodger, we know little, beyond name and date. The following excerpt from the Presbytery Records, however, has reference to his coming to the parish; "February 13th, 1649 William Rodger accepts a call from the parishioners of West Kilbride to be the minister; and the parishioners are to help to repair the Manse which is ruinous."

His successor, William Cuningham, was deprived of his benefice by the Act of Parliament of 1662. "His insicht and plenishing were estimat at j. c. lib."

The next on the list, Alexander Irvine A. M., was an Aberdonian. He was translated to Greyfriar's, Edinburgh, in 1672. After being denuded of his charge, he served himself heir to his brother William, who was the first minister of Udny, Aberdeenshire.

The next two upon the list, Robert Boyd A.M., and Gilbert Hamilton Crawford, are entered as "Indulged," in that although they had probably taken the "Test Oath" which recognised Episcopacy as the ecclesiastical polity of the National Church, they were, "yet permitted to cling to the old Presbyterian faith, continue the old Presbyterian worship, and meet in their old Presbyterian Courts." They may also have been of the number who took advantage of the, "Act of Indulgence" of James II., which granted liberty of conscience and worship to all religious sects. Still, if there is any reliance to be placed on the tradition, that the minister of West Kilbride was one of the two hundred clergymen, who were rabbled out of their Manses, parishes and livings about the time of the Revolution, either of there or both, may have known what it was to have been carried about in mock procession by an infuriated rabble, with their gowns torn over their heads, and their prayer-books burned before their eyes, ere they were expelled from the parish, and told never to return.

Robert Boyd was translated from Linton parish in Teviotdale—indulged by the Privy Council—summoned before the Justiciary Court in 1683, though the diet was deserted on finding "that he is known to have been notoriously loyal, and to have refused to read the rebels' declaration"—and restored to his old parish at Linton in 1693.

Gilbert Hamilton Crawford was indulged along with Robert Boyd, and cited before the Privy Council in 1677 for not keeping the rules.

On the next incumbent's career, considerable light is thrown by extracts such as these from the Presbytery Records:—"June 17th, 1687, The qk day a call was presented to the parish of Kilbryd to Mr. Robert Hunter to the exercise of the ministrie amongst them with a desire that the presbrie would putt him to his tryalls in order to his ordination, whilk desire the presbrie took to their consideration till the next day, and appointed Mr. John Wallace to go to Kilbryd and preach. That according to the order of the Church, the call might be before a minister subscrybed or assented to. And the said Mr. John Wallace to make report aga the next presbrie day; and appoints Mr. Robert Hunter to preach at Kilwinning, that day Mr. John Wallace preaches at Kilbryd." On September 28th, of the same year, we however, find that Mr. Hunter's ordination is delayed until the next "presbrie" day, and Mr. Gabriel Cunningham is to speak to my lord Montgomerie and Auchenharvey anent removing of some report concerning him. On November 2nd, 1687, the "presbrie" find there is no ground to delay his "tryalls," and he is ordained on April 28th, 1688.

His ten years ministry in the parish does not seem to have been a very happy one, either for himself, or his parishioners. His experiences with Robert Boyd of "Pencross" appear to have been specially disagreeable, as may be gathered from references thereto in the Presbytery Records

"On April 21st, 1692, the Rev. R. Hunter informs the presbrie that Robert Boyd and Antonia Montgomerie his spouse had been very offensive in their carriage before marriage, in that they had gone away to Belfast, and there been irregularly married by a Nonconformist. On September 27th, 1692, the presbrie appoints Mr. R. Hunter to bring in one extract of Boyd's process before the Session of Kilbryd again the next presbrie day. On December 21st, 1692, R. Hunter reports Boyd guilty of drunkenness, swearing, dishaunting of the ordinances and cohabitation. On February 21st, 1693, Boyd confesses to drunkenness,—but not a whole night at a

time,—to swearing 'By God,' in the minister's parlour—
to disturbing the worship of God, and to antenuptial
fornication.—And on July 25th, 1693, Boyd and his wife
are appointed by the Presbytery to appear before the
Session, which appearance is delayed until October 24th,
when they are duly absolved."

   But Presbytery troubles soon begin to gather around
Mr. Hunter's own head, for on October 26th, 1697, there
is a record of the privy censure of Mr. Hunter, because of
the Presbytery's doubts as to his oath on the will of the
late Mr. Hunter of Hunterston, and on February 8th,
1698, we have still further evidence of the Presbytery's
suspicions that Mr. Hunter's deposition does not agree
with documents seen in Edinburgh by a commission
appointed by the Presbytery. Then on March 1st, 1698,
we find Mr. Hunter preaching before the Presbytery upon
his ordinary (Matthew v. 12.), but not well approven.
Evidence also goes to shew that he had not visited the
families of his congregation for two years past; that he
had further become slack in examinations and visiting of
the sick;—was at law with his brethren—was suspected
of perjury as to his father's will—whilst the Session
Records were incorrectly kept and blanky. Apparently
finding the situation uncomfortable, we find him demit-
ting office on April 5th, 1698, assigning as his reason for
doing so—"Discouragement in the work of the Lord
from certain persons in the parish; but with this reason
the Presbytery does not express itself as well satisfied."
Towards the close of his ministry the parish would
appear to have been in somewhat destitute circumstances
both ecclesiastically and scholastically, since on March
2nd, 1698, we find the Minister, Elders and Heritors
reporting to the Presbytery that they had no church

utensils except a session table, five fourmes and table-cloths for the communion—that they had no mortification for the poor, and only £4 in the box,—that they had no school-house, schoolmaster, or salary for one—that the fabric of the church was in good case, but its yard dyke unbuilt. Then the Minister reports that neither the loft of the Manse nor the office-houses were in good case;—that the glebe and yard only measured three acres twenty falls. The Heritors are accordingly recommended to repair the Manse, augment the glebe, built a school-house, and provide one hundred merks for the School-master's salary.

Of Mr. George Rennie, A.M. Mr. Hunter's successor, the only notice we have seen in the Presbytery Records is, that on January 10th, 1699, he is "appointed to preach at Kilwinning, because of the interest my lord Montgomery and Major Buntine have in the parish of Kilbryde." From other sources we learn that he was in earlier life a teacher at Borrowstonness, and in 1692, teacher of the Scotch school at Rotterdam. He was licensed in 1698.

By the time of his death in 1713, the Patronage Act of Queen Ann had become law, and it soon made its pernicious effects felt in this parish by a protracted vacancy, due to the inability of the patron, Lord Eglinton to see eye to eye, either with the parishioners or Presbytery in the selection of a successor to Mr. Rennie. The nature of this collision will be best seen by a reference to the Presbytery Minutes of the time, which shew that on July 14th, 1713, John Stewart, Minister of Eaglesham was presented to the parish, the Presbytery strenuously protesting against the exercise of such patronage. In September the Session and Heritors are in favour of a Mr.

Carlisle, and in November Lord Eglinton promises to the Presbytery to be easy as to planting of vacant congregations where he had any interest. On January 12th, 1714, a Servitour from Lord Eglinton appears at the Presbytery with a presentation in favour of Mr. John Glasgow of Kilbirnie, and on February 9th, 1714, Lord Eglinton won't consent to the appointment of Mr. Carlisle, though the parishioners want him. Again on June 8th, 1714, there is a presentation in favour of G. Chalmers, minister of Kilwinning, when the Presbytery again remonstrates against such exercise of patronage, as also on November 4th. On November 9th, a deputation of the Presbytery waits on Lord Eglinton, but without success, but on December 14th, Kilwinning petitions Lord Eglinton and the Presbytery to retain Mr. Chalmers, and on December 19th, Mr. Chalmers himself protests against translation, and maintains that the appointment has now fallen into the hands of the Presbytery. On January 11th, 1715, the Session and Heritors petition for the appointment of Mr. John Adam, who is at the same time the object of Dreghorn's desire. The Presbytery sustains Mr. Chalmers' declinature.

As the parish has now been two years vacant, on February 8th, 1715 the Presbytery claims the "Jus Devolutum." On April 20th, 1715 Lord Eglinton presents a Mr. W. Hunter, whereupon the Session again present a petition in favour of Mr. Adam on May 10th, and on June 14th Lord Eglinton gives indication of consent, but not with a very good grace. His language is—"He would endeavour to comply." At length the "desolate" congregation at a meeting of Heritors held on August 16th, 1715, has Mr. Adam's election confirmed, and a most appropriate text for a trial sermon prescribed: "Pray for the peace of Jerusalem." Mr. Adam is ordained February, 15th, 1716.

It was during his incumbency that the church was thoroughly renovated, as noticed in last chapter. In his day, too, we have a record of a Presbyterial visitation to the parish, which shews it to have been by no means a mere nominal thing. Such visitations had apparently been carried on for a long time, as we find the following entry in the Presbytery Records of date December 7th, 1647. "Mr. Robert Bell is excused from being at the visitation at Kilbride from his inibilitie to travall." At the visitation on February 8th, 1733, many heritors, elders and heads of families were present. *First.* The minister was removed, when the elders and heads of families reported approval of his doctrine, life, conversation and pastoral work. The minister was then called in and encouraged to go on with the work of the Lord. Then the elders were similarly dealt with and satisfaction expressed with them. On its being reported that there are no deacons, exhortation is given to appoint fit persons as such. Heads of families then pass through the Presbyterial fire, and on their being recalled, they are encouraged to give attendance upon ordinances, and to be circumspect in their whole conversation.

As there is now a legal salary for a schoolmaster, David Biggar, the dominie, is subjected to the same scrutiny, and satisfaction is expressed with him also. So minute are they in their investigations, that they come down to David Bone, the Kirk-Officer, who also appears to have given satisfaction. The Church Utensils are reported as two silver Communion Cups, two flagons, Communion table, cloths, and a Baptismal basin. There are no mortifications, but two bonds, for the poor (one of three hundred merks, and the other of one hundred and ten lib. Scots). The collections are given to the poor as soon as received. The Session-Records are ordered to be sent to Dalry for revisal by Messrs Fullerton and Smith. It is further reported that nine hundred and sixty-six lib. Scots are needed for Church repairs, and that Mr. Robert Hunter of Kirkland is to get forty-eight lib. Scots for his commission as collector. The schoolmaster is appointed to apportion the rates. Cases of discipline are then dealt with.

Notwithstanding the favourable report then given as to Mr. Adam's ministrations, his teaching has been handed down as that of cold moderatism capable of being summed up in such words as these: "Be ye guid, and do ye guid, and guid 'll come o' ye' doon, doon to the end of time," nor, if all stories be true, does he appear to have been too scrupulously regular in his pulpit ministrations, since it is said that the ringing of the Church-bell at eight o'clock on the Saturday evenings owes its origin to Mr. Adams adopting this method of letting his parishioners know whether there was to be service on the following Sunday or not—no bell, no sermon. Of the two Adams and Oughtersons on list, the latter was the son of the former.

Of all the incumbencies since the Reformation, that of the Rev. Arthur Oughterson was considerably the longest, nearly fifty-two years. He is said to have had a special antipathy to the Irish, and thought that the only cure for Ireland was ten minutes under the water. On one occasion, a man who had a fancy for two sisters and would fain have married both, came to consult Mr. Oughterson what he would advise him to do:—
whereupon he received the counsel to marry one of them, and afterwards return and give him his experience. This

the ardent suitor is said to have done, with the sad confession, "If I had kenned, what I ken noo, half a ane would have dune for me."

Mr. Oughterson, junr., was much more evangelical in his teaching than his father, to whom he acted as Assistant and Successor for seven years, when he was translated to Monkton, ten years before his father's death. This translation may have been advantageous to both, since owing to difference of views, their intercourse was not always marked by the greatest harmony. Besides John, Mr. Oughterson had another son Arthur, who became minister of Greenock. One of his sons, who was fond of fishing, adopted a novel expedient wherewith to overcome his somnolent tendencies in the morning, which were apt to interfere with his prosecution of the gentle art, viz., this, He had a string tied to his big toe, and let over the window with a weight. This string the beadle pulled on his way to his work, with the result of arousing the sleeper betimes.

For some time before his death, Mr. Oughterson was in failing health. He was succeeded by the Rev William Vassie, who had formerly been a chaplain in the Navy, and was accordingly wont to speak of his study as his cabin. The furnishings of that study, which appear to have been all the equipment he considered necessary for the preparation of his sermons, were by no means munificent, if the story is true, that they simply consisted of a Bible, a Church Warden, a few books of Divinity, a jar of whisky, and some tobacco. In early life he had been a student of Mansion House Academy, Camberwell, London. In 1813 he was minister in Thropton, and there is a tradition that he was appointed to West Kilbride, on condition that he should marry a certain person, which he did. He is said to have been very proud and pompous, sometimes going about in his ministerial robes during the week. He was often an object of popular sport, especially at election times, when, for his high Toryism, he is said to have been pelted with mud, rotten eggs, etc., and forced to seek shelter in the Manse. On one occasion, he got into difficulties with Mr. H——, one of the heritors, as to the bellringer. Mr. H——, wished to retain the services of Mr. Malcolm, the old official, whilst Mr. Vassie desired Mr. Duncan, a younger and more efficient man. The minister declared, as the congregation was retiring at the conclusion of his Sunday service, that he had been insulted by a magistrate in the parish. Thereupon the heritor's sister is reported to have waylaid him on his egress from church, and belaboured him with her umbrella, telling him that, if he had aught against her brother, he should have come and spoken to him privately. Neither was her wrath easily appeased, for she is further reported to have come to the Manse next day with a whip, in order to administer further castigation. The minister, however, duly forewarned, and believing in discretion as the better part of valour, had barred all entrance against her, and thus thwarted her designs. Chafed and enraged, she is said to have entertained the thought of accomplishing her purpose on the following Sunday, but was dissuaded therefrom by her brother. Mr. Vassie was the author of a published sermon entitled "The Necessity of Religion and Virtue to National Happiness and Prosperity."

Mr. Vassie was succeeded in 1831 by the Rev. T. Findlay, who had acted as assistant and successor since 1832, and who continued to hold the charge until the Disruption in 1843, when he became the first minister of the Free Church in the parish, and survived until 1875. Then came the Rev. Alexander King, whose name and service still linger fresh in the memories of many of the present generation. He died in 1882. As to the Personel of the other members of Kirk Session in bygone generations we have not been able to glean much information. In 1817 we find the Session composed of the Minister and the following eight Elders, Messrs Cochrane, Lockhart, Spiers, Simson, Ritchie, Caldwell, Pinkerton, and Ken; and in 1819 we find a special district of the parish assigned to each for supervision. In addition to the administration of finance, the Session's energies would seem to have been mainly directed to the maintenance of Church Discipline and that especially with regard to breaches of the seventh commandment. Page after page of their records is occupied with the sickening tale of such painful cases, indicative of a zeal in the direction of ferreting out information in doubtful instances by the citation of witnesses from far and near, not unworthy of an Inquisition. One serious case actually extends over the greater part of three years (1804-1807). Discipline for this sin was for long carried out in the face of the congregation, so that even in 1803 when a request was presented by an offender, that a line of confession of guilt should take the place of the public appearance, the petition was not granted. This practice of public ecclesiastical discipline seems to have been continued until 1833 or thereby.

As custodiers of the morals of the parish, the Session's attention was, however by no means confined to this one sin, as, especially in earlier days, we find cases of Sabbath desecration, profanity, smuggling, etc., coming under the cognizance of their scrutinizing and reproving authority, with all its attendant public discipline. The following extracts from Sessional and Presbyterial Records will illustrate this point:—

1707. A tattered and somewhat illegible fragment refers to a case of Sabbath desecration which came before the Session, as to the gathering of Wrack or Seaweed, before the expiry of the Sabbath. Some of the witnesses are, however, inclined to think it was Monday morning, as the cock had crowed; but one Hugh Tarbert says that he had gone out at 2 a.m., and they were there before him.

1716. April 19th. "It being represented to the Session that one Colin Black quho has for some time resided in this paroch, had sometime after harvest last, driven cattle belonging to Mr. Crawford on Sabbath day, from Caldwell Law to Crosbie Park, and that the said Colin being to leave the place, desired a testificate from the Session, he having brought one with him to the paroch and produced it to the elder of the quarter. The Session appointed their officer to cite him the next Session, and withal recommended it to the minister to advise with the Presbytery anent the censure due for such a transgression, in regard the Session, on some considerations was not unanimous thairanent." About a month after, we find Black rebuked in Session and obtaining his certificate.

1716. May 13th. "It being represented to the Session that the Sabbath was much profaned in several places of the paroch, especially Arneil, by children meeting and playing together, and by persons come to age, flocking together and feeding their cattle, the Session unanimously agreed that the several elders upon the Sabbath day after last sermon should go through their respective quarters, and take notice of persons guilty of such abuses, in order to their being informed against; and that intimation of this Act be made to the congregation Sabbath next by the minister from the pulpit."

1717. May 22nd. "This day, the Session was informed by one of the elders of a bark coming to the Little Isle on Sabbath se'en night—wherein there were two belonging to the paroch, viz., James Or and Hugh Thomson, and that they, with the rest of the crew, came on shore about 9 of the clock at night, and that they, with the help of some people in the isle, viz, William Harper, Patrick Montgomerie, Jane Moor and Elspa Tyre, did draw down a boat in order to transport one of their crew to the Fairley. The Session taking this to their consideration as a gross prophanation of the Lord's Day, appointed the minister to enquire into the truth and circumstances of the business, and to cause summon the foresaid persons against next meeting of the Session."

1718. August 20th. "This day it was represented to the Session, that William King, Couper and Ann Cunningham his wife, had been guilty of horrid cursing and imprecation against James Bole, etc."

1720. May 25th. This day the Session was informed that some person was seen lately carrying off brandy upon Sabbath morning, etc., etc.

1721. October 22nd. "This day compeared William King, and was examined about baking bread in his house on the Lord's Day. He did not deny that it might be done; but neither he nor his wife knew anything of it. He told that there was a great confusion about his house that day with soldiers and custom house officers, who came up to take brandy on that day, etc.

1722. January 17th. "This day the Session was informed of Robert M'Caltyre in Broomcraig, of Hunterston, his having abused with reproachful names, Jean Kell, and particularly for calling her a "d——d hypocrite in a public company, and on a Sabbath morning in his own barn, where Archibald M'Killop was brought in dead, having killed himself with drinking of brandy the night before."

1722. January 31st. Robert M'Altyre, being called compeared, and being asked how he came to fall on his neighbour with such foul language and reproachful names, and particularly for calling her "a d——d hypocrite," he answered, he said nothing but what she deserved, and was provoked to, because she charged him with Archibald M'Killop's death. The said Jean told that as she was coming to the church on the Sabbath morning, she saw, a gathering of people about the said Robert's barn; she drew near to see what it was, and understanding the occasion of the gathering, all she said was, "'Fye upon you Robert, and your brandy." He was rebuked.

1724. August 29th. The Session, being informed that it is become a practice for young women to carry loads of brandy, some twelve, some sixteen miles out of the parish, etc.

1725. September 1st. "This day there was a report of the Sabbath being lately profaned by persons concerned in the brandy trade. Ordered that inquiry be made into it by the elders against their next meeting."

1725, October 3rd. "This day reported that the rise of the last Session day's information concerning the profanation of the Sabbath, was that some herds falling on some casks of brandy that was hidden on the moss, and abusing themselves with it."

1725. October 25th. "Sabbath—This day compeared Robert Miller and others, who owned that about twintie days ago they were at Corsbie, in time of public worship, but pretended they were seeking a horse which had wandered away. It being suggested by one of the members that they were digging potatoes at Corsbie, and were likewise heard railing and making a noise in the hall. They denied it."

1727. May 31st. "This day information was given in against William Cochran, in Brakenlie, weaver, by his gross forgetfulness of the Sabbath in working at his employment."

1727. August 27th. "This day information is given in against Margaret King, spouse to James Rankine, her grievous cursing her master to the laird of Mountain, by sitting down upon her knees, and wissing him nor his never to do well in a world." She is ordered to be cited.

As late as 1802 we find a similar watchfulness manifested by the Session. Hence the following:—

1802. September 26th. "The Moderator acquainted the Session that he had received information that the following persons, David Rayside, etc., had gone out in a boat upon Sabbath last, being the 19th inst., and gone aboard a ship passing up to Greenock in the afternoon of that day. After remaining some hours aboard, they brought out of that ship five casks of rum, etc., which they carried in their boat and brought them on shore, betwixt nine and ten o'clock that night. The officer is ordered to summon four of them, who compeared. One of them declared that the articles, though brought ashore, had not been bought, and that he had gone to see a friend. The others are summoned in October, acknowledge their sin, express sorrow, are rebuked and admonished by

Session, and their sentence intimated from the pulpit on October 31st, for the satisfaction of the congregation. Doubtless when the Kirk Session took up such matters as those referred to in the foregoing extracts, and endeavoured to enforce their authority in the punishment of such backslidings, their hands would be kept pretty full. From these extracts, we also learn that rather more was expected from elders in those days than now, in that a more or less familiar acquaintance with the life and manners of those in their respective districts or quarters was expected from them. The pulpit, then, was also expected to be a medium of information about many things now regarded as beyond its province, *e.g.*, Civil Acts, Roups, etc.

About other church officials in the parish, we cannot glean very much from the old records still available. So far back as 1693, we find "William Or, Haplands" appointed Treasurer to the Session, "To continue half a year from the date hereof, to be countable at the end of the half-year for receipts and disbursements." About a century later (1770-1802) we find Robert Starret, Schoolmaster, occupying the same post, and he is followed by Alexander Ritchie. The office of Session Clerk seems generally to have been in the hands of the Schoolmaster. Hence we find Robert Starret, Hugh Workman, Robert Pinkerton, and William Smith successively holding that office. We find the following names of Church Officers, Beadles, Bellmen, and Sextons:—John Workman, (1771), Robert Dickie, (1800), William Motion, (1816)—Malcolm—Duncan, (1830), (whose wife is said to have been the village barber of the day), William King, (1842), Thomas Workman, (1860), James Workman, (1893), Robert M'Lellan, (1895).

The emoluments attached in bygone days to these and other church-offices, give us an idea of the greater value of money in those times. Thus, the Session Clerk receives in 1780, £1 per annum; in 1786, £1 5s; in 1803, £2; in 1814 £3:—the Kirk Treasurer in 1780, 10s; in 1803, £1; in 1861, £2:—the Kirk Officer in 1771, 10s; in 1799, 15s 6d; in 1801, £1 11s:—the Precentor in 1809, £2 2s; in 1811, £4 4s:—the Presbytery Clerk from each parish within the bounds, in 1792, 6s 8d; in 1804, 10s 6d; in 1811, 19s; in 1815, £1 1s:—the Synod Clerk in 1810, 4s; in 1812, 6s:—Gravedigger in 1801, 1s 6d for each grave.

From 1823 at least, services in connection with the Relief Kirk, afterwards a portion of the U.P. Church, would seem to have been conducted in the parish on alternate Sundays by Mr. Ellis of Saltcoats and others. Previously, adherents of that persuasion, used to go to Saltcoats, taking lanterns with them, which were utilized for the lighting of the Meeting House at evening Service. In 1794, Dissenters in the parish are said to have numbered about fifty, part of them belonging to the Relief Church, and part to the Secession. Their Services in West Kilbride were at first held in a joiner's shop near Gateside, which was tidied up for the purpose on the previous Saturday evening. Such Services led about 1825 or thereby to a settled Seccession Ministry in the parish, The first minister, the Rev. Mr. Mather, was ordained on the Castle Green about that time. On his demission of office in 1837, he became the founder and first minister of the E.U. Church in Ardrossan, and afterwards the editor of "The Christian News." He was succeeded at West Kilbride by the Rev. Mr. Sprott, under whom the congregation became somewhat diminished in numbers.

On his departure, there was a vacancy for some months, and then its prosperity was revived under the late Dr. Boyd who came from Ireland in 1848 and continued in its ministry until 1866, when he retired and was succeeded by the present incumbent, the Rev. J.C. Balderston. The first Church of the "United Associate Congregation" seems to have been erected by subscriptions both in money and manual labour about 1828, which date is inscribed upon the first tokens therein used. It had 434 sittings. It stood behind the present U.P. Manse, with its front gable to the public road, until its removal a few years ago. It was considerably improved in 1859 by the enclosure of its outside stair and other repairs, The present United Presbyterian Church in Ritchie Street was erected in 1882, and the present U.P. Manse about twenty years ago.

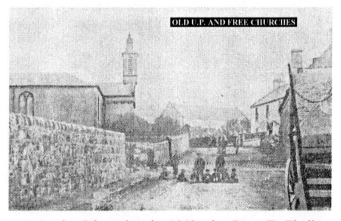

OLD U.P. AND FREE CHURCHES

At the Disruption in 1843, the Rev. T. Findlay, parish minister, became the first minister of the Free Church congregation, which met for a short time at first in Simpson's Hall, Damlug. The first Free Church, now

Rosevale Cottage, stood near the Railway Station. The present Free Church was opened for public worship in August, 1881. The present incumbent, the Rev. W. M'Kenzie, was first appointed Assistant to the Rev. T. Findlay in 1871, then Assistant and Successor in 1873, and attained to the full charge in 1875.

The erection of the Episcopalian charge at Ardrossan in 1873 originated from an Episcopalian Mission, begun in West Kilbride in 1851, and still continued at Kirktonhall in the form of an Anglican Service on the third Sabbath of each month. Roman Catholics also have a monthly service in a hall near Gateside.

Previous to the passing of the "Education Act" of 1872, the bond linking the Parish School to the Parish Church was a very close one; for, whilst the Schoolmaster might be elected at a meeting of Heritors' the Parish Minister had generally a considerable amount of influence in his selection. The Annual Presbyterial examination of the schools also helped considerably to strengthen the bond. So far back as 1603; we find the name of John Lowrie, schoolmaster in Kilbride West, as witness to a Will of that year. The Presbytery Records show a Mr. Johnson to have been parish schoolmaster at Kilbride in 1688. In 1717 we find the following entry in the Parochial Records: May 1st, 1717. "The said day, the gentlemen heritors residing in the paroch,. viz., Hunterston, Carlung, and Kirkland, waited on the Session and chose Mr. Alexander Glas to be their Schoolmaster." Again on May 22nd, 1717. "The said day, the Session unanimously chose Mr. Glas to he their Session Clerk and ordered the registers to be committed to his care." Item, they appointed William King, Wright, to repair the school, to put up a bed, a clay brace and a partition. We have already seen the dominie of 1757, Mr. Kennedy seeking to augment his regular emoluments by engaging in the running trade. The succession of parish School-masters since his day would seem to have been, Messrs Robert Starret, (1802), Hugh Workman, (1802-1809), Robert Pinkerton (1809-1828), William Smith, (1828-1860), Peter M'Conchie, (1860-1896).

One of Mr. Starret's sons went to the West Indies where he amassed a considerable fortune; his grand-daughter was married to Major Graham in a sort of run-a-way match, the window in Hawbill House by which she eloped, being still pointed out. H. Workman is said to have been noted as a Land Surveyor, and the constructor of an organ—a remarkable feat for those days.

The qualifications required of parochial schoolmas-ters in the earlier part of this century may be gathered from the fact, that when Mr. Smith was appointed, he was examined by the Presbytery and found qualified to teach English, Latin, French, Greek, Writing, Arithmetic, Book-keeping, Navigation, and Geography. In 1809 the emoluments of the office seem to have been 400 Merks (Scots), the school fees, a house and two bolls of oatmeal in lieu of a garden, and the election seems to have been made by the Session. Towards the close of last century the school stood on the glebe just behind the Old Build-ings near the Village Cross. It was a mean, single-roomed, low, thatched-roofed building, with a single window, a latch-door, and an earthen floor. This build-ing was demolished by order of the Presbytery about 1805, when the school was removed to the Old Manse, which in turn was supplanted about 1846 by the old parochial school, converted in 1884 into the Parish Church Mission Hall. The present Public School was built in 1876, and has since been twice enlarged. The schoolmaster's house has occupied different sites. It was once in the Session's house on the glebe, at another time in a house on Castle Green, and then beside the School.

In addition to the Parish School, there have existed at various dates, other schools, *e.g.*, one at Underbank, kept in a room of Lord Sempill's house after it had been let to humbler tenants. The walls of this school-room are said to have been covered with printed and gilt leather, probably of Dutch manufacture. In 1820 Robertson tells us there were two schools in the parish attended by 126 scholars. At a later date there were—the Free Church School, erected shortly after the Disruption, on the site now occupied by Woodbine Cottage;—its Schoolmaster's house, now forming the dwelling-house of the Station Master;—the Female Industrial School and house on a site contiguous to the present Public School, intended for girls and very young boys, and erected in 1855 by means of subscriptions and grants from Government, and Ferguson Bequest. It was managed by the Parish Kirk Session. There was also a school in Ritchie Street taught by Mr. Craig.

From the late Dr. Edgar's "Old Church Life in Scotland," we learn that there was a Sabbath School in this parish about a century ago, one of six then to be found in the Presbytery. The Presbytery of Irvine in 1798, were greatly exercised about the spread of Sunday Schools, and accordingly cited all Sabbath School teachers before them with a view to testing their qualifications. The following questions were put to them: (1) Are you willing to subject yourself to the doctrine and discipline of the Church as by law established? (2) Are you willing to take the oaths to Government, and to have your school

registered in the County Books? (3) Do you receive
payment from your scholars or any other person? (4)
Have you any commission from, or connection with, any
Missionary Society, or any Society beyond your own
parish, *e.g.*, the Haldanites? In 1799, two Nathanaels
from West Kilbride took instant alarm and wrote to the
Presbytery, "That they had come to the full determination
of ceasing from this date, to attend the Sunday evening
Schools in assisting to catechize the few children who
have for a very few Sunday evenings attended in this
place."

If we might judge from the number of ecclesiastical
names, fabrics, relics, and traditions associated with the
parish in bygone days, we might be inclined to say, that
up to the light of the age in which they lived, the forefathers of this village hamlet, and rural district, were
characteristically a religious and devout people, but the
evidence supplied by Presbytery and Session Records to
which our attention has been called, seems to show that
not a little superstition and worldly-mindedness were
intermingled therewith. Church discipline was harsh and
inquisitive, and practical Christianity, as associated with
special church agencies, largely at a discount. Still, home
piety and family devotions were somewhat more in
evidence than they are now, although, such devotions
were sometimes rather protracted and diffuse, as the
following anecdote may show:—A Mr. F——when
lodging in one of the inns of the place, about the beginning of this century, happened to go out for a stroll about
the time of evening worship; he met in with a neighbour
of the innkeeper's. On their return some time after, they
found the evening exercises still unfinished. "Hoo far's
he on noo?" said the one to the other. "Weel, he's at

Constantinople," was the reply. "Weel, then, we need not be in a hurry to go in, it'll be a gey blink before he gets to Jerusalem." His prayer was very comprehensive— dealing with the Pope, the False Prophet, and many other topics. About a century ago, some of those attending church are reported to have taken considerable liberties during public worship—even leaving the church for a time to take a stroll or fill their pipes.

Still, among these worshippers of bygone centuries, there were not a few specimens of the peasant-saint, that class which so excited the enthusiastic admiration of a Carlyle, and led his thoughts backward to the Carpenter of Nazareth. As we stand today on the ground they occupied, all we would in conclusion say is this: "Other men laboured, and we have entered into their labours."

# CHAPTER VIII.
## PAROCHIAL LIFE OF THE PARISH.

"THE short and simple annals of the poor" present a phase
of parochial life, that is at once intrinsically interesting,
and capable of shedding some rays of light further afield
than their own narrow bounds. They remind us how true
it is, that the poor we have always with us; and even in
the meagre entries of Parochial Records they supply us
with the framework of many a pathetically absorbing
tale. They link the present to a remote past, the days of
toil and nights of sorrow, that enter so largely into the lot
of the obscure and humble poor. To reproduce aright a
life-like picture of their experience, we need a wisely
directed and carefully guarded use of the historical
imagination, to clothe with flesh and blood the somewhat
dry skeleton whose various bones require to be disinterred from the musty records of a Kirk Treasurer's
Account Books, or the Minute Book of a Parochial
Board. In such records we find the earlier life of traditions, habits, and customs, some of which are now
extinct, and others barely traceable in lingering relics. As
we ponder such records, with telling force there recurs to
our minds the truth of the familiar sayings, "Distance
lends enchantment to the view," and, "Our little systems
have their day." The substance may still be the same, but
the form is different. The outward may be changed, but
the inward abides. The hopes, the fears, the joys, the
sorrows, the social customs, the complexions of thought,

the modes of speech, the occupations, and even the fashions of attire that still prevail in our midst, link themselves to this past and lend an enhanced interest to it.

The material extant for such a delineation as we propose, is by no means abundant; yet, it is sufficient to inspire the desire to save from oblivion a few of the more curious entries to be found in these old Parochial Records, which may be deemed suitable to the elucidation of the parochial life of bygone generations. One of the oldest of these Records extant was brought to light about two years ago from an attic above a baker's shop in the village. It was in the form of a few scattered leaves of a Kirk Treasurer's Account Book between the years 1788 and 1818. Since then, under the guidance of the present Inspector of Poor, we have succeeded in discovering in what is humorously called "West Kilbride Municipal Buildings," the predecessor to the above Kirk Treasurer's Book, ranging from the years 1770 to 1788. Within this book there were a very few faded leaves of Sessional Records of poor relief, of registers of baptisms, and of proclamation of banns, reaching as far back as the close of the preceding century. Entries in these two Kirk Treasurer's Books throw a considerable amount of curious and interesting light upon persons and practices, ecclesiastical and parochial, during the years embraced within them; and just as Browning developed the well-known poem of "The Ring and the Book," from an old record of a criminal trial picked up at a bookstall in Florence, so will we assay a humbler flight, and endeavour from these entries, combined with information derived from other sources, to produce a sketch of parochial life in this parish upwards of a century ago.

From such sources we learn that the care of the poor was at that time the joint interest of the Kirk Session and Heritors, a system which the late Dr. Edgar tells us began in 1672. Previous to that date the Kirk Session alone had been entrusted with that charge. The relief granted to the poor, he further tells us, was generally distributed either in face of, or under the surveillance of the Kirk Session. When sent the Kirk Officer generally made a charge of one penny for delivery. The deacons were the formal inspectors of poor; and the post of Kirk Treasurer was often a gratuitous one, although not always so in this parish. In 1797, we find Robert Starret, schoolmaster, holding this latter office. The money contributed by the heritors towards the maintenance of the poor would seem to have been raised by voluntary assessment, or Stent, as it was called. This Stent was irregularly levied, and still more irregularly paid. According to the Kirk Session Minute Book, the heritors seem to have first voluntarily assessed themselves for the relief of the poor in 1834, as the following entry shews: "February 27th, 1834. The Heritors agreed to assess themselves at the rate of Twopence upon the Pound of Valued Rent for the support of the poor and other general parish uses, and also recommend that the farmers, householders and others not being Heritors, should subscribe for the support of the poor; and that all prudent measures be taken for the improvement of the Collections at the Church Doors, and thus avert, if possible, that worst of modes for their support, a legal assessment." This worst of modes, a legal assessment, was begun in this parish in 1846. It was at first levied upon "Means and Substance," the value of which would seem to have been ascertained by a process of mutual inquisition, akin to our present Income Tax System. Hence such entries as these:—

"July 7th, 1849. Archibald Malcolm, fisherman, Ritchie Street, charged on heritages, £13 11s; Means and Substance, £31. The charge for Means and Substance departed from."

"Same date. Mr. Thomas Rutherford, Dykes, charged on £45, Means and Substance. Half of charge to be abated on account of sickness in the family."

The assessment on Rental dates from 1861.

The Kirk Session's principal sources of revenue for the support of the poor, were the ordinary church door collections, special collections at Communion seasons; interest on bills, mortcloth dues, fees for proclamation of Banns, fines from delinquents, rents of certain pews, and special benefactions.

Of the ordinary collections at different periods we have given specimens in a previous chapter. Suffice it now to add, that in 1788, they seem to have averaged about 5s 6d a day, and that at the beginning of the present century, they vary from 4s to 10s a day, and occasionally a little more. The Special Collections at Communion Seasons, which, two centuries or more ago, were taken in some parishes on retiring from the Table, were not greatly inferior to those of the present day. This was largely owing to the greater number of services then prevalent at such seasons. They generally amounted to about £4, and in 1793, we find one of £5 7s. These collections, or at least a portion of them, appear to have been specially distributed among the poor. Of the revenue derived from interest on Bills, the following may be taken as specimens:—in 1772, £3 16s 9d; in 1773, £7; in 1777, £1 15s 0½d; in 1785, £2 17s 6d.

Money seems to have been lent to various persons, so that even the minister found refuge in his day of need in the resources of the Session, as the following instance will shew:—1772. To Mr. Oughterston, his bill, £6, and again £16 17s. The Session's funds would also seem to have been lent for various periods of time. Hence, the bills uplifted in different years vary, e,g., in 1771, £4; in 1776, £42 2s. The following entries will throw further light on this matter:—"November 26th, 1800. Received the interest of the Session's Bank Bill, £4 9s 7d. September 22nd, 1802, of Cash Gott from irvin of interest and part of the Bill, £13 8s 3d. November 12th, 1802. Received £2 10s of Mister Miller's Bill."

Monetary transactions with Todd and Montgomery, the then bankers of the place, are also of frequent occurrence. The rate of interest charged for the advance of money on loan, was generally about four per cent. Thus, were the Kirk Session the parochial bankers, pawnbrokers, and bill exchangers of the time.

Another source of revenue, long since discontinued under the influence of the despotic sway of fashion, was the hiring out of mortcloths at funerals. Of these, three qualities were at one time kept, which were hired out at different dates at diverse rates. Thus in 1771, the rates are five shillings for the best, and three shillings for the second; but these rates are afterwards raised to eight shillings for the best, and four shillings for the second, and three shillings for the third, in the case of an adult; and one shilling and eightpence and one shilling and tenpence for a child. In the case of a person of special wealth or importance, however, the Kirk Session knew how to apply the screw; in such instances we sometimes find ten shillings charged. The revenue derived from such a source naturally varied according to the number of deaths per annum, and the wealth of their relatives, *e.g.*, in 1771, £2 17s 10d; in 1772, £2 4s; in 1775, 12 7s; in 1786, £1 18s 4d; in 1788, 16s 10d; in 1801, £2 11s 8d. The Church Officer was allowed twopence for taking care of it each time it was hired out. The original cost of a mortcloth was considerable, as the following entry will shew:—1788, May 7th. To Mr. John M'Indoe, merchant in Glasgow, for 61 yards Genoa Velvet for a Mortcloth, condescended upon by Minister and Session, with linen and silk for the fringes, amounts to as per receipt £13 8s. October 30th, 1788. To John Miller for making the new Mortcloth, 3s, and to Mary Melville for working the fringes to the Mortcloth 10s; so, that when complete, the mortcloth must have cost £14 1s. Other entries bearing upon this subject are such as these;—1788, October 30th. To John Miller for mending an old Mortcloth and silk, 8d. 1803, February 21st. Mister Stirret for the best Mortcloth, 8s. 1803, March 26th. James Simson, Mortcloth, 3s. 1806, August 27th. To Mortcloth for M'Leish's child 10d.

The Mortcloth was sometimes brought to the house and left upon the corpse until burial. The names entered as hiring the Mortcloths, are those still large ly common in the district—Boyds, Wilsons, Montgomeries, Crawfords, Hunters, Caldwells, Workmans, Millers, Tyres, Baillies, Gemmells, etc. A few less familiar or altogether extinct names are also found, *e.g.*, Service, Rayside, Ferry, Sharp, Tamey, etc. In default of a duly authenticated register, the list of those hiring the Mortcloths, throws not a little light upon the dates of the decease of the ancestral relatives of some of the present inhabitants of the district.

About the beginning of this century, the charges made for the use of the Mortcloths would seem to have been regarded by some as excessive, and hence the co-operative system was called into requisition as a remedy. This we gather from the following letter addressed to the minister and Heritors on February 16th, 1826: "The subscribers for the morecloath, etc. in this place have to intamate that they discontinue to use it any longer, and have agreed to make a present of it, the Session—and hope, Gentlemen, on that account you will can give it on easier terms than the old. Archibald Miller, Pres." This letter appears to have been the result of a prosecution of the shareholders by the Session, on the ground of the loss accruing to the Poors' Fund from the use of the Co-operative Mortcloth. The legal expenses of that prosecution amounted to £2 3s 10d. The prayer of the petitioners for a reduced rate would seem, however, to have been efficacious, as shortly thereafter, we find the following scale of charges for use of the best Mortcloth, 5/-; of second 2/6; of third 1/6, whilst one was kept for the poor gratis. After 1835 the sole charge is 2/6. The Kirk Session's next source of revenue for the poor, was fees for the proclamation of banns, which were at the rate of 10/6 for one day, and 5/- for two days. These, of course, also yielded variable sums according to the number of proclamations in a year, e.g., in 1802, £3 2s. 0d.; in 1803, £2 17s. 0d. In addition thereto, collections were also made in behoof of the poor, at the celebration of the marriage, whether in public (i.e., in Church or at a penny wedding) or in private. Hence such entries as these: 1773, December 26th, To a private marriage 2/-; 1775, March 1st, To a publick marriage 1/11; 1786, March 2nd, To a publick marriage 3/7½; 1810, September, 18th, Collected at William Scot's and Mary Galbreth's Marage 3/6. The amount derived from this source was also necessarily variable, being in 1776, 10/3$_{1/2}$; in 1780, 5/10$_{1/2}$; In 1786, 0/-; in 1787, 5/4$_{1/2}$; and it seems to have died away altogether after 1810. The following further entries will illustrate a rare source of additional revenue from irregular marriages:—

1783, July 17th. Received from Mr. F— M— and spouse for their Irregular Marriage, £2.

1825, June. £5 from M— G— on irregular marriage (before a Magistrate, though afterwards iu Church,) with Miss M— L—.

Fees or fines for delinquency would also seem to have found their way into the coffers of the poor. Entries under this head are generally amusing, and in one instance at least, savour too much of the nature of a Sale of Indulgence. Specimens are these:—

1777, August 31st. Received 5/- sterling, from William Simson and John Paterson for the behoof of the poor. In token they have put up some Difference which was betwixt them.

1796, April 6th. John Tarbert, Saylor in Overton, paid a fine for fornication and absolved £2 10s.

1802, December 7th. Received from Hunterston as a fine of one of his servants for neglect of dutie, £2 3s.

1840, September 2nd. Received from Ad. Meller iu Third Millie, 4/6, being his part of the Mony Gott Bak from Volenters.

1805, July 24th. Received a donation from Mrs. Colonel Hyndman, (Carlung) by the hands of Miss Margaret Boyd of Orchard, being the fee due to one of her servants who run off, 10/6,

1826, February. £1 for shooting a pheasant upon Lady Montgomery's lands, handed to Session for behoof of poor.

1836, September 14th. Proceeds of fine for trespassing, 4/4.

1839, November 3rd. Proceeds of fine for poaching, 7/-

Another source of revenue to the Kirk Session's Poor Fund was the rental of a house once known as the Schoolmaster's house and situated to the West of the churchyard. In 1771, it yielded £1 5s. per annum, 1822, £2 2s., when it was let to W. Logan, Wright, who still tenanted it in 1840, at a rental of £2 10s. It was probably transferred to the Parochial Board iu 1845, and was swept away with the other old buildings near the Cross, in 1865.

Next to collections, the principal source of revenue was the proceeds of certain pews in Loft, and Big or Lang Seat, let by annual roup and yielding such variable sums as £6 0s. 6d. in 1798; £8 11s. 6d. in 1802; £5 9s. in 1803; £7 in 1805, £12 2s. in 1807; £17 16s. 6d. in 1808; and £19 9s. in 1810, at which date individual sittings began to be let, as may be seen from such entries as these:—

May, 1810. By Cash from 7 sittings on Lang Seat at 4 /- £ 1 8s.

1810. Rent of Seat for Mrs. Pinkerton, 4/-.

1812, December 13th. Money for Sittings in Big Seat, £1 4s.

In 1818, A. Ritchie receives 5/- as his commission for the rouping of these seats. The annual rental of each sitting seems to have been 2/- 3/- or 4/-. The legality of thus deriving revenue from seat letting seems to have been questioned in May, 1830, and, after the erection of the Feuars' Gallery in 1834, the income therefrom seems to have gradually decreased; the sum realized that year being £2 13s. 1½d., and in 1839 £2 19s. 3d.

Ever and anon the Session's Funds were also Enriched by special donations to the poor. Thus, from Presbytery Records we learn that in 1767, Dr. Hugh Baylie sent £6 16s. as a charitable donation to be distributed unto two old women in each of the seventeen parishes of the Presbytery of Irvine, after November 1st next, in the way of buying coals for them, and some oyl for sight to enable them to spin at night for their better subsistence. And, at even an earlier date, February 8th, 1727, we find the minister acquainting the Session that Mr. Wm. Young, late Schoolmaster in Largs had left in legacy twelve copies of Mr. Guthrie's Treatise, to the poor of the parish of West Kilbride. Other curious and interesting entries under this heading are these:—

April 14th, 1772. Received from Mr. Robert Adam in Virginia, £1 1s. 6d.

1786, November 27th. The deceased Wm. Wyllie, in Cowberryshaw left as a donation to the poor of this parish, £5.

1793, March 9th. Bequeathed to the poor of this parish by the late Peter John Hunter, £31 10s.

1796, April 17th. Miss Hunter of Hunterston, and Miss Hunter (younger) sent 5 Guineas each, at Hunterston's death.

1799, October. Mr. James Russell who stayed in the Minister's, gave to the poor when he went away 5/-.

1804, July 31st. There was paid to the Rev. Mr. Arthur Oughterston by Mr. William Parker, Merchant in Kilmarnock, by the hands of Mr. John Henry, preacher of the gospel, upon the fifth of June last, the sum of £20, sterling, being a legacy bequeathed to the poor, by the deceased Mr. Robert Adam (father of Mr. Adam of Tours) merchant in North Carolina, and devoted in trust to the said Mr. Oughterston, to be by him distributed as he shall see most proper and needful.

1812, November 22nd. Received by the hands of Miss Boyd from Mrs. Hunter, £1.

During the years 1788 to 1818, we find special donations from the Craufurds of Auchenames to the amount of £24 9s.; from the Hunterston family, £13 4s. 6d.; from Lord Eglinton, £5 5s.; from Mrs. Boyd, for poor of Carlung, £1 Is.; from J. and A. Oughterston, £1 3s.; from Mrs. Oswald, Shieldhall, £1 Is.; from F. Tarbert, Fairley, 4s.; from Robert Starret, Junr, £2 2s.; from Captain J. Meller, £1 1s. Francis Ritchie, Kirkton-hall, £3 3s, one Guinea of which was on the occasion of his marriage in 1808; from Mrs. Reddie, £1 2s.; from Lady Mary Montgomery, £15. During those years there was distributed amongst the poor of this parish as the produce of special benefactions, at least, the sum of £132 10s. 6d., or an average of £4 8s. 4d. per annum. Subsidiary sources of revenue were, the Bell-penny at funerals, and small sums occasionally realized from the sale of paupers' effects. Of the latter the following may be taken as examples:—

1801, April 27th. To Cash received from Janet Starret, being the price of cloth received in barter, for the the deceased Margaret Gray's Cloaths, 8s.

1810, June 30th. By Cash for Sundries at the roup of the deceased Janet Sharp, £4 9s. l0d.

1812, June 5th. Amount of Hannah Service's roup clear of King's dues and other expenses, £2 19s. 2d.

While, such were the Sources of the Kirk Session's revenue for the poor, the income derivable therefrom was slightly depreciated by two untoward facts, viz., the large amount of bad copper coins, then in circulation, not a little of which seems to have found its way to the Kirk plate,—and the occasional closing of the Church doors on Sunday, when no service, no collection. Evidence of the injurious effects of the former upon the Kirk Session's revenue we find in such entries as these:—

1785, March 16th. To halfpennies which will not go current, 5/-.

1786, March 6th. Loss of three dollars got before they fell, 1/-.

1800, September 3rd. Bad half-pence this last month, 1/8.

1801, February 13th. Sold the poor's bad halfpennies per the Minister and Session, 27 1/2 lbs. at 10d. per lb., £1 2s. 11d.

The loss accruing from closed church doors may be gathered from the entry, "No Sermon," occurring in 1770, 12 times; in 1771, 10 times, in 1772, 4 times; in 1773, 6 times; in 1782, 6 times; in 1786, 5 times; in 1794, 8 times, &c.,

Rarely is any reason assigned for the lack of Sabbath service. Exceptions are:—

1804, October 7th. No Sermon, Minister not well; and 1817, July 20th to September 14th. Church under repair.

Ministers were then apparently allowed to take it somewhat easier than now. Over against this latter source of deduction we ought, however, to place the fact, that about a century ago, Week-day services, (generally on a Wednesday), were more common than now, and at these, collections, were taken. In 1770 we find three such services yielding a revenue of 18/11¼; in 1771, five, with a revenue of £1 19s. 6½d. in 1775, six, with collections amounting to £1 12s. 11½d. After this date, these Week-day services gradually become less numerous, so that in 1782 there are only two, with a revenue of £1 1s 8½d.

Upon another source of diminished income, the following Minute of June 19th, 1823, will throw some light:— "At a joint meeting of Heritors and Kirk Session, it was moved by Mr. Hunter of Hunterston, and seconded by Mr. Hunter of Kirkland, that as some Inhabitants of the parish have of late employed Seceding Clergymen to preach each alternate Sunday, whom they pay out of the collections then made, by which means the Poors' Funds are considerably lessened, the Elders are therefore requested, wherever any application shall be made to them for relief, to take particular pains to ascertain whether the Applicant be of the Established Church, and if it shall appear that he is not, or that he has been in the constant practice of attending these seceding meetings, the Elders shall without loss of time report the same to the Session, and the Session to the Heritors, and shall in the meantime not order any more money to be paid to such applicant than is barely sufficient to keep him or her unbeggant." This was unanimously agreed to.

But even subject to all such deductions, the revenue derived from these various sources of income seems to have been amply sufficient for the purpose, the number of pensioners being small and the expenses of management a mere trifle. We think the statement may be risked that those, then requiring parochial relief, were no worse off than now.

Having thus seen the sources of revenue, let us now mark the light thrown by these old records upon the disbursement of this revenue. Then as now, the two main objects upon which expenditure was incurred, were the relief of enrolled, and of casual poor. From a loose scrap in the older Kirk Treasurer's book, of date, 1691, we learn that relief was distributed according to districts, *e.g.*,

### SOUTHENDAND POOR.

Margarat boyd, - - - - - - - - - - - -01 00 00
marion King, - - - - - - - - - - - - -01 00 00
jannet baylli, - - - - - - - - - - - - -01 00 00
thomas workman, - - - - - - - - - - -01 00 00

### HUNTERSTON GROUND.

isob'll Reed, - - - - - - - - - - - - -01 00 00
jannat Hunter, - - - - - - - - - - - - -01 00 00
Margarat Hunter, - - - - - - - - - - -01 00 00
margarat boyd, - - - - - - - - - - - -01 00 00
martha Steinstoun,- - - - - - - - - - -01 00 00
jannat jamie, - - - - - - - - - - - - -01 00 00

and similarly, Portincross ground with two pensioners; Carlung ground with eight pensioners; Corsby ground with one pensioner; Law ground with three pensioners. The allowance mentioned is probably monthly, and stated in pounds, Scots.

Those obtaining relief are then styled pensioners, a somewhat milder term than the modern word, pauper. Whilst dealing with these few scattered leaves of two centuries ago, we may notice the following curious entries therein found:—

1693, January 1st. Given out to a poor woman living in Dalry, 1/-.

1693, February 22nd. Given Out to Margarat
Glasgow in Corsmuir, 1/-.

1693, February 22nd. Jannat Miller in bally, 8d.

1693, March 28th. The minister, 04 00 00 whereof
he gave Two pond for the Clerk's faill (fee) of the prisbritry, and the rest was given before the prisbritry upon the
Session's accompt.

1693, March. Given to Thomas Craig in Corsby who
has a horse dead, 02 00 00.

With difficulty we decipher such an entry as this:
"This day, (1663) the minister and elders have appointed
William Or, of Hapland, to be Treasurer to the Session,
and to continue half a year from this date hereof, to be
countable at the end of the half year for receipts and
debursements."

Do not such entries as these point to the depopulation,
since then, of the rural parts of the parish, and to a practical interest in the temporal well-being of the poor, that
can concern itself even with the loss of a horse!

The number of enrolled pensioners in 1788 was
small, only five, whose names were: Jean Kell, Jean
Rayside, Mary Biggart, Archibald Stewart and John
Wilson.

In 1800, they numbered seven and nine; in 1810,
nine and ten. Sometimes the same name continues on the
roll for a considerable number of years, that of Hannah
Service, *e.g.* from 1792 to 1812. Aliment would seem to
have been paid at first monthly, afterwards fortnightly.
The average weekly allowance was in 1800 about 1s 6d,
but unnamed poor boys at Holehouse, Glenside and
Halfway generally receive £1 per month. Special allowances were sometimes made during times of sickness.
Hence such entries as these:—

1783. June 3rd. To John Wilson, a poor man, a pair of blankets, to be returned to Session again, 5s 11½d.— (Mark the Kirk Session's forethought and thrift.)

1788. November 25th. To Catherine M'Millan as a donation in her present situation, and the orphans, 10s.

1792. June 15th. To Hannah Service, who has been some time ailing, and was applying to a doctor for some medicine, but was reduced,—had nothing to pay for't 2s. Extra allowances were also made for clothing, blankets, etc. *e.g.*

1782. September 2nd. To Robert Steel for cloth to make a pair of breeches to William Shedden, a poor boy, ordered by Session, 2s 4d.

1789. January 26th. To James Hogarth for five old shirts bought for the use of poor John Wilson and Thomas Tyre, 3s 9d.

1789. March 2nd. To Thomas Tyre, a pair of stockings and a wig got at a roup, 5d.

1789. March 2nd. To Robert Steel for one pair of blankets to Thomas Tyre, a poor man, 8 yards at 10d, per yard, 6s 8d.

1789. November 5th. To Thomas Tyre, for a covering as per receipt 3s 9d.

1796. February 16th. To John Malcom, for buying a coat to the poor boy in Holehouse, and he got 2s 6d from a gentleman to pay the making of said coat, the 5s was ordered some time ago, by a Donation, this 1s added to the 5s buys the coat, 1s.

The death and burial expenses of pensioners are also an item of expenditure in the Kirk Treasurer's Books, *e.g.*

1771. June 19th. To John King for a coffin for Alexander Adam's wife, 6s 6d.

1810. July 30th. Funeral charges of J. Sharp, *viz.* Grave-digging and proclaiming roup 2s, Whisky and Biskets 2s 6d, Coffin and Service 18s, £1 2s 6d.

1812. January 23rd. Funeral charges of Hannah Service, to candle 3d, to whisky 2s, to the coffin 16s, grave-digging is 6d, warning to the Buril 3d., £1 2s 0d.

Such charges remind us that, until this present century, relics of the Roman Catholic Wake or Watch night still lingered in our midst, and they bring up, before the mind's eye, the humbly furnished room—the white-sheeted corpse in one corner, the deal table in another, with its whisky and biscuits slowly disappearing, as the lonely watchers beguile the eerie hours with memories of the departed, and with the gossip of the day. It is a scene in which the sad and the hilarious strangely intermingle, and reminds us of days departed never to return. Even then, however, there was some improvement upon the usage of an earlier date, when sometimes no coffin whatever was provided for a pensioner,—merely a winding sheet, with the uncoffined corpse carried to the place of burial on a bier, known as the "Parish Coffin." But while such scenes are sufficient to lead the thoughts backward to that ruder age, when orgies were by no means uncommon at funerals; tobacco pipes, which they were won't to stick in their hats, being distributed amongst the assembled mourners; they are also suffi-cient to point forward to a better state of matters in more modern times, and to make us thankful, that all such relics of a fanciful superstition have vanished beneath the influx of a fuller light and a higher hope.

The revenues of the Session's Poor Fund were further burdened with the payment of school fees for poor children, as such entries as,—"1770, J. W. a poor scholar, 2s or 2s 6d a quarter, frequently shew. Another charge was that for the nursing of sick pensioners, which does not seem to have been always very liberal, as the following entries shew:—"1784. December 16th. To Jean King for washing and cleansing poor John Wilson in bed cloths and body, cloths, which was in a very miserable condition, and she took her own coals, one day 2s. To 1½lb soap for the above at 7½d per lb, 11½. For one Stone of Straw to put into the said John Wilson's bed, 3½d. Again on May 25th, 1794, the same Jean King only gets 12s for taking care of the deceased John Wilson for twelve weeks. This Jean King would appear to have been Washer and Scrubber to the Session as on October 5th, 1790, we find this further entry:—"To Jean King for cleansing poor John Wilson, washing, soap and time 2s 6d." We can well imagine what a regular good scrubbing poor John would get for that money. The allowance for constant sick-nursing would seem to have been afterwards somewhat more munificent, as in 1810 Elizabeth Renfrae gets 7s per week for taking care of Jennet Sharp.

Lawyers too come in for their share in the spoil; *e.g.* 1774. August 2nd. Given to a Lawyer for advice about M'Quaker's child, an orphan, who was offering to be thrust into this parish from another:—9s 4d.

1788. June 24th. To a Lawyer in Ayr, counsel about Catherine M'Millan 3s 6d. To Dinner, horse corn and drink in Ayr and hay is 10d. Horse corn at Irvine and bottle ale 6d. Two bottles ale at Irvine in return from Ayr 4d, and 2d for Tolls.

"Cases of lunacy are of rare occurrence, but, there is at least one instance upon which the following entries cast a sad and lurid light. It is the case of J.W. who appears upon the Session Records in 1802 as applying for the payment of her boy's school wages, which is granted, although the payment of her house rent is refused."

1810. September 24th. pied for taking care of J.W., for Board and washing, one week 9s.

1810. September 27th. pied for taking care of J.W., four days 5s 6d.

1810. September 28th. Pied for goieng to Glasgow with J.W., £1 1s.

1810. November 6th. pied James Workman for a strit Jaciket got to J.W., June 1810, 6s 6d.

(Same date.) pied for 7 pins of Gless l0d per pain, Brok by J.W., 5s l0d.

1811. February 22nd. Pied to the poor-house in Glasgow for J.W., for Bordin and funrel charges £6 13s. Thus ends the sad and sorrowful case of J.W.

Vagrancy seems to have been very prevalent towards the close of last century and the earlier part of this one, especially amongst discharged soldiers, many of whom, after the close of the Peninsular and French wars, were not able to find employment.

Neither is this prevalence of vagrancy to be wondered at, when we remember that it was the practice of Kirk-Sessions in earlier days, to grant badges to certain privileged parishioners entitling them to beg throughout the district. This was with a view to the relief of the Stent and their own poor-fund. On the breasts of these licensed beggars there was sometimes branded, with a stamp of lead, the name of the parish to which they belonged. It was sometimes also the practice to give assistance to deserving beggars at the Church door. The Kirk Treasurer's books of this, parish do not exactly bear out the Statement of the Old Statistical Account of 1794, that, whilst there were seven paupers, there were no wandering beggars. The licensed beggary referred to above may serve to explain frequent entries of this nature:—To a sailor etc. "*with a pass.*" Thus, although efforts more or less strenuous were put forth from time to time to suppress unlicensed vagrancy, a system of licensed beggary soon produced its natural fruit in a plentiful crop of blue-gowns, who, with staff in hand, and wallet on back, found a precarious, but by no means stinted sustenance and shelter amongst the more generous of their supporters. In this way, every parish came to have its representatives of the Edie Ochiltree class, whose visits with the news of the outside world, were far from being always unwelcome. One privileged Vagrant of this class, who perambulated this and other parishes about a century ago, was Colie Locks, a seller of old books. He would sometimes put up at a farm-place for a considerable time; he was but a type of several who were always sure of a bite of supper and a bed in the barn, when they paid their periodical visits. An instance of this we ourselves came across a few years ago at a farm in the parish. A century ago, there were no Mendicity Societies with their tickets for bed and bread, to inspire such vagrants either with terror or scorn; and when they became well known by their regular visits, they were often generously treated.

Casual, unknown, and unlicensed beggars were, however, no more favourites in the parish, then, than now. The main effort of the Kirk-Session was to get such as speedily as possible out of their borders, by passing them on to a neighbouring parish, or by helping them a stage on their destined way. When temporary relief was granted to them, it was always small, and often at the intercession of the minister, as such an entry as this may suggest, "1808. September 2nd. pied a poor trevlin women, Miniester Being not at home, 6d." Many of the entries bearing upon the relief of the casual poor are most amusing, as the following illustrative specimens will shew:—

"1779. March 3rd. To a reduced gentleman from America, 1s 6d.

1779. August 3rd. To a poor man reduced, who was taken by the rattlesnake, and was taken with Fitts etc. 6d.

1780. April 10th. To a poor object and reduced, 3d.

1781. March 10th. To a stranger with a good character, poor and indigent with a small family, 5d.

1786. March 25th. To a Saylor who was cast away near Dundee, 6d.

1787. November 1st. To a poor woman from Greenock going to Colonel Montgomery to get a protection for her husband from the Press, 6d."

The Kirk-Treasurer is evidently anxious that the Session should see that there is good reason for his munificent donations to the casual poor; although we are not altogether certain that the poor and indigent stranger of good character and with a small family, did not turn away from his door with a feeling of disappointment and chagrin, as he tried to picture to his own mind how much fivepence would do to provide bed and board for himself and Dependents. It is also evidently the fact, that another recipient of the Treasurer's charity is a *gentleman* from America, which opens his purse strings somewhat wider than usual. Neither is this hard-fisted official much more liberal to those he employs to do his work, as may be seen from the following entries:

1789. March 2nd. To Robert Scott for taking a poor cripple to the Largs, who came here on a carriers cart from Saltcoats, who had nothing but his knees to walk with, 1s.

1791. November 16th. To a carrier to take up a a poor insane person who will not walk to the Largs, who came with a carrier to this place from Saltcoats, to carry her from one parish to another, till she arrived to her parish or to some place where she is known, 3s 6d.

1791. November 22nd. To James Fullarton, for keeping the poor object above all night, who was sent back from the Largs to be sent to Saltcoats. They sat up with her all night. Give her before she went away some punch, 1s.

1791. November 28th. To Francis Tarbert, for taking down the poor dying woman to Saltcoats, but he says he must have more (And do we wonder at it!) 1s.

1806. February 30th. (Mark the date) pied Nill Mackelvie and Alexander Macmillan for tarring a man Drenged to Dalry, 5s.

1802. June 29th. By cash, paid John Allan for conveyence for a lame woman to Largs, with horse and cart, 3s.

The Kirk Treasurer does not appear to be altogether sorry either, when a regular pensioner is removed from the Roll, be the cause what it may, as this entry shews:

1773. March 8th. To Elizabeth Kyle, she is dead from this date, 1s. Further specimens of how he dealt with his casual and wandering visitors are these:

1790. March 5th. To a poor traveller and his family going home, 6d.

1790. May 30th. To a stranger in great necessity, well recommended, 4s. 6d.

1793. September 6th. To a poor sailor, to carry him to Greenock, 6d.

1800. June 29th. Paid to a soldier from Holland, who was wounded and discharged, with a large family, on their way home to Rothesay, where they were born, is. We scarcely think this soldier would be highly impressed with the generosity or gratitude of the country in whose cause he had bled, as he tried to find a passage for himself and family from West Kilbride to Rothesay, with only 1s. to pay for it.

In nearly all cases in which money is given to the casual poor, some special reason is assigned for doing so, *e.g.* "In present necessity,"—"In her advanced need,"—"A poor woman in trouble not a pensioner,"—"To a family in need, to be repaid when able,"—"Deranged of mind,"—"Travelling to Dublin, Dundee, etc.,"—"Three women going home,"—"Soldier's wife and child," and such like. The treatment meted out to the casual poor illustrates vividly the truth of the wise King's proverb, "The poor is hated even of his own neighbour," and shews the great object of each parish in all such cases to have been the lifting of the burden off its own shoulders, and the placing of it upon those of some other parish. Ill deserving, though some of them may have been, can we wonder that, thus tossed about from place to place, they generally became the very waifs of society, dragging out a weary life with a sore grudge against their more fortunate fellowmen? We further learn from these old Parish Records that there was not the same restriction then as now, upon relief in kind, as the following illustrations shew:—

1789. January 2nd. To a poor man in distress and reduced, (P. Ewing in Hunterston) to help to buy some little cordial for him, 2s.

1789. February 15th. To John Malcolm for a pair of shoes to Jean Renfrew, Netherton, formerly ordered by the Session, 3s.

1789. March 2nd. To John Wilson, a poor man, to one pair stockings at a roup, 3 1/2 d.

1789. November 5th. To 3 yards plaiding for a coat to a poor boy in Holehouse at 11d. per yard, for making and thread to W. Smith, 3d., 3s.

1793. March 19th. To Elizabeth Renfrew in Hunterston, a poor woman and a small family, to help to buy some lint to work on, 15s,

1803. January 17th. Plidin for an apron for Wm. Robson, Is. 10 1/2 d, pid R. Gemmell for making cloths for W. Robson, 2s.

1809. December 16th. A gill of whisky to Janet Sharp, 5d.

1810. February 12th. A bottle of Ale to Janet Sharp, 2 1/2 d.

Dr. Edgar further tells us that a common method of relief was the giving of meal, generally at the rate of half a peck per week for each. The Kirk Treasurer's books seem to have been by no means regularly audited or attested. We find them, however, examined on May 2nd, 1744, when the remark is made that amongst other Monies the Treasurer had in his hands, there was a ten-pound bank-note, whether Scots or Sterling we know not, but plainly a rarity in those parts at that time. The following may be taken as a specimen of the mode of audit of the Treasurer's books then prevalent.

Kilbryde, 23rd March, 1774.

The Sess mete and having cleared wt the Treasurer from 2nd March, 1773, to this date—and find there was collected at the Church Doors in yt time

|  | £16 11 6¾ |
|---|---|

£16 11 6$_{3/4}$

Int. of Bills in that time, - - - - - - - -   7 10 0
Profits of Mortcloths in that time,  - - -   1 12 8
Uplifted of the Stock in Bills in yt time,   42   4 2$_{1/4}$
Balance in the Treasurer's bands
at the last compting, - - - - - - - - - -   5 15  4$_{1/4}$

£73   3  9$_{1/4}$

Deburst to the several poor
                    in that time, - - - - -£31 13  0$_{1/4}$
Lent of the Stock in that time,  - - - - - 20   0  0
Balance in the Treasurer's hands,- - - - 21 10  8$_{3/4}$

                  Attested by Arthur Oughterson, Modr.

Similar Attestations follow at irregular intervals, often accompanied with the words, "For the above balance I hold myself and heirs responsible to the Kirk Session of Kilbride. Alex. Ritchie Treasurer."

The Treasurer would seem to have kept a sharp enough look-out against imposition or the relief of unnecessitous poor, as in 1805, we find Mary Wilson struck off the Poll, because he has come to know that she has eight guineas, which have been entrusted to Janet Whiteford.

Interesting references of a more modern date are such as these:—

In 1847, Mr. Fullarton made a motion in the Parochial Board that the introduction of politics at meetings of said Board should be avoided, which motion was not carried.

In 1848, those rated at £20 and upwards are the recognised members of the Parochial Board.

In 1849, there is a cholera scare, when a sanitary inspection of the village is ordered, the examinators to have their attention directed not merely to nuisances, but also to the state of the lower orders of the population, as to food and physical comfort. They report a few cases of excessive filth and overcrowding. There would appear to have been twenty cases of cholera in the parish at that time.

In January, 1866, the Inspector reports that the general health, condition, and circumstances of the parish's ordinary paupers, as far as he could discover, are in a satisfactory condition, and, although there were not any high gratulations for an excessive liberality, there was upon the whole a pleasing evidence and expression of gratitude and kindly feeling to the Board for their allowances, which were evidently regarded by the paupers more as the emanation of a spontaneous and free, than a constrained generosity; and which, whilst it was pleasing for him to witness,. and doubtless is gratifying for the Board to be informed of, is at the same time dutiful in him to record.

In 1848, we find work provided for the unemployed, as also in 1858, at the making of the cemetery road. What a picture of life amongst the poor in this parish upwards of a century ago, does the perusal of such facts as those we have now recorded, summon up before the mind. We see the widow at Hunterston with her large family spinning busily at her wheel to keep the wolf from the door, and scarcely able to get the lint to spin. We think of her sending her silent prayer for help to the Father of the fatherless, the widow's Stay, and the orphan's Help. We conjure up her little ones, early inured to labour, doing what they can to help their toiling mother. We imagine the feeling of heart-felt gratitude wherewith she brings the fifteen shillings worth of lint home to spin, and how her fingers work the faster when her heart is lighter. And

so the days and years of hard work and scanty fare fly
past, until her family becomes more able to relieve the
hard struggle of life. Or again, it is our old and honest
friend the pedlar we gaze upon, as he trudges with his
pack on his shoulder through "dub and mire," arrayed in
stockings and wig bought at a roup for fivepence. We
think of the homely bargaining, as with joke and banter
he displays his wares to view in some farmer's kitchen,
and seeks to tempt the wary purchasers. We see him
asleep in his pew under the influence of something wet
on the Saturday night, and something dry on the Sunday
forenoon. With difficulty we restrain the feeling of regret
that it should come to this at the end, a parish covering
for 3s. 9d,, a cart of coals for 3s. 6d., and a pauper's
burial to close the scene. Or again, it is the poor boy at
Holehouse, that moves across the stage, thinking himself
rich with the half crown he has got from a gentleman to
pay for the making of his coat. Or, yet again, it is Janet
Sharp with her shilling a week, drawing near the end of
her rough and thorny path through this world, getting in
the month of February 6s. 7d. as she is not in her
ordinary; in December a gill of whiskey, in the following
February a bottle of ale, and at last in July her 10s. coffin.
We picture the homely gathering at her funeral, the half-
crown's worth of whiskey and biscuits handed round the
assembled company of mourners, and finished by those
who are left behind. We hear the bellman proclaim the
roup of her effects. We mark the few simple articles
exposed for sale, and scattered over the homes of her
kindred poor. We note the proceeds, £4 9s. 10d, handed
over to the Kirk Session to help to meet the advances
made on her behalf; and very possibly those present at
that sale on June 30th, 1810, might think that that was the

last of Janet Sharp in so far, as this world was concerned, little dreaming that, at least, her name and these facts about her life would be heard and spoken of, when the names and lives of many, then residing in the parish, in much more affluent circumstances than she, would be entirely forgot—little dreaming that a few matter-of-fact details, entered into a Kirk Treasurer's books, with regard to relief granted to her, would be brought under the notice of those residing in the same place about a century afterwards. How many of us will have our names mentioned in the parish where we have spent our lives, a century after we are dead?

There are many other pictures of a kindred character outlined in these old parochial records on which we would fain have dwelt, but space forbids. In these short and simple annals of the poor, we have a record of homely joys and destinies obscure. In the light of the present some may be apt to think that the phase of parochial life in West Kilbride a century ago, here brought under review, reveals a mode of life comparatively rude and uncouth; but whilst allowance must be made for that enchantment which distance lends to the view, was it not less sophisticated than that of modern times; more simple and natural; were there not less artificiality and officialism than there are in these days; less envy and jealousy; greater contentment and happiness; less of the feuds between rich and poor; less contention between master and servant, employer and employed; more of the larger heart and the kindlier hand? The artificialities and courtesies of a later day may have rubbed down many idiosyncracies and angularities of that earlier time, but the solid and substantial are there—the blocks out of which were reared the earlier courses of that social structure whose upbuilding is still in progress, and we shall not go far amiss, if in our day and generation we produce as stable a basis for the super-structure of the future; as that past has for this present.

# CHAPTER IX.
## THE INDUSTRIAL AND SOCIAL LIFE
## OF THE PARISH.

IN the Industrial Life of a parish mainly rural, the principal occupation of the bulk of the inhabitants is bound to be pastoral and agricultural; and if under the term "pastoral" we include the feeding and rearing of cattle as well as sheep, we may venture the statement, that, until about the middle of last century, the parish may be said to have been more pastoral than agricultural; and that probably to as great an extent, as it is now more agricultural than pastoral. It is especially since the introduction of tile-draining, that so much of its soil has been reclaimed for agricultural purposes. The prevalence of such agricultural and pastoral pursuits, as well as the general wants of the community, naturally called for the presence in the village, as a centre, of such craftsmen as were necessary to minister to their wants, such as, masons, smiths, joiners, &c. As man for long has derived a portion of his sustenance from the sea as well as the land, a seaboard parish, such as this, was bound to have its quota of sailors and fishermen who braved the perils of the deep. In days gone by, these were found within our borders in larger numbers than now. A class is now also extinct in our midst, who once derived not a little of their livelihood from Neptune's domains, viz., Kelp-burners and Saltmakers. In so far as we know, the only other pursuits widely prevalent in the parish during the bygone centuries, have been weaving, and flowering, *i.e.*, the sewing of the once fashionable Ayrshire work. Other pursuits, which engaged a few in the days that are past, were tanning, candle-making, lint spinning, charcoal grinding, millering, lime burning, millstone making, tailoring, shoemaking, &c. In more modern times, and especially since the introduction of the railway, house-letting and the erection of houses for that purpose, have taken a prominent place as sources of revenue to the inhabitants. We shall endeavour to take a general survey of these pursuits as carried on in this parish. We begin with agriculture.

The soil and climate of the district appear particularly well adapted to dairy-farming. Hence milk, butter and cheese may be regarded as the staple agricultural products of the parish. The kind of cheese made is Scotch Cheddar, which may now be regarded as having superseded the once far-famed Dunlop variety. The milk produced in the parish is by no means, however, all used in the making of butter or cheese. A considerable quantity of it is retailed in Largs, Fairlie, West Kilbride, and Ardrossan, whilst some is sent per rail to Glasgow. Next to dairy-produce, early potatoes may be regarded as the most characteristic product of the parish. These were not grown in any quantity until after 1740. They are now principally grown along the sea-board, and central valley of the parish. For the excellence and earliness of this crop, West Kilbride ranks next to Girvan and surrounding district. Earliness is specially fostered by the well known boxing system, *i.e.*, the sprouting during winter of the seedling potatoes in boxes stored above the stable, or byre, or in some other outhouse. In this way they have secured a considerable start before being planted. They are generally ready for lifting about the end of June, or beginning of July, and before the close of the year, crops of rape, green barley, or turnips are not infrequently raised from the fields thus early cleared. Next to grass and potatoes, oats is the crop chiefly grown, with a view to supply fodder to the cows during winter, as well as for the feeding of horses and men. Wheat is only grown to a limited extent, as the climate is not too well adapted to its thorough ripening. Barley and rye are occasionally to be seen in small quantities. Beans have rather increased in acreage, although they are by no means extensively culti- vated. There is a fair acreage of turnips, used for the feeding of cattle during winter and spring. Mangold wurzel and late cabbage are grown to a less extent fir the same purpose. The former is valuable as less injuring the taste of the milk than turnips. Carrots are grown to a small extent, and with considerable profit. A few patches of beetroot, artichokes and other market vegetables are occasionally to be seen; but these are so few and far between, as scarcely to be worthy of mention. The hill pastures, largely interspersed with bracken, whin, and heather, supply abundant food to flocks of sheep and herds of small cattle.

Amongst the stock reared, the prime place must be given to the well known Ayrshire breed of cows, somewhat delicate through narrowness of chest, but affording an abundant supply of milk. The fattening of bullocks for the market is only carried on to a limited extent. The breeding and rearing of Clydesdale horses occupies, however, a considerable amount of attention, and of these some studs have acquired an extensive fame. Pigs, frequently brought from Ireland, are fattened on the whey produced in cheese making. Poultry are abundant and profitable, but do not include many turkeys or geese. Farm houses and steadings may be described as fairly good—a few good, but some capable of improvement. Farm implements in all departments may be regarded as abreast of the age. They include ingenious presses for the turning of several cheeses at once, low wheeled frames for the lifting of whole ricks of hay, self-delivery reaping machines, potato lifting machines, &c, Most of the grain is now thrashed by travelling thrashing machines, and not a little of the churning is done by steam, water, or horse power. Milking machines, though tried, cannot be said to have met with popular favour, and would require to be greatly simplified and improved before being generally adopted.

The farmers are generally industrious and enterprizing, but have of late years had to fight a stern battle with diminishing prices for all their produce, even that of the dairy being now threatened with colonial competition.

Much of the land now under high cultivation was up to the middle of last century, or even later, little better than moorland covered with scrub or heather, and not a little of it undrained morass. What cultivation there was, was very defective, whilst accommodation and implements were equally rude. In his "Rural Recollections," (1829), Robertson gives us a picture of it. He tells us that, up to 1750, there was hardly a passable road in the county. The farm houses were mere hovels moated with clay, with a dunghill at the door, and an open fire-place in the middle of the apartment. The cattle were lean and ill-thriven, the people wretched. Much of the land was covered with reeds and rushes, whilst ditches and hedges were ill made and worse kept. Where rude cultivation was, the soil was on the top of the ridge and water in the furrows. There was no fallow, no green crop, no sown grass. Carts and waggons were unknown, and strawyards also. Scarcely a potato or other esculent root was grown, and little but Bail was to be seen in the garden plot. Milk and oatmeal formed the staple elements in the diet of the people. Straw was scarce and little used and what there was, was got from the bags. The little manure used was conveyed to the field on cars or sledges, or a rude kind of framework, or vehicle called "Tumbler Wheels," in which the wheels turned with the axle tree, and the whole supported a wretched vehicle hardly able to draw five cwts. Oats after oats was the constant crop, until the exhausted soil became overrun with thistles. The common size of a farm was a plough gate of four horses, but that was sometimes held by two or three farmers conjointly, each with his own rig, but dwelling in the same house. Leases were frequently drawn out for three times nineteen years. Rent was sometimes paid in kind, or by steel-bow tenants, in what was called "Half Labour," i.e., one half of the crop going to the land, the other half to the tenant, for the maintenance of his family and the cultivation of his farm. Leases were often hampered by a multitude of vexatious servitudes, such as ploughing and leading for the landlord, working his hay, &c. The farm was generally divided into the croft or infield land, and the outfield. The former got all the manure. The starved cattle were allowed to poach and roam over the fields from harvest to seed time. The natural grass was either cut up on all the clay lands, or drowned with water in the cattle's footsteps. Horses were poorly fed on straw, boiled chaff, weak corn, or coarse bay. The plough was never yoked until after Candlemas; and there were generally three men to each plough, one to lead, one to drive, and one to clean the mud boards and keep the irons in the ground. Late oats were seldom sown before April, and bere before the end of May. During the summer months, the horses were allowed to feed on tether, or under the charge of a boy and dog.

Moor farmers occupied extensive tracts of land, destitute of plantations or enclosures. Their Stock generally consisted of black cattle,—weighing not more than 16 to 20 stones per head,—and blackfaced sheep. Up to 1710, farm produce, was carried to market on horseback, hay and straw crosswise in cadges; corn in sacks; butter, cheese, and eggs in creels. There was a man alive in this parish in 1829, who remembered when there was not a cart or carriage on wheels in it. Horses brechams were frequently made of straw and ropes.

The finest land was rented at from 2/- to 3/- per acre. The Old Statistical Account further tells us that, at the close of last century, lime was much needed, that oats and bere, yielding from five to seven bolls per acre, were the principal crops,—and that much flax was sown after potatoes.

The picture thus presented to our view of the state of agriculture in this parish upwards of a century ago, cannot, with modern conceptions, be regarded as an attractive one; but even it was doubtless an improvement upon that of earlier days. At the beginning of this century the 7924 acres in the parish are represented as thus distributed:—Lands under tillage 1455 acres; Cultivated grass land and Meadow 3302 acres; Hill pastures 2935 acres; Woodlands and gardens 232 acres, Of the lands under tillage, two thirds were devoted to oats, one eleventh to wheat, clover, and ryegrass, and the remainder to barley, rye, beans, potatoes, turnips and flax. With regard to potatoes, as then cultivated, the remark is made, that "their cultivation was extensive, considering the small demand for them outside of the parish, and that they were largely consumed by cattle and horses." The flax grown was only in small patches for family use, often a mere head-rig, yielding two or three stimpards (a stimpard being the eighth part of a bushel) by each farmer. The steps connected with its growth were clodding, weeding, and pulling. Its fibres were converted into lint at the mill at Glenbride, and afterwards spun into yarn, in the farmer's or crofter's kitchen, during the long winter evenings. Towards the beginning of this century, there were forty farms in the parish varying in annual rent from £36 to 300, and in rate per acre from 12/10 to 20/4. The Live Stock of the parish is then enumerated as, 162 horses, 601 milch cows, 794 other cattle, 2373 sheep, and 218 pigs. The wool of the sheep fed on the shore land was finer than that of the tarred hill fed sheep. The yearly crop of wool in 1794 was 625 stones.

Next to agriculture, weaving was for long the main industry of the parish. Now, it is rapidly drawing towards a vanishing point, as the number of weavers' shops being converted into dwelling houses may shew. The Old Statistical Account informs us, that the manufacture of coarse linen then employed many hands during winter, as many as 7000 yards being sometimes made in a year. This linen was bleached at home, and sold, at an annual fair in June, to Glasgow and Paisley merchants at 1/- or 1/3 per yard. Most of it went to the West Indies.

The steps through which the flax passed from flax to cloth were:—rippling, steeping, drying, cloving, scutching, heckling, spinning, weaving, and bleaching. The Lint mill at Glenbride was in operation up to little more than sixty years ago, when the late Mr. R. Gemmell's grandfather was miller. Joseph Weiss, at Portincross, was a noted weaver of linen yarns into table-cloths, etc.

In 1838 there were no fewer than 85 harness looms and 5 plain looms in the parish. These were employed in the making of a great variety of cotton, woollen, and silken fabrics, inclusive of the long celebrated Paisley plaids and shawls. Remuneration for such work was then much higher than now, and we have heard present-day weavers talk of the days when £200 of weekly wages for weaving would be coming into the village. Many women were also employed as winders of yarn, and, until improvements in loom-construction dispensed with their services, a drawboy was required for each loom, whose duty it was to lift a certain portion of the loom at every stroke of the shuttle so as to allow it to pass through amongst the warp. This draw-boy's wage was commonly 2/6 per week. Glasgow and Paisley manufacturers have been the principal employers, but a few looms have occasionally been engaged in the making of blankets, tweeds, &c., for local use,—or, in weaving customers' own wool for home needs.

Those engaged in this last, were called "Customer-weavers." As many as 120 looms are said to have been in existence at one time in the place, every available corner of a shop being occupied with them. The art of weaving the famous plaids and shawls was learned at Paisley by a few who taught it in turn to others. In the palmiest of those times a diligent weaver is said to have been capable of earning upwards of £2 per week. The products of the few looms still employed, are chiefly table covers, curtains, and shoulder shawls, but their employment is fitful and irregular.

Next to farming and weaving, fishing may be regarded as the most important industrial pursuit of the parish, but it was much more important a century ago than now, as is evidenced by the many little boat ports still observable along the coast, as well as by the fact that a certain quantity of herring was sometimes wont to appear as a stipulation in the payment of rent. Accordingly in the Commissary Records of Glasgow, a tenant at Fairlie is represented at his decease in 1601, as indebted to the Lady Fairly, "Twa hundrith half hundrith mail herring," whilst another in Largs owes the Lady Robertland, "Sax thousand salt herring, pryce of the thousand vi lib, to be paid it yeirlie betwixt Yuill and Candlemas, &c."

In the latter part of last century, we find no fewer than 150 people occasionally employed in fishing. Portincross' natural harbour then formed a place of shelter for the fishing wherries, and had a considerable export and import trade, being capable of admitting boats of 50 tons burthen. By 1820, however, this important branch of industry has fallen into such decay that it only gives employment to seven wherries with nineteen hands. At present there are only four or five families regularly engaged therein. A great contrast truly! to the year 1700 when the herring fishing alone, whose season lasted from July to October employed thirty boats with four men each, yielding £600 per annum. Last century, Sandilands near Seamill, and Netherton on the Hunterston estate, seem to have been considerable fishing hamlets. In 1782, we find West Kilbride supplying no fewer than 63 hands either to the Navy or to trading vessels. Now, the herring fishing is but irregularly resorted to; trawling in the Firth and local fishing for say the, salmon, sea trout, lobsters,

&c., being the main objects of attention. In seasons of scarcity of outdoor employment, a considerable number, especially of women, procure a precarious livelihood from the gathering of whelks and other shell fish, which are generally sold by the cwt. to buyers in London and other English towns. The Old Statistical Account informs us that at one time, ten tons of Kelp, valued at £3 5s. 0d. per ton, were made annually, especially at Seamill, where in the neighbourhood of the Hydropathic, the remains of kilns used in the burning of it, were recently removed. The sea yielded yet another product in the salt made from its waters at Hunterston; and to this we may add small quantities of Barilla, black ashes, and soda.

In the earlier part of this century, a considerable number of females found employment in Ayrshire sewed work, otherwise known as "Flowering," and "Tambour-ing"' an art of which lingering specimens have come down to the present day.

Another industry still carried on at Fence Bay, though not to such an extent as formerely, is the making of millstones from a kind of hard close-grained white sandstone mixed with quartz found on the upper western slope of Kaim Hill, and nowhere else in Scotland. It is somewhat like, though inferior to, the famous French Burr. At first these millstones were made in one piece, and brought down from the quarry by means of a long rough pole or tree, thrust through the centre by which their course was guided. If, inadvertently, it fell into any rut or hole, a horse was used to pull it out. Now, the stones are generally made of four or eight pieces bound together with Roman cement around a central stone, the whole being firmly welded together with iron hoops bound round the circumference. Roughly dressed at the quarry, they are generally brought down to the factory at Fence Bay, to be fitted and finished. They vary in diameter from three to five feet. Their average value may be about £12. At one time they were shipped as far as America, and the West Indies; but the introduction of steel rollers for grinding purposes has greatly diminished the demand for them. When a specially large one was despatched, it was frequently done with great rejoicing, a piper sitting on the top of it and playing.

A few other industries now extinct, were once carried on to a small extent in the parish, such as, a tannery, where the present gas work is, employing some eight or ten hands, and carried on by Mr. Duncan; a brick and tile work near Highthorn; a lime work near Ardneil; starch-making at Nethermil as also grinding charcoal for foundries; and candle-making in Halfway Street. This last art was also carried on, somewhat surreptitiously in farm kitchens as a precaution against payment of duty, where dips and moulds were made for home consumpt, while the females of the household wiled away the long winter evenings with spinning, and the gudeman made his maunds or baskets from Sough willows by the fire.

Ordinary occupations, such as masons, joiners, smiths, millers, shoemakers, tailors, and shopkeepers, &c., have, of course, for long found a livelihood within the parish, but in bygone centuries in smaller numbers than now. Thus in 1794 we find 2 joiners, 3 blacksmiths, 2 shoemakers, 5 tailors, 17 linen weavers, 19 cotton weavers, and 3 silk weavers. By 1820 there were 24 weavers, 7 tailors, 11 shoemakers, 24 wrights, 5 masons, 9 smiths, 2 bakers, 1 butcher. A century ago there was only one shop in the village kept by a "Johnnie a' things," called Robert Steel, a man with a cleek hand.

This shop stood upon a site nearly opposite the present Free Church. A century ago butcher's meat was brought into the parish from Dalry, and baker's bread in small quantities from Sercots, (Saltcoats).

In those days, when the inhabitants of our parish are constantly rubbing shoulders with the outside world, and when the introduction of the railway has brought in its train both the advantages and disadvantages of modern civilization, it is, perhaps, somewhat difficult for us truly to delineate the plain, primitive, and unsophisticated social life of those earlier days, when to be in Kilbride was to be out of the world. For the most part plain and homely, sometimes even rough and wild, the rude forefathers of this village hamlet infused not a little happiness into their simple lot. They toiled, they rested; they laughed, they wept; they mingled their mourning with their mirth, they served their day and generation in their own unostentatious way, and their homely joys and destinies obscure are left for us more to imagine than depict. Still, there are some relics of their past which have come down to our present, which may help us to form some imperfect idea of what the past social life of our parish was. Old wills, inferences from meagre statements in old parochial records, and more or less well authenticated traditions are the principal sources of information upon which we have to rely,—the material out of which we have to endeavour to reconstruct the social fabric of bygone days. The Social life of a people is, in its widest sense, a most comprehensive subject; and includes such topics as, the home-life of the people, their everyday customs and habits, their mental, moral, and spiritual characteristics, their mutual intercourse and inter-relationships, their quaint humours and idiosyncracies, their modes of speech, their dwellings and furnishings, their food, their work, their recreations, the incidents that ruffled the ordinary tenor of their way, the eccentricities of those popularly known as "Characters," their wages, and a multitude more of other things too manifold to enumerate.

Specimens of the old Wills or Testaments of some of the heritors of the parish towards the beginning of the seventeenth century may be found in such works as Fullerton's Appendix to "Pont's, Cunningham," or "Paterson's History of Ayrshire." By way of illustration the following brief one must suffice here:—

"The Testament dative and Inventar of the guidis geir etc., quhilks pertenit to umle, Robert Huntar of Hunterstoune, within the parochin of Kilbryd, the time of his deceis, quha deceist in the monethe of Maiy, the zeir of God 1616 zeiris, ffaitbfullie maid and gevin vp be Patrik Huntar, now of Hunterstoune, executor dative etc. Inventar, Item: the defunct had the time foirsaid perteining to him, as his owin proper guide and geir, and in his possessioune, the guide and geir vnderwrittin of the availlis, qualities, and pryces eftirspecifit, *viz.*, Twa ky, pryse of the piece x lib, inde xx lib. Item, in the borne, four bolls beir, pryce of the boll vi lib inde xxiiii lib. Item, the insicht of the house in vtincills and domicills, with the abuilzement of the defuncts bodie, estimat to xxxvii lib via viii d. Summa of the Inventar lxxvii lib visviiid."

From such Wills we learn that many of the conveniences of modern times, which are now to be found in all ordinary middle class houses, were then altogether unknown even in the homes of the wealthier and propertied classes, whilst their household plenishings were by no means superior to those of their tenants at the present day. Neither kitchen nor napery press of the mansions of those days appear to have been superabundantly stored, if we may judge from such testaments. They also shew us that oats and beir were in those days, the main crops of the farm, and horses and cattle the principal classes of Live Stock. Some light is also thrown by such Wills upon the intercourse then kept up with Ireland; upon salt. making as au industry of the parish. From the number of "hogsheids, pynt stoppis, and choppein stoppis" Archibald Boyd is represented as leaving behind him, we may gather that considerable use for such articles must have been found within the precincts of Portincross Castle. From such Wills, we also learn the money value, in pounds Scots doubtless, of many common articles in those days, and, if we take into account the depreciation of money since then, we at once perceive that prices for farm produce were relatively better in those days, than now. We further learn that it took four "Auld naigis" to be equal in value to one good horse;—that a cow was worth £12, a quay £5, and a stirk £2. They also represent farmers as then paying their rents either wholly or partially in kind. A few articles, such as a skout or a caddy, appear, with which under such names, at least, we are not in these times familiar. We have further evidence from such Wills, that debt was not always scrupulously avoided by the ladies of the period, as the "Debtis awand out" at their decease too plainly indicate. The minister's subscription shows him the will-maker of the period. From the "inventar of the guidis perteint to umquhile Jeans Montgomerie, spous to Robert Boyd of Portincross," of date 1621, we learn that such articles as these made up the household plenishings of the wealthy of the period, viz.—"feddir beddis, bowsters, blankettis, caddayis, coveringis, courtingis, lyning scheittis, round scheittis, hardin claith, heid scheittis, codwaris, buird-claithis, serveittis, breid claithis, lang towallis, compter claith, cutihornis, chaneleris, bassingis, lawer, pewldier stoip, plaithis, truncheours, salsours, saltfalt, watter potts, pottis, speitts, skis, caldroune, kettill, panniss, girdill, cruiks, chimnoy, kistis, beddis, other inspret." And, if such was the state of plenishing in the houses of the wealthy, in those of the tenantry, and still more in those of their servants, the furnishings were proportionately inferior. Even up to the middle of last century, Robertson tells us, that out of 165 farm-houses on Eglinton Estate, there were not twelve in which a stranger could have been provided with a separate bedroom.

The byres, stables, and other outhouses generally stood in a row with the farmer's cottage. This cottage was roofed with thatch, and often consisted of one apartment, with two beds, a table, a chest of drawers, two or three wooden stools, and a few smaller articles. "The but and the ben were a product of later days. Even the houses of the larger heritors, which generally took the form of square towers, were then incommodious and badly lighted. Many of them had no stairs; access to the upper storeys being gained by ladders."

By slow degrees, gooseberries, currants, strawberries, rasps, and all the ordinary garden fruits and vegetables of the present day were added to, and largely displaced the almost universal Kail. Whilst oatmeal and milk formed the staple elements in the general diet, a little butcher-meat was used by the country-folk, but this more frequently, in a salted than a fresh state. Because of its being salted at Martinmas, it was called their "Mart."

The broth made from it during winter, was mixed with groats made from oats, or barley made from beir.

The daily routine of life in our parish, as lived in these bygone centuries, was, (owing to defective means of communication with the outer world), much more self-enclosed than now. In contrast to modern ideas, it might be humble and homely, but still it may be questioned if fully as kindly a feeling did not permeate the social relationships of the parishioners then as now; a kindness, doubtless, helped by the more frequent intercourse between landlord and tenant, as fostered by the more constant residence in the parish of those who held so large a landed interest in it.

Whilst attention to the needs of their estates, hunting, fishing, services as yeomen, and a somewhat boisterous form of conviviality occupied much of the time of the upper classes; stern toil, relieved by a somewhat rude jocularity and kindly homeliness, formed the daily lot of the working classes.

The picture of the gathering in the farmer's kitchen on a long winter evening is by no means void of interest. By the light of the fire, or the oil cruizie, or the penny-dip, the gude man sits with his willow-wands around him weaving the baskets his Summer's toil will need. The gude wife, as she plies her needle and thread, is striving to "Make the auld look a' maist as weil's the new." The daughters spin the lint grown on the farm. The sons find some useful work, too, wherewith to close the day's toil. Lively conversation, merry with joke and banter, circles round,—made all the merrier when some inmate of a neighbouring farm arrived, bringer her spinning-wheel with her, just as the ladies of to-day bring their knitting or other work; and thus improving with useful work the social hour or two she had come to spend. We can well imagine how the local crack and gossip of the day would relieve the tedium of the busy hours and rob monotonous toil of much of its weariness;—how keenly the state of the markets and the prospects of the year would be discussed—how the females of the company would have their comments to make upon the last marriage that had taken place in the district, or the next one that was expected to take place;—upon the latest article of furniture or attire that had found an entrance into some neighbour's home, as an indication of a tendency to "upsetting pride." And, when the cackle of their own little bourg was for a time lulled, and the busy hum of the outside world was heard from afar, methinks we still can mark the lively interest, and the plain but shrewd speculation, wherewith the rise and fall of political parties and the fate of contending nations were discussed. Doubtless, in many a home in our midst, as well as in the parishes of Kyle, our national bard might have found a sitting for that masterpiece of his art:—"The Cotter's Saturday Night."

It cannot be denied that the social life of a by-gone century had its uncouth and unlovely aspects too, as the prevalence of smuggling, Sabbath desecration, intemperance, and other no less objectionable forms of carnal indulgence referred to in previous chapters, but too plainly shew. It is impossible for that romance of the past which lends enchantment to the view entirely to hide these black spots from our gaze. But on these we do not dwell, preferring to linger over the honest toil, the dry and caustic humour, the simple joys and sorrows, the somewhat severe but earnest piety that cluster round the ancestral homes of our parish.

Many social customs now extinct have lingered in the memories of the older inhabitants of the parish. Specimens of these are:—the assembling on New Year's Day of the men and boys, in the district at Ardneil Bank, for the purpose of fox hunting;—a gala-day of Shintie in the village at the same time;—the "Riding of the Braes or Brooze" at Weddings, when the first of the guests to reach the home of the newly wedded pair was the recipient of a bottle of whisky, which he probably shared with his less speedy companions,—festivities at "Booking," *i.e.* the giving in of names for the proclamation of Banns;—at the Fairday, when farmers and others repaired on horseback, and in procession to the home of one of their number whom they had chosen as Captain for the year, where they were served with refreshments;—the Races after the Fair, variously said to have been run at Ardneil, or on the Kilruskin road.

Closely akin to extinct customs is the memory of those who in bygone days were known as "Characters," in that peculiar sense so familiar in all country districts, which recognizes them as a sort of privileged class because of their eccentricities. Conspicuous amongst these in our parish was Thomas Tyre, the pedlar, to whom, because of the indigence of his later years, we slightly referred in our last chapter. From notes left behind by the late Dr. Ritchie and other sources, we learn that he was a man rather under the middle size—that his garb consisted of blue plaiding knees breeches, a short coat, a blue bonnet, or sometimes a cocked hat on his head, huggers on his legs, and nature's clothing on his feet. His occupation was that of packman, but he also sometimes carried webs for the silk-weavers to Dalry. He lived alone in an old house at the head of Halfway Street, a "hallanwa" separating his dwelling from that of Baldy Malcolm. The late Miss Dunn was wont to describe him as a "Kin' o' wake judgment man," and we are told he was very irritable. He is said to have had a strong predilection for the ministry, and on occasion of the Presbytery's visitation of the parish for the purpose of examining the Parish School, he was wont to present himself before them for examination. On one of these occasions he was asked by a member of that reverend body, "Whether the world was burned or drowned at the flood?" to which the pedlar's reply was, "Surely it was the tane o' them." He generally lived off other people, at one time ate to excess, at another suffered from want,— we know that "Whiles at Yule he sipped a drap." He had great delight in anticipating or enjoying the gratification of his appetite, and by way of restraining his inordinate desire for food, his mother is said to have sometimes made his brose with oak-bark water. Lads desirous of taking their fun off him would tickle his imagination with mountains of porridge and seas of milk; or a mill-dam of porridge and milk.

Some amusing anecdotes are still told with regard to him. On one occasion, when he went to one of his generous friends in the parish for some peats, he was told, as she was busy, just to go to the Stack and take them, but, although he had come purposely for them, he went away without them, as they had not been duly given him. On another occasion, he found on the public road, a purse with some money. After counting its contents he laid it down again, saying he would have nothing to do with what was not his own.

From the entries in the Kirk Treasurer's books with regard to him, to which we referred in our last chapter, he would seem rather to have been the recipient of occasional relief than a regular pensioner. Still we cannot but regret that so honest a man, should in the closing days of his earthly pilgrimage have felt so keenly the chill blasts of extreme poverty. The quaint inscription on his tombstone, which has been credited to the Rev. A. Oughterston, the then minister of the parish, has frequently appeared in newspapers and other public prints. It attracts the attention of many visitors to our old Churchyard, and. is to the following effect:—

> "Here lie the banes of Thomas Tyre,
> Wha lang had trudged tbro' dub and mire
> In carrying bundles and eik like;
> His task performing wi' sma' fyke.
> To deal his snuff Tam ay was free,
> And serv'd his friend for little fee,
> His life obscure was naething new.
> Yet we must own his faults were few;
> Altho' at Yule he sip'd a drap
> And in the Kirk whiles took a nap;
> True to his word in every case
> Tam scorned to cheet for lucre base.
> Now he is gone to taste the fare
> Which none but honest men will share.
> He died January 2nd, 1795, aged 72
> Years and a half."

Of a somewhat earlier date and of a different rank was old Spens, as he was called, *i.e.* Robert Boyd, whom we had already seen as a witness in the Crawford case (See page 182.) He is said to have been remarkable for his humour and outspoken brusqueness. He died in the earlier part of last century at the advanced age of upwards of 100 years.

Another "character" was lord Lisle of Springside, who lived in an old house on the Castle Green. His moral integrity could by no means bear strict investigation. When sent, on one occasion, in a cart to Irvine to be tried on a charge of incendiarism, so careless a surveillance did John Glass, the special constable, to which care he was entrusted, exercise over him, that his prisoner was back in West Kilbride as soon as be.

Another worthy was "Slaverin' Baldie," who lived, about the beginning of this century, along with his sister in a tumble-down cottage near the present entrance to Overton quarry. As his name indicates, he was filthy in his habits. He was in the habit of frequenting sales and other places of public resort, when there was likely to be anything going that would gratify his intemperate appetite.

Then there was Prophet Boyd, to whose deprada-tions at Law Castle we have already referred. He was suspected of complicity in the death of James Duncan, the tanner, who was found lying on the shore near Chapelton; and was himself killed when quarrying stones in Kilruskin Wood.

Some still alive may remember Johnnie Hamilton, the weaver, whose blackbird kept him at his work as it ever and anon whistled in his hearing, "Whip on Johnnie"—Nelly Biggart, with her cow in the pit—Duncan M'Caig, who was wont to go without a hat, but who, on one day donning one, said he had gone out without his bare head—Heather Jock, the wandering musician, with his hat adorned with bells and heather, singing "Annie Laurie," and suiting the action to the word, especially when he came to the line, "For bonnie Annie Laurie I'd lay me doon and dee"—Willie Watt and his mangle, whom all the servants in the place were to marry, in return for some simple favour,—John Bone, so long Free Church beadle—David Craig, with his barrow old and new, with his "As lee at the Station, not known to be the same lee at the other end o' the toun." His shrewd method of exposing an unintentional fraud by changing a shilling received in payment for the carriage of fourteen bags of shavings, (for which be was to receive a penny a bag), and returning and placing a penny over against each bag, thus gave ocular demonstration that two were wanting.

Other matters having a bearing upon the Social life of the parish are:—the Language of the people—the Population and Valuation of the parish at different dates—the Varying Prices of commodities at sundry times—characteristic anecdotes illustrative of the mental and moral complexion of the inhabitants of a bygone day, etc. Up to 1600, Gaelic was the language of Ayrshire, and would therefore be familiarly spoken in this parish. It has now entirely disappeared; Lowland Scotch, largely Anglified since the days of Burns, having taken its place. Many of our national Bard's terms and modes of expression are now but very imperfectly understood, even in this county of his birth. There are not many words or modes of expression that may be considered peculiar to the district. Possibly a few are such as these, "Aughts (owns), Buit (lantern), Maun (manage), Onct (once), Scurrs (water insects), Seirkint (too critical), Taigle (hinder), I seen it (I saw it), etc." It is more the tone or twang which strikes the ear of a stranger, and reminds him that he is at no great distance both from the Highlands and Ireland.

The Population of the parish has varied considerably during the last two centuries. Sometimes it has been on the increase, at other times on the decrease, as the following Statistics will shew:—In 1755 we find it as low as 885, a depopulation to the extent of a hundred families, having taken place after 1740, at which date grazing largely supplanted ploughing for a time. In 1792 it is lower still, viz. 698. From the beginning of the present century, it shews an upward tendency:—795 in 1801, 1015 in 1811, 1371 in 1821, 1675 in 1831, 1885 in 1841, 1968 in 1861, 2301 in 1891. The variations of population are also discernible from the differences of average birth rate, which from 1692 to 1718 is 42, from 1801 to 1806, 19, and from 1826 to 1831, 51.

The Valuation of the parish has also had vicissitudes, but it is generally on the increase. In 1640 it was £2,297 11s. 4d., in 1815 £7,006, in 1841 £9,805, in 1860 £13,115, and now it is nearly £23,000.

The development of some literary taste is discernible from the starting of a Public Library in 1830, which in 1837 had about 400 volumes, and has now upwards of 1,700. Friendly Societies had found an existence in our midst even from an earlier date, the oldest going back to 1796.

Prices of ordinary commodities seem to have varied. The following culled from the old Kirk Treasurer's books may suffice as specimens:—Coals in 1779 cost 3s. per cart, in 1801 4s., in 1809 7s., and in 1811, 7s. 4d. Shoes in 1779 cost 3s. 8d. per pair, in 1809 8s. In 1779 a trap-ladder cost 2s. 6d. In 1784 soap is sixpence per lb. In 1783 whiskey is twopence per gill, and straw 3 1/2 per stone. In estimating the relative value of such prices, we must, of course, bear in mind the lower wages of ordinary workmen, and the comparatively higher value of money. The Old Statistical Account was published about 1794, and was largely due to the energy of Sir John Sinclair acting through the clergy of the period,—an unsuccessful attempt to produce such an account of each parish having been made in the previous century. It tells us, that, for some years previous, the prices of labour and provisions had been on the increase; that the wages of an artist, *i.e.* of a skilled tradesman had risen from 1s. 3d. to 1s. 6d. per day; those of an ordinary labourer from 1s. to 1s. 3d. or even 1s. 6d. per day; that sheep formerly worth 10s. a head now bring 16s. and £1 each, and that owing to the better style of living, butter had advanced from 6d. to 9d. and 11d. per pound.

In the early years of this century, the national turmoil due to the French Revolution and Buonaparte's ambition sent a ripple even to our distant shore, and made its influence felt in a two-fold way; (1) in the stirring up of a spirit of national enthusiasm and patriotism, which manifested itself in the 300,000 Volunteers then in the land, to which West Kilbride supplied its contingent, and (2) in that enforced system of service in the army and navy,—known as the press-gang. Hence, we find one of the Wilsons of Kaimhill quarry rescuing himself by dint of courage and swiftness of foot, from the blue-jackets that had come to arrest him; and the late Mrs. Lindsay's father (J. Taylor) actually press-ganged, serving against Napoleon and forming one of his guards at St. Helena.

But days have changed since then in West Kilbride as elsewhere, and if the Old Statistical Account is correct, not much for the better, since this is the remark it has to make about our village and parish at the close of last century:—"Seclusion has saved the inhabitants from the encroaching influence of that corruption which in other places of more business and resort has produced so great a change in the morals of the people. They still are characterized by industry, sobriety, and decency, and the oldest man living does not recollect an instance of one convicted of a Capital crime. They are punctual in the payment of their debts, at two seasons in the year. Their feasts are conducted with rural gaiety, but without riot. They are regular, attentive, and neatly dressed in their attendance on public worship. Happiness, contentment, and independence generally prevail, and the inhabitants are well adopted for husbandmen and sailors; but the change from the frankness of the sailor to the factiousness of the manufacturer is by no means an improvement."

Still the tide of change will not brook to be stemmed by any, and so the luxuries of an advancing civilization and refinement find their way even into West Kilbride, an instance of which may be seen in the cupboard of Mrs. Boyd, of Highthorn, in the first China Cups, small and handless, brought to the parish by Captain Clark (father of the late Miss Agnes Clark, Halfway Street). With a few anecdotes, illustrative of the mother wit, enterprize, shrewdness, and caustic humour of parishioners of a bygone day we draw these chapters to a close:—On one occasion a farmer on the borders of Dalry parish was examining of a Sunday evening, the members of his family, on the tenth commandment. He asked if any of them could tell why the coveting of a neighbour's *house* was forbidden first. After a pause, the youngest at length volunteered this answer, "Faither, I ken." Repressed for a time with the reprimand, "Haud yer tongue, Jock, it's no yer turn," he was at length encouraged with, "Weel, my callan' what's the reason," to give his answer, which was to this effect, "Faither, mony a body wud like oor house, that wudna' like tae leeve wi' my Mither." As the farmer's wife, rather a contentious woman, was present, there was no further explanation of the tenth commandment asked that night.

The wife of a former tenant of Stairlie knew well how to practice generalship upon her somewhat birsy and cantakerous gudeman. When she thought her daughters would be the better of new hats, she addressed him as follows:—"The lassies'll no need a bonnet this year, but their mither needs ane." "Ay, but they'll get bonnets, and brow anes tae," replied John Grumlie, "and we'll get them at Kilmarnock on Friday first."

Another parochial worthy, when told by an elder with whom he was discussing some religious topic, that in matters of religion we must lay aside common sense, gave the somewhat ungracious reply, "If ye dae that, ye'll no be ony lichter."

A new way to pay old debts, or rather to escape personal seizure for them, was once adopted by one of the smaller proprietors in the parish, when he ensconed himself in a barrel, which. with its contents, was purchased by his betrothed wife, previous to marriage, and afterwards married in it.

An interesting tale is also told of how Yonderton came into the possession of one of its former proprietors. In the war between England and America in 1812, a large ship with a very valuable cargo was commanded by the father of the previous proprietor. It was captured by an American frigate and manned by an American crew, the captain and one sailor being left on board to help to navigate the ship to an American port. Somehow or other all the Americans were induced to go below, when the hatches were quietly and quickly battened down, whilst the captain and sailor stood over them with loaded guns. One American sailor was however, allowed to come on board to help to work the vessel. The captain and sailor watched and wrought alternately, but, on one occasion, the exhausted captain fell asleep when on watch, and dreamt that the American sailor was standing over him with a marling spike ready to kill him. He awoke in a fright to find his dream too true. Without uttering a word he sprang into a sitting posture, pulled the Yankee down by the legs and overmastered him. He made him swear that he would loyally assist him in bringing the vessel to England, which was duly done. With the handsome reward given by the owners of the vessel to the captain he purchased Yonderton.

Thus have we endeavored to give a sketch of the physical and topographical features of this Ayrshire parish, as also to delineate its antiquarian, ecclesiastical, parochial, industrial, and social life, in the hope that our humble efforts may serve to lend a somewhat fuller and more intelligent interest to the scenes upon which its inhabitants are daily looking, and towards which, because of their natural beauty, an ever increasing number of visitors are being yearly attracted. Much more doubtless remains to be learned, and to be told about the life and history of West Kilbride. We have merely attempted to make a humble contribution to that object, hoping to save from passing into oblivion relics that are becoming faded and worn, and to encourage others, by further research, to give still fuller development to the "Annals of this Ayrshire Parish."

Printed in the United Kingdom
by Lightning Source UK Ltd.
119097UK00001B/1-9

**15** Una o minuti!

# Martina il ciclone

Illustrazioni di Raffaella Bolaffio

© 2016 Edizioni EL, San Dorligo della Valle (Trieste)
ISBN 978-88-6714-573-7

www.edizioniel.com

# Martina il ciclone

Testo di **Stefano Bordiglioni**

**EMME EDIZIONI**

La sveglia squillò e Martina, senza
svegliarsi, si rigirò e cercò di spegnerla.
Urtò con la mano il fastidioso
apparecchietto sul comodino e lo
fece cadere. La sveglia scricchiolò
rimbalzando e poi tacque, fracassata a
terra. Non era la prima che si rompeva:
forse era la quarta o la quinta. O magari
la decima. La bambina ne aveva rotte cosí
tante che neppure se lo ricordava piú.
Comunque non se ne preoccupò affatto:
si riavvolse nelle coperte e nei suoi
riccioli, e si rimise a dormire.

Fu la mamma, come tutte le mattine, a svegliarla: – Martina, un'altra sveglia rotta! Io non so proprio come fare con te! La bambina poteva ignorare il suono della sveglia, ma di certo era impossibile far finta di niente di fronte a una mamma arrabbiata. Improvvisamente sveglia, saltò giú dal letto e piombò sopra la bambola di pezza abbandonata la sera prima sul pavimento. La bambola fece un rumore strano, una specie di sospiro rassegnato, e poi scivolò sotto il letto di Martina.

La bambina intanto si era liberata del pigiama, spedendo la maglietta nello scatolone dei giochi e i calzoncini sulla lampada del comodino.

Quindi rimestò fra gli indumenti che si ammucchiavano in grande disordine nel suo armadio alla ricerca del vestito giusto per quella mattina.

Voleva la maglietta rossa, quella con sopra l'immagine di un panda, ma non riusciva a trovarla. Dovette rovesciare tutti i vestiti perché era proprio in fondo al mucchio.

Soddisfatta, alla fine Martina si infilò la
maglietta con il panda, un paio di jeans e
finí di vestirsi in fretta. Quindi corse
a lavarsi.
Nel corridoio urtò inavvertitamente il
geranio della mamma, il vaso cadde

e si sbeccò, e la pianta perse un bel po'
di fiori e di foglie.
Entrando nel bagno, sbatté la porta cosí
forte che i vicini di casa pensarono che ci
fosse un temporale e guardarono il cielo
preoccupati.

Martina si lavò la faccia con una spruzzatina d'acqua. Ben di piú fu quella che finí a terra, tutt'intorno ai suoi piedi. Poi svitò il tappo del dentifricio che subito le cadde e scomparve sulle mattonelle colorate del pavimento.

La bambina strizzò un po' troppo il tubetto, e la pasta dentifricia si distribuí un po' sullo spazzolino e molta di piú sul lavandino. Poi Martina, dopo una dura battaglia, sconfisse a colpi di spazzola la ribellione dei suoi riccioli. Quando finalmente uscí dal bagno, lasciò dietro di sé un laghetto attorno al lavandino, il dentifricio aperto, la spazzola nella doccia, l'asciugamano per terra e il sapone che si era rintanato chissà dove.

Quindi Martina si sedette a tavola e fece colazione come sempre, guardando la televisione e conversando con la mamma. Distratta dalle immagini, la bambina inzuppò il tovagliolo di carta nel latte al posto dei biscotti e lo morse con gusto. Con il gomito poi, rovesciò il tè di suo fratello Matteo, senza farci caso più di tanto.

La mamma sospirò e rinunciò a sgridare quella specie di ciclone di sua figlia, tanto scombinata che sembrava avere due mani sinistre e due piedi destri.

Poi Martina prese la cartella e uscí di casa. Salendo in macchina pestò senza accorgersene il piede destro del suo papà, che gemette, meravigliato di quanto potesse pesare una bambina cosí piccola.

Durante il tragitto in auto, giocando con Matteo, l'anellino nuovo regalatole per per il compleanno andò a impigliarsi nella tappezzeria del sedile. Martina tirò con energia eccessiva e fece un bello strappo.

Inoltre urtò Matteo, che cadde finendo sul pavimento dell'auto, incastrato fra il suo sedile e lo schienale di quello del papà. Martina lo guardò stupita, senza capire che cosa ci facesse lí suo fratello.

Il papà fermò l'auto e lui e la mamma
liberarono il piccolo da quella scomoda
posizione.

Davanti alla scuola, la bambina si mise
lo zaino in spalla e scese dalla macchina.
Baciò il papà, pestandogli stavolta il
piede sinistro, poi si girò a salutare
la mamma e con lo zaino investí il
fratellino.

Il piccolo Matteo franò al suolo tra le lacrime. Martina lo aiutò a rialzarsi e gli raccomandò di stare piú attento.

Quando finalmente entrò in classe la bambina-ciclone abbandonò il suo zaino in mezzo ai banchi appena in tempo per permettere a Emilia, una delle sue compagne, di inciamparvi sopra.

Poi Martina corse a raccontare al maestro tutto quello che, il giorno prima, aveva fatto, visto, giocato, sognato, comprato, venduto, tenuto, lasciato, sgonfiato, incartato, attaccato, pestato, colorato, telefonato, mangiato, bevuto, sentito, detto o solo immaginato.

Siccome parlando si agitava, capitò che facesse cadere a terra il quaderno di Enrico e la penna di Franco.

La povera penna rotolò disgraziatamente proprio davanti ai piedi di Rosa, che senza volerlo ci camminò sopra e la sbriciolò con uno scricchiolio sinistro.

Nello stesso momento, Martina urtava involontariamente Luca, che finí a terra a sua volta.

A questo punto i bambini protestarono
con il maestro, ma a lui venne da ridere
e non riuscí a rimproverare Martina.
Quel ciclone di bambina rovesciava
penne, quaderni e bambini, però era
anche una bambina tanto simpatica.

# Tre passi
## tra i giochi...

IN QUALE ORDINE MARTINA COMPIE QUESTE AZIONI? INSERISCI IL NUMERO GIUSTO IN OGNI CERCHIETTO.

( ) PIOMBA SOPRA LA BAMBOLA DI PEZZA.

( ) RIMESTA FRA I VESTITI DEL SUO ARMADIO.

( ) URTA LA SVEGLIA CON LA MANO.

( ) SI INFILA LA MAGLIETTA CON IL PANDA.

( ) SI RIAVVOLGE NELLE COPERTE.

RIORDINA LE SILLABE SULLE SVEGLIE PER

FORMARE LE PAROLE PRESENTI NELLA STORIA.

IN QUESTA FRASE LE PAROLE SI SONO INCOLLATE LE

UNE ALLE ALTRE. PROVA A METTERLE IN ORDINE E

POI SCRIVI LA FRASE SOTTO.

LABAMBINAINTANTOSIERALIBERATADELPIGIAMA,

SPEDENDOLAMAGLIETTANELLOSCATOLONE

DEIGIOCHIEICALZONCINISULLA

LAMPADADELCOMODINO.

_____

_____

_____

COME SONO I PERSONAGGI DELLA STORIA?

COLLEGA CIASCUN PERSONAGGIO ALLE PAROLE

GIUSTE.

IN LACRIME

MERAVIGLIATO

SIMPATICA

ARRABBIATA

5° gioco

HAI LETTO BENE LA STORIA? METTI UNA CROCETTA
ACCANTO ALLA RISPOSTA GIUSTA.

1) IL TAPPO DEL TUBETTO DI DENTIFRICIO FINISCE...

   A ☐ NEL LAVANDINO      B ☐ SUL PAVIMENTO

2) MARTINA LASCIA LA SPAZZOLA...

   A ☐ NELLA DOCCIA       B ☐ NELL'ARMADIO

3) DI QUALE COLORE È LA MAGLIETTA CON IL PANDA?

   A ☐ ROSA               B ☐ ROSSA

4) QUALE PIEDE DEL PAPÀ MARTINA PESTA PER PRIMO?

   A ☐ IL DESTRO          B ☐ IL SINISTRO

5) A CHI APPARTIENE LA PENNA SU CUI ROSA CAMMINA?

   A ☐ A FRANCO           B ☐ A ENRICO

UNISCI CIASCUN PERSONAGGIO ALL'AZIONE
CHE COMPIE.

EMILIA...     RIDE E NON RIESCE A RIMPROVERARE MARTINA.

MATTEO...     RACCONTA QUELLO CHE HA FATTO IL GIORNO PRIMA.

LA MAMMA...     INCIAMPA SULLO ZAINO IN MEZZO AI BANCHI.

IL PAPÀ...     FINISCE SUL PAVIMENTO DELL'AUTO.

MARTINA...     SVEGLIA MARTINA, COME TUTTE LE MATTINE.

IL MAESTRO...     GEME PERCHÉ MARTINA GLI PESTA UN PIEDE.

# L'autore

Stefano Bordiglioni è nato a Roma piú di sessant'anni fa e ha insegnato nella scuola primaria. Ha pubblicato tantissimi libri per ragazzi e ha ricevuto numerosi riconoscimenti. Molti dei suoi libri sono stati tradotti e distribuiti all'estero. È anche autore di canzoni per ragazzi ed è stato autore di programmi televisivi.

# Tre passi

Finito di stampare nel mese di settembre 2016
per conto delle Edizioni EL
presso G. Canale & C. S.p.A., Borgaro Torinese (Torino)